America's Local Service Airlines

David H. Stringer

Published by the American Aviation Historical Society, Huntington Beach, CA

First Edition 2016

ISBN: 978-0-9801092-1-4

Library of Congress Control Number: 2016932935

All rights reserved. No part of this work covered by the copyright hereon may be reproduced or used in any form or by any means – graphic, electronic, or mechanical, including photocopying, recording, taping or information storage and retrieval systems – without written permission of the author or publisher.

Cover Image: One of two Mohawk Airlines Douglas DC-3s that were painted in Gas Light Service livery. Photographed at Albany, New York, by Jim Shaughnessy. (Photo via George Hamlin)

Copyright © 2016 David H. Stringer
All rights reserved

Published by the American Aviation Historical Society in cooperation with APT Collectibles.

American Aviation Historical Society
P.O. Box 3023
Huntington Beach, CA 92605-3023
www.aahs-online.org

APT Collectibles
P.O. Box 788
Bonsall, CA 92003-0788
www.aptcollectibles.com

Dedicated to the memory of

R.E.G. (Ron) Davies,

the dean of airline historians.

CONTENTS

Acknowledgements	9
INTRODUCTION	11
Chapter 1 - BIRTH OF THE LOCALS	13
Chapter 2 - ALLEGHENY AIRLINES	17
Chapter 3 - BONANZA AIR LINES	24
Chapter 4- CENTRAL AIRLINES	28
Chapter 5 - FRONTIER AIRLINES	37
Chapter 6 - LAKE CENTRAL AIRLINES	44
Chapter 7 - MOHAWK AIRLINES	51
Chapter 8 - NORTH CENTRAL AIRLINES	58
Chapter 9 - OZARK AIR LINES	62
Chapter 10 - PACIFIC AIR LINES	74
Chapter 11 - PIEDMONT AIRLINES	80
Chapter 12 - SOUTHERN AIRWAYS	86
Chapter 13 - TRANS-TEXAS AIRWAYS	97
Chapter 14- WEST COAST AIRLINES	106
Chapter 15 - NOT TO BE FORGOTTEN	112
Bibliography	117

Acknowledgements

This author would like to thank the network of professionals who helped him to bring this book to a finished product fit for the reader.

My thanks to Hayden Hamilton, Tim Williams, and the late Kase Dekker of the American Aviation Historical Society (AAHS), who have given me free rein on this project. Kase approached me via email to ask if I would like to contribute any articles to the AAHS Journal. That led to a five-part series presenting the histories of each of the "thirteen Locals," followed by Hayden's encouragement of my idea to turn the series into a book. Tim has been very gracious in opening up his vast collection of airliner photos for my use.

I'd also like to thank the other editors who have helped me along the way in my effort to tell the stories of the world's airlines. First and foremost, I extend my gratitude to John Wegg, the founder of AIRWAYS magazine, who first published my work and continued to do so. Taking up John's torch has been Enrique Perrella. I am humbled that Enrique had the faith in me to make me the History Editor of his magazine.

And then there are Nick Stroud and Mick Oakey in London who publish the outstanding quarterly journal, THE AVIATION HISTORIAN (TAH). Nick encouraged me to write an overview history of America's Local Service Airlines for his readers, and that assignment helped me in my preparation of this project.

Along with my editors, I must extend a sincere "thank you" to the librarians and library staff who have been so kind and generous in fulfilling my requests for research material: Julie Takata, Tomohiko Aono and the late Christine Harris of the San Francisco Airport Commission Aviation Library (associated with the SFO Museum), and Roberto Sarmiento and Kay Geary of the Northwestern University Transportation Library, and all of their associates. Thank you for your gracious assistance and for making me feel welcome.

To my fellow airline historians and enthusiasts who knew that I was working on this project (Dacre Watson, Jon Proctor, Dr. Charles Quarles, Bruce Kitt, John Corpening, Perry A. Sloan, Bjorn Larsson, Troy Kimmel, Edward C. King, Jack Harty and Philip Chuang), thank you for your encouragement and my sincere apologies to anyone whose name I have inadvertently left out.

My gratitude to the photographers and to the photo collectors who have brought the story of the Locals to vivid life with their pictures: again, thank you to Tim Williams and Jon Proctor, and thanks to George Hamlin, Ed Davies, Ed Coates and David L. Weatherford.

I owe a special debt of gratitude to R. Dean Denton of St. Louis, Missouri, who single-handedly has saved the largest archive of historical material related to Ozark Air Lines. Dean entrusted me with reams of valuable documents that helped me to tell the Ozark story in the most complete way possible.

Finally, "thank you" to my family and friends, who have put up with me talking about "the book" for a couple of years now: Dennis Michael Raybuck, Linda Tiboni, Herb Pohlman, Loretta Randolph, Bill Hurley, and all the rest of you. You are saints. And here is the book!

David H. Stringer
San Francisco, California
November 2015

INTRODUCTION

In the 1950s and 1960s, the United States was blanketed by a group of air carriers that served virtually every nook and cranny of the 'Lower 48' states. Residents of smaller cities, such as Hazleton, Penn.; Moultrie, Ga.; and Gallup, N.M., could board a 21-28 passenger Douglas DC-3 at their hometown airport and be on their way to any place else in the world. The 13 airlines selected to provide this convenience eventually wound up serving 580 cities in the U.S. with a fleet of more than 400 aircraft. These were America's permanently-certificated Local Service Airlines.

The Locals, as they were called, received public service revenue, or "subsidy", from the federal government to cover the losses they incurred from providing transportation to places that did not generate enough passenger traffic to cover expenses.

In his book, *Airlines of the United States Since 1914*, Ron Davies remarks that "the ever-increasing amount of government subsidy that was required to keep the Local Service Airlines serving the small cities of America" (or 'Main Street, USA' as the carriers themselves liked to refer to their destinations) "persuaded those who cherished a vision of an ideal transport world to come to terms with economic realities." That was the crux of the local airline conundrum.

The basic cost of operating short haul air service, with its many takeoffs and landings, is high. Operate that service with aging airliners staffed by a crew of three (captain, first officer, and flight attendant) supported by the required employees and equipment on the ground, and it becomes more expensive. Add the fact that most cities being served by Local Airlines were not big enough to generate the traffic necessary to support the service provided and it is easy to see why the Locals would never be able to perform the task that they were created for without some sort of government aid.

In the United States, if you talk about programs subsidized by the government for the social welfare of a certain group of citizens, in this case the residents of smaller cities, you will immediately have some people accusing the bureaucracy in Washington of overstepping its bounds and promoting socialism. Throw in the word "regulation", and a chorus will rise up decrying the constraints placed on free-market capitalism by government interference with private companies. But Congress and the Civil Aeronautics Board (CAB) believed that the need for subsidy would diminish over the years as more people became acquainted with, and started using, the service provided by the Locals. That did not happen. For a number of reasons, the subsidy bill kept going up even as more passengers patronized the Locals.

Just one year after President Eisenhower validated the Local Service Airlines, giving them 'permanence' in America's great transportation system in 1955, he signed

another piece of legislation that would drive a nail into the coffin of the local airline network. On June 29, "Ike" signed into law the Federal Aid Highway Act of 1956, paving the way for 41,000 miles of "superhighway" to be built over the course of the next 13 years. Officially called the National System of Interstate and Defense Highways, the framework was laid and the funding was authorized for what would become America's Interstate Highway System. The goal was to create a "safe and efficient highway network" that would "be essential to America's military and civil defense". These were the days of the Cold War and Eisenhower declared that the new road network would provide for "the personal safety, the general prosperity (and) the national security of the American people." The Interstates would be there to assist in the evacuation of cities, if necessary, just as the Local Airlines were supposed to help by transporting soldiers and staff among the hundreds of military installations throughout the country. The Interstates would also make the drive to a neighboring city more appealing than relying on scheduled transportation because such a trip could be accomplished at relatively high speed on one's own schedule.

In 1958, the 13 Locals employed a total of 242 aircraft, the vast majority of them Douglas DC-3s. By 1966, there were 410 aircraft in the Locals' fleets, 160 of which were turbojets and turboprops. The remaining 250 were piston-engine Convair and Martin twins and a rapidly dwindling number of DC-3s. With the introduction of jets, some Locals started calling themselves Regionals. And now that they had those jets, they had to fill them with passengers flying long enough stages to make money.

In 1972, George C. Eads of The Brookings Institution published a book entitled, *The Local Service Airline Experiment*. The conclusion he reached was that the "experiment" had been a failure. Quoting Eads, "And at many isolated points, unsubsidized air taxis would fill in the gap if the service were discontinued." Unsubsidized air taxis, or Third Level Carriers, as they were called, were sometimes financially-shaky ventures that could be here today and gone tomorrow. Often, when they did replace the Locals at isolated points, the independent Third Level operators would try to make a go of it with their Cessnas or Beechcrafts for a few months and then give up when income did not cover expenses.

The substitution of smaller aircraft operating more frequent schedules did help to boost patronage in some markets, notably among the early Allegheny Commuter services. But it is this author's belief that a large aircraft (one with 20 seats or more) represents safety in the minds of the general public. The presence of a flight attendant aboard reinforces the feeling of security. People feel comfortable about patronizing a service that makes them feel safe and secure.

The purpose of this book is to preserve the history of the airlines that did succeed in bringing commercial air service to the small cities of the United States, using big aircraft: DC-3s, Convairs, Martins, and Fairchilds. They succeeded because the United States government subsidized their service through the agencies of the CAB and the United States Post Office Department (today's U.S. Postal Service). During the roughly 34 years that regulated local service was in play, from the announcement of the feeder airline experiment (1944) to the signing of the Airline Deregulation Act (1978), America's certificated Local Service Airlines provided small cities in the continental United States with dependable scheduled air service and a level of reliable, attractive and comfortable transportation that most of those cities have not seen since.

It can be argued that the zenith of that service was reached between 1958 (the year of the CAB's Seven States Case Decision) and 1964, when the number of individual airports served by The Locals reached its peak. Yet for many cities, the zenith was reached after pure jet service was inaugurated. Tuscaloosa, Ala., hosted daily Southern Airways DC-9 flights while Utica, N.Y., served as the headquarters city for Mohawk Airlines, enjoying that carrier's daily BAC-111 jet flights. Neither city has any scheduled air service today.

Some of the cities once served by the Local Airlines continue to receive airline service today under the U.S. Department of Transportation's Essential Air Service (EAS) program. A variety of aircraft types are used under the program, from single-engine Cessnas to Regional Jets. But places like Anniston, Ala.; Red Bluff, Calif.; Valentine, Neb.; and Marion, Ohio, all of which were once served by certificated airlines operating DC-3 aircraft and larger, have no scheduled air service today and probably won't again in the foreseeable future.

This is a record of those companies that provided a social service to the small cities of the United States. Here is the history of a major component of America's air transportation system at one of its finest hours. ➔

CHAPTER 1

BIRTH of the LOCALS

The "Local Service Airlines," as they eventually became known, were given birth by the Civil Aeronautics Board (CAB). In 1943, the CAB undertook a mission to investigate the possibility of extending scheduled air service to smaller cities and towns throughout the United States even if the service to some of those communities might not be economically viable. This was an incredibly progressive undertaking for a government agency. America was in the midst of World War Two. The nation was becoming "air-minded" and the members of the Board knew that, once the war was over, every city and town would want to be on the airline map with this new industry carrying the weight of importance that the railroads had shouldered in the 19th century. Providing transportation to isolated towns and implementing air service to communities near military installations in support of national defense were additional reasons for examining the potential of this new type of air carrier.

In order to make routes into smaller cities attractive to airline entrepreneurs, government aid would be offered in the form of subsidy for carrying the U.S. air mail. When the war ended there would be hundreds of freshly-trained pilots returning to civilian life looking for jobs. There would also be an assortment of war surplus aircraft available. With these three forces at work, subsidy, manpower and affordable aircraft, the seeds were planted and the timing was right.

The Board issued its opinion in the summer of 1944 stating that, indeed, this new level of air service should be instituted on an experimental basis. There would be a whole new category of certificated carriers to be called "Feeder Airlines" because their primary purpose would be to transport passengers from smaller cities and towns to the big airports where those passengers would be "fed" to the trunk airlines for their onward journeys. By this time there were already hundreds of applications on file to provide different forms of air service to small cities and towns. In addition to feeder airline proposals using fixed-wing aircraft, there were helicopter service presentations, plans for mail pick-up service and schemes by railroads and bus lines to provide air service coordinated with their primary businesses. In addition, the established trunk airlines were very wary of creating a whole new set of air carriers when they felt that they themselves could handle the need for feeder service.

But the CAB wisely decided that an entirely new and experimental concept should be carried out by new outfits that would have to prove themselves capable. Their operations would be scrutinized every few years to determine if their certificates should be renewed. The Board felt that large carriers concentrating on bigger markets would not offer the kind of service envisioned for smaller, less productive stations.

The process began. Regular Civil Aeronautics Board hearings scheduled to cover service proposals in specific parts of the country would now include applications for feeder air service. Presentations were made in these "cases," oral arguments were heard, proposals were reviewed and an examiner from the Board's staff would make recommendations for awards. After the recommendations were announced, rebuttals to the examiner's report would be filed and arguments from those with opposing views would be heard.

Then, after deliberation among the Board's five members, awards would be granted based on a majority polling of those members. Oftentimes, after an award was announced, there would be further appeals.

When the process had run its course, most applicants had been eliminated and one company that had shown itself to be particularly "fit, willing and able" to provide feeder service in a particular part of the country walked away with the coveted Certificate of Public Convenience and Necessity.

Most of the time the CAB got it right. They chose an outfit that could take the concept from drawing board to reality and America's Local Service Airline network began to take shape.

THE FIRST FEEDER AIRLINES

The honor of being the first of the certificated feeder carriers to get off of the ground goes to a company calling itself Essair, which had previously operated an intra-state service within Texas. The "ESS" in the company's name stood for Efficiency, Safety and Speed.

On August 25, 1945, under the authority of its newly-issued feeder certificate, Essair began service between Houston and Amarillo, Tex., via four intermediate stops, using Lockheed L-10A Electras. The following year Douglas DC-3s were introduced to replace the Electras and the company management wisely changed the outfit's name to Pioneer Air Lines. Pioneer would become the first of the local service carriers to operate aircraft larger than the DC-3 when it replaced its fleet of *Gooney Birds* with Martin 202s in 1952. Unfortunately for Pioneer, the upgrade of its entire fleet to Martins did not sit well with the CAB and the company was eventually forced to reinstate an all-DC-3 operation (see Chapter 15: "Not to be Forgotten").

The 25 Feeder Airline Certificates Issued by the CAB, 1945 – 1950

AIR COMMUTING
ALL AMERICAN AIRWAYS
ARIZONA AIRWAYS
BONANZA AIR LINES
CENTRAL AIRLINES
CHALLENGER AIRLINES (formerly SUMMIT AIRWAYS)
EMPIRE AIR LINES (formerly ZIMMERLY AIR LINES)
ESSAIR (name changed to PIONEER AIR LINES)
FLORIDA AIRWAYS (formerly Thomas E. Gordon d/b/a ORLANDO AIRLINES)
ISLAND AIR FERRIES
MID-WEST AIRLINES (formerly IOWA AIRPLANE CO.)
MONARCH AIR LINES (formerly RAY WILSON, INC.)
OZARK AIR LINES
PARKS AIR TRANSPORT
PIEDMONT AIRLINES
PURDUE AERONAUTICS CORP.
ROBINSON AIRLINES
SOUTHERN AIRWAYS
SOUTHWEST AIRWAYS
TRANS-TEXAS AIRWAYS (formerly AVIATION ENTERPRISES, INC.)
TURNER AIRLINES (formerly ROSCOE TURNER AERONAUTICAL CORP.)
WEST COAST AIRLINES
WIGGINS AIRWAYS (officially E.W. WIGGINS AIRWAYS)
WISCONSIN CENTRAL AIRLINES
YELLOW CAB COMPANY OF CLEVELAND

In addition to the above, Mid-Continent Airlines, one of the existing 'trunk' carriers, was issued a feeder certificate in 1950 for the one segment of the Parks Air Transport (Parks Air Lines) system that was awarded to Mid-Continent when the CAB revoked Parks' certificate. That segment extended from Sioux City, Iowa, to the terminal points of Chicago and Milwaukee via several intermediate stops. The remainder of the Parks system went to Ozark Air Lines.

Pioneer reintroduced the Martin 202 into its fleet before finally succumbing to a merger with Continental Air Lines in April 1955. By that time Pioneer was serving 21 stations in Texas and New Mexico.

Next up was Florida Airways, originally called Orlando Airlines. This company was awarded routes within its namesake state in the CAB's Florida Case, decided in March 1946. The airline operated Beechcraft D-18s to 10 airports in the northern part of Florida on routes reaching from Orlando to Jacksonville and Tallahassee. Service was planned as far south as Miami and as far west as Pensacola. But Florida Airways could not make a go of it on such a small network and went out of business in 1949.

Empire Air Lines, formerly known as Zimmerly Air Lines, was already operating in Idaho when it received its certificate on May 22, 1946, to operate from Idaho Falls, Idaho, to Spokane, Wash., via a string of intermediate cities. Empire operated Boeing 247Ds, eventually replacing them with five DC-3s. Empire merged with West Coast Airlines in 1952, with West Coast prevailing as the surviving carrier.

Other CAB route cases in 1946 gave birth to more feeder airlines. Ray Wilson, Inc., an applicant from Denver, Colo., was awarded routes from Denver and Salt Lake City south to Albuquerque via intermediate stops in the Rocky Mountain States Case. When the company inaugurated service in November of that year it had taken on the name Monarch Air Lines. In that same case, Summit Airways was chosen to operate from a northern terminus of Billings, Mont., southward to Salt Lake City and Denver via intermediate points. By the time Summit began operations in the spring of 1947, it had rechristened itself Challenger Airlines. Monarch and Challenger would eventually merge and absorb the certificate of yet another feeder, Arizona

Airways, in 1950. The amalgamated enterprise would proudly call itself Frontier Airlines.

In the CAB's West Coast Case, also heard in 1946, two more feeders received their certificates: Leland Hayward's Southwest Airways was awarded a system that stretched from Los Angeles northward through many cities in California to Medford, Oregon. Nick Bez's West Coast Airlines received authority to operate from northernmost Washington State (Bellingham) southward to Medford, where it met up with Southwest. Both airlines began service in December 1946. Southwest Airways would change its name to Pacific Air Lines in 1958.

By the end of May 1947, seven feeder airlines were operating under their new CAB certificates: Challenger, Empire, Florida, Monarch, Pioneer, Southwest and West Coast. Two airlines, Bonanza and Robinson, were conducting intrastate operations, in Nevada and New York state respectively, but both would be operating under full CAB feeder certificates before long. One more company, All American Aviation, was flying air mail and express only on a unique air 'pick up' system in the Middle Atlantic states. All American Aviation would eventually abandon this type of operation for a full-fledged passenger, mail and express feeder certificate as All American Airways, ultimately to be renamed Allegheny Airlines.

All in all, between 1945 and 1950, 25 'new' airlines were issued Certificates of Public Convenience and Necessity to operate as Feeders. Hundreds more were rejected in their

By 1956, successes, failures, and consolidation had resulted in 13 local service carriers, each with its own niche market as indicated in this period route map. (From the author's collection)

America's Local Service Airlines

bids for certification. The term "feeder" was losing favor as the definition of this new type of air carrier was evolving. In addition to 'feeding' passengers to the trunk airlines, the new carriers were expected to connect big cities with the smaller cities and towns within their market sphere of interest allowing a person to travel from the big city to the small city in the morning, conduct business, then return home later the same day. The ability for an opposite transaction was also provided: a person could leave their small city residence in the morning, fly to the big city, conduct business or go shopping, and then return home late that same afternoon or evening. To provide this level of service a minimum of two round-trips per day over each route would be necessary, one outbound from the big city or 'hub' airport in the morning, another in the late afternoon or evening and one inbound in the morning, another later in the day. The ideal route would have big city airports at both ends with smaller cities linked along the route between the two like a chain. That way flights proceeding in both directions would have a large terminal city at either end to serve as a shopping or business destination and as a transfer point for passengers connecting to trunk airline flights. The title "Local Service Airline" conveyed this concept better than the moniker "Feeder Airline," and it became the standard term for these new companies.

THE CONCEPT COMES OF AGE

The feeder airline concept was an experimental proposition and the CAB exercised tight control over the rules of what these carriers could and could not do. The Board's goal was not only to protect, nurture and grow the new Locals but also to protect the interests of the trunk airlines assuring that they would not suffer undue competition from this new breed. When the Board announced its approval of the feeder concept in 1944, it issued guidelines for certification of the new carriers. Each certificate would state specifically what a company could and could not do with regards to non-stop or skip-stop service. And even though only the companies that were meticulously scrutinized and found to be the most "fit, willing and able" were selected to perform the new service, their certificates were subject to renewal after three years following another thorough review of their operations. Everything about the feeder airline concept was 'temporary' and 'experimental'.

By 1955, the original 25 certificated companies had been whittled down. Of the 25, five had never gotten airborne under the terms of their certificates (Air Commuting, Arizona, Island Air Ferries, Purdue Aeronautics and the proposed helicopter operations of the Yellow Cab. Co. of Cleveland) and three more had their certificates cancelled by the CAB after their first three year review (Florida, Mid-West and E.W. Wiggins). Mergers between two different sets of Locals (West Coast / Empire, Monarch / Challenger) had reduced the number of operating certificates by another two and one (Parks) had its certificate revoked after a lengthy investigation during which it tried to establish service. One more (Pioneer) merged with, and was absorbed by, a trunk carrier, Continental Air Lines.

THE SURVIVORS

THE 13 LOCAL SERVICE CARRIERS GRANTED PERMANENT CERTIFICATES IN 1955

Allegheny Airlines (formerly All-American Airways)
Bonanza Air Lines
Central Airlines
Frontier Airlines (formerly Arizona Airways, Challenger Airlines and Monarch Air Lines)
Lake Central Airlines (formerly Turner Airlines)
Mohawk Airlines (formerly Robinson Airlines)
North Central Airlines (formerly Wisconsin Central Airlines)
Ozark Air Lines
Piedmont Airlines
Southern Airways
Southwest Airways (later Pacific Air Lines)
Trans-Texas Airways
West Coast Airlines

That left 13 operating companies in business as of May 19, 1955. The 13 each operated in their own territory and together they did a good job of covering most of the continental United States. On the date mentioned above, U.S. President Dwight D. Eisenhower signed legislation which gave permanent certification to the 13 remaining Local Service Carriers. No longer would their certificates come up for renewal every few years. With assurance from the United States Government that these airlines would be around for awhile, they now became much more attractive to financiers. They became stable investments instead of risky ventures. The employees of the airlines could now breathe a little easier knowing that their jobs were more secure.

Each of these 13 carriers became familiar to the residents of the territory that they served. These were their hometown airlines. Because of the regular and reliable schedules that the local airlines offered to the communities that they served, businesses and industries were more willing to establish offices and locate manufacturing plants in smaller cities. The Local Service Airlines connected "Main Street USA" to the rest of the world and gave many of the small cities and towns on their networks better inter-city commercial transportation than they would ever see again.

What follows in the chapters of this book, in alphabetical order, are the individual stories of each of the 13 'survivors', followed by a chapter about the Locals that also flew for a short time but did not survive long enough to receive a permanent certificate in 1955. ✈

CHAPTER 2

ALLEGHENY AIRLINES

Although Allegheny's first flight as a passenger-carrying feeder airline (under the name All American Airways) took place in March of 1949, the company's heritage was rooted in a unique commercial operation that took to the air in 1939 from its original home in Wilmington, Delaware. All American Aviation, backed by the prestigious DuPont family, established a mail pick-up service that did not require landings and takeoffs at intermediate points but, rather, a low fly-by of the field where the outgoing mail pouch was secured to a wire strung between two posts. A cable that extended from the aircraft would snag the outgoing mail sack with a hook while the inbound mail was deposited in another pouch dropped from the plane. This clever procedure brought air mail service to dozens of small communities in the Mid-Atlantic states, and in West Virginia and Ohio.

The air mail pick-up system was almost written off as just an interesting experiment. One of the biggest problems was a lack of nighttime service due to the danger involved in the low altitude fly-bys. It was considered too hazardous to perform such maneuvers after dark. Most correspondence is mailed and postmarked at the end of the business day so the nighttime restriction was a handicap to the development of the service. Then World War II broke out and the volume of air mail skyrocketed with civilians on the home front writing to their loved ones overseas. All American's revenues multiplied and many other companies around the country also applied for air mail pick-up route certificates. All American Aviation applied for more pick-up routes too, in New England, the Great Lakes region, and the Southeast. The requests for air mail pick-up authority were heard by the CAB in conjunction with the requests of other carriers for feeder certificates and certificates for helicopter service.

But the end of the war saw a decline in mail transported by All American. The flow of correspondence to servicemen decreased and highway improvements accommodated the use of more mobile postal units by the Post Office Department.

Like the new feeder carriers, the company was dependent on air mail subsidy. However, the feeders also generated revenue from passenger operations, a source of income not available to All American. Feeder airlines carried air mail aboard their passenger flights; All American considered doing the opposite. The company proposed combining passenger service with the air mail pick-up, landing the aircraft at airports in between the pick-up points to accommodate passenger boarding and deplaning. At first the CAB was optimistic about the prospect, if and when an aircraft suitable for such operations became

Allegheny Airlines DC-3 (C-47A-30-DL), N151A, ex 42-23609. (From the Charles E. Stewart collection, AAHS-P006019)

available. But as time passed the proposal lost favor. The numerous quick descents and ascents required for pick-up service at smaller towns between the airports would not be conducive to passenger comfort and the CAB wisely questioned the safety of the concept. The idea was shelved.

At its zenith after the war, All American Aviation provided air mail pick-up service to 121 communities in six states, from Delaware to Ohio, serving many small cities and towns embedded in the mountainous terrain of The Appalachians. While the executive offices remained in Wilmington, the operations base was more centrally located in Pittsburgh. The company's primary fleet type was the Stinson Reliant. In addition, All American had purchased two Beech D-18Cs in anticipation of joint passenger/air mail pick-up flights. But the low-altitude air mail pick-up scheme turned out to be a short-lived phenomenon and applications for expansion into other regions were denied by the CAB, as were air mail pick-up proposals by other applicants. All American's unique type of operation was losing money hand over fist. The CAB determined that the needs of the travelling public and the Post Office Department were better served by conventional passenger carrying operations and by late 1947 it was obvious that All American's future lay in the hopes of establishing a traditional feeder service.

In 1948, the CAB looked favorably upon All American's nine years of experience operating a complicated aviation enterprise throughout the Mid-Atlantic states and selected the company over other applicants to provide feeder airline service in the region. The routes to be operated stretched west to Cincinnati, north to Buffalo, and covered the mountainous terrain of Pennsylvania reaching eastward to Philadelphia and Washington, basically the same area that had been served by the pick-up operation. Each route included several intermediate small cities, the primary reason for the airline's existence. In addition, All American was certificated to provide feeder service east to Atlantic City, N.J., and to cities in Maryland and Delaware on the Delmarva Peninsula. War-surplus C-47s, converted to passenger DC-3 standards, would be the aircraft employed. The name of the company was changed from All American Aviation to the more suitable All American Airways, and the airline's executive offices were moved to Washington National Airport.

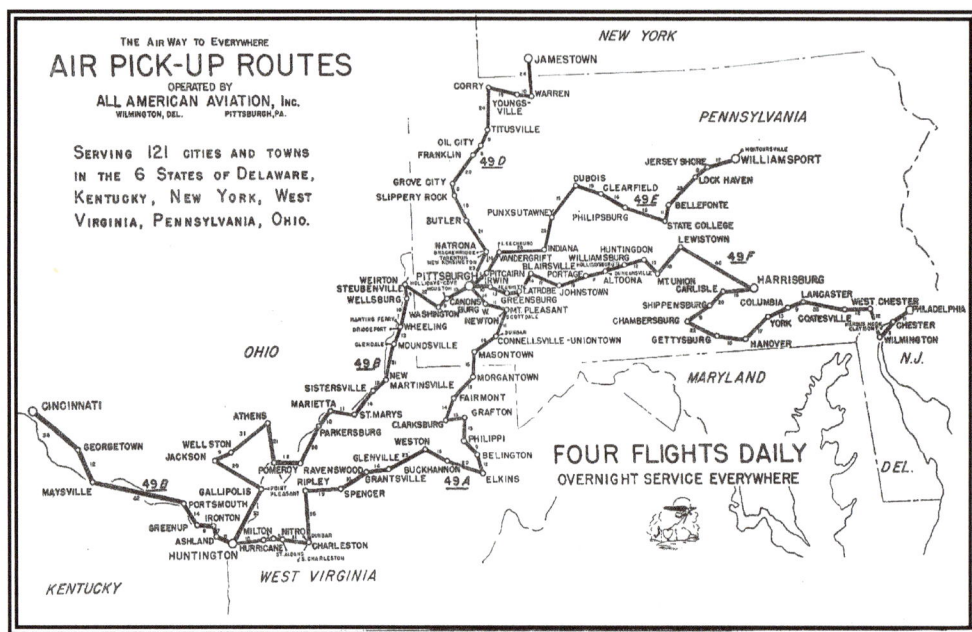

Route map showing the various pick-up points of All American Aviation's mail service. Most of these "stops" were low fly-bys snagging the mail pouch with a cable and hook. (From the author's collection)

Meanwhile, All American's engineering division, which had developed and manufactured the mail pick-up equipment, continued to function in Wilmington. The knowledge gained from developing the pick-up apparatus was employed by the engineering division to develop applications for the military, including pick-up apparatus to save downed flyers.

Allegheny DC-3 N150A (C-47 c/n 6178) taxis away from the gate at Newark Airport in this 1959 photo. (Photo from the Tim Williams collection)

Allegheny timetables from December 1955, April 1959, and August 1965, spanning the period from introduction of the Martin 202 to the announcement of service with "jet-powered" Convair 580s. (From the author's collection)

Before starting passenger service, the company was awarded one more route by the CAB - a link between Pittsburgh and New York (Newark, N.J.) via several cities in central and northern Pennsylvania.

All American Airways operated its first scheduled passenger flight as a feeder carrier on March 7, 1949, over the route between Washington and Pittsburgh via intermediate points. The airline's other certificated routes were phased into service with a fleet of 11 DC-3s during the course of the spring and summer until the entire system was operational by July 25. Meanwhile, the air mail pick-up service was being phased out, route-by-route. On June 30, 1949, the last Stinson-operated pick-up flight took place over old Route 49D from Jamestown, N.Y., to Pittsburgh with many descents to scoop up air mail pouches in between. The innovative pick-up service had come to an end. The company had completed its transition.

Not only had All American Aviation pioneered the air mail pick-up service, the company's engineering and research division had invented all of the equipment used in the operation. By 1952, it was apparent that the development and manufacturing of equipment undertaken by All American Aviation's engineering division had little in common with All American Airways, the feeder airline. The two companies were separated, each becoming an autonomous entity.

To mark this new era and to signify the carrier's independence from the engineering division, the airline's board of directors decided on a name change. As of January 1, 1953, All American Airways officially became Allegheny Airlines.

Shortly after the name change, a new leader was selected to help transform Allegheny into an airline that could make the most of the strategic territory that it served. Leslie O. Barnes took over as president of Allegheny in April 1953, and he spent the next 22 years at the helm, developing Allegheny into one of the top performers in America's local service field.

Like all of the Locals, Allegheny grew slowly and steadily under the CAB's watchful guidance. The first adjustments came in 1953 as service to Cincinnati was terminated and Huntington, W.V. / Ashland, Ky., became the terminal for that segment. Cleveland, Ohio, was made the western terminus of the system at the same time. Later in the decade Allegheny's system would be extended further west to Detroit.

As early as 1953, Les Barnes was aware that Allegheny needed some larger aircraft. To quote the company's annual report from that year, "In many respects your company has outgrown the DC-3. Many flights consistently operate at maximum capacity... it is not always possible to meet either passenger or express demands except through the operation of additional schedules." Certainly, some of the other local service carriers wished that they had that problem!

Barnes's team acquired three 40-passenger Martin 202s from the assets of defunct California Central Airlines and a fourth from Pioneer Air Lines. The Martins were placed into service beginning June 1, 1955. Allegheny christened the 'new' aircraft Martin "Executives," never using the '202' designation in publicity material. The public could make the assumption that the Martins were the more advanced, pressurized 404 model, which was similar in appearance. Allegheny eventually operated a total of 18 model 202s.

Concurrent with the arrival of the Martin *Executives*, the company adopted the slogan, "Airline of the Executives."

Allegheny Martin 202 Executive N172A, named "The Ohio Valley." (Photo by Ira Ward from the George Hamlin collection)

Allegheny Convair 540 "Leilani," N440EL, seen at Pittsburgh in June 1959. (Charles E. Stewart photo from the AAHS photo archives, AAHS-P012420)

In 1956, Allegheny's crew complement included 114 pilots and 55 flight attendants, all men. In a marketing arrangement with Air France, 15 of that company's most junior hostesses were 'loaned' to Allegheny for six months to work aboard the Martins. For all of them it was their first assignment with Air France, which paid their salaries during the sales promotion project. The French female cabin attendants brought the desired public attention to Allegheny.

By the end of 1958, the company operated a fleet of 10 Martin 202s and 13 DC-3s, all 23 aircraft decked out in the company's dark green livery with red titles. Most of the other Locals were still operating all-DC-3 fleets while just beginning to sign contracts for aircraft the size of Allegheny's Martins. But Barnes was already looking at his next move, toward aircraft with even greater capacity, not to replace the Martins and DC-3s but to augment them.

Consequently, on July 1, 1959, Allegheny put its first turbo-prop aircraft into service, on an experimental basis. Allegheny was the launch customer for Napier's Eland-powered 'jet-prop' conversion of the popular Convair 340 twin. Dubbed the Convair 540, a single example was leased from Napier and introduced on services to Atlantic City and Cape May, N.J., from Pittsburgh and Washington. To celebrate Hawaii becoming the 50th state in the Union that year, Allegheny's management decided to paint the exterior of the aircraft with some festive markings and staff them with Hawaiian hostesses wearing "colorful island garb." Dubbed Leilani Service, snacks were offered from a 'Hukilau' food tray. The company reported that "all previous sales records on these route segments were exceeded by a wide margin as a direct result of this colorful service."

At the end of the summer season, the Convair 540 was deployed on an innovative new non-stop commuter run between Pittsburgh and Philadelphia. Eventually called "Commuter Express," Allegheny offered such advancements as walk-up no-reservation service, booklets of multiple commuter tickets at a reduced rate, and the ability to pay your fare on board. The service became popular and competed favorably against the trunk carriers flying larger aircraft on the route and was eventually expanded into other markets. Eastern Air Lines copied and refined the concept for the Northeast Corridor when that company introduced its famous "Air Shuttle" in 1961.

After the initial Hawaiian Islands-themed livery had served its purpose on the single leased Convair 540, Allegheny's management decided that it was time to refresh the whole fleet and the corporate image. New colors of red and royal blue were selected and a new paint scheme was applied to aircraft featuring a stylized arrow logo (the flying wedge).

Allegheny ordered five Convair 540s from Napier and also arranged for the acquisition of 11 unconverted, piston-engine Convair 440s. The 440s and 540s were all outfitted with 52 passenger seats.

1959 would see Allegheny suffer its first fatal accident when a Martin 202 crashed on approach to Williamsport, Penn., on December 1.

With the inauguration of new routes into southern New England in the spring of 1960, Convair 440s were placed into service. Allegheny was replacing American Airlines at some of the stations and on some of the routes in southern New England, which were more suited to service by a local airline than by a trunk.

Allegheny was a strong carrier, always ranking at or near the top in boarding and revenue statistics among the 13 Locals. The territory served was economically thriving, rich in industry, with a large population base. On the Pittsburgh to Philadelphia route alone, Allegheny's share of the market jumped from one percent in 1959, prior to the inauguration of *Commuter Express*

An advertisement from a brochure prepared by Douglas Aircraft. The text describes Allegheny's order for 100-passenger DC-9-30s, but shows a sketch of the smaller dash 10 variety in Allegheny colors. (From the author's collection)

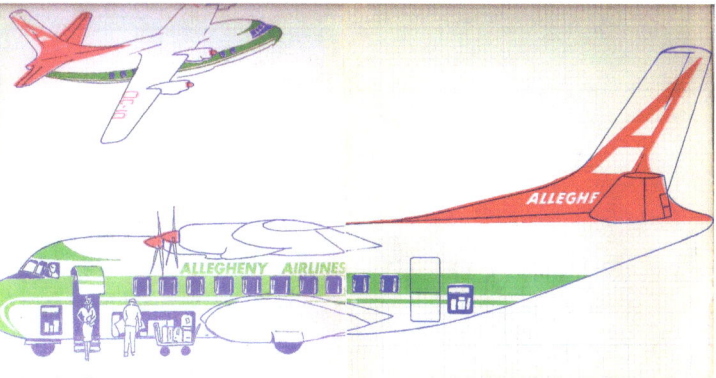

The cover of Allegheny's employee magazine, "Air Commuter," Feb.-March 1957 issue, showing the sketch for a planned "DC-3 replacement" to be built by Douglas Aircraft Co., tentatively to be called the DC-10. As we know, that never happened. (From the author's collection)

service, to 61 percent in 1961. Again, some of the other local service carriers would have been grateful to serve such profitable markets.

When Napier, now under the banner of Rolls Royce, cancelled the Eland 540 project altogether, the turboprops were removed from the fleet in 1962. The venerable DC-3, which had served the company since 1949, also flew for Allegheny for the last time that year.

In 1963, Allegheny converted one of its Convair 440s to a cargo-carrying configuration, becoming the first local service airline to place an all-cargo aircraft into operation. The success of the service prompted the company to convert a second aircraft, this time a Martin 202, to cargoliner specifications. The company settled on the 202 as its standard for all-cargo service and two more of the type were eventually converted as they were retired from passenger service.

While the federal government grappled with the issue of public service revenue (subsidy) for the Locals, the payment of which far exceeded what the CAB had ever envisioned when initiating the feeder airline experiment, Allegheny's management noted that, in 1963, 14 of the airline's 38 certificated stations produced 84 percent of total passenger and cargo revenues while the other 24 airports produced only 16 percent. This was a fact of life for the Locals, one that Congress and the CAB would have to live with if they wanted these airlines to continue their mission of serving smaller cities. Les Barnes insisted that the CAB needed an affirmative plan for strengthening the Locals if the CAB wanted to reduce subsidy payments without a reduction of "public service" flights. The CAB would respond over the ensuing years by relaxing route restrictions and granting the Locals innovative new non-stop authorities.

In his 1964 report to stockholders, Les Barnes noted that "There is no question but that the local service airlines are steadily assuming more of the characteristics of regional airlines; but in accomplishing this desirable transition these airlines must not ignore their obligation to serve the intermediate smaller cities."

Always looking ahead in anticipation of upcoming equipment needs, the company began its examination of jets for future use on "highly competitive routes," and decided to replace the engines on its Convairs with turbo-prop power plants. The Allison-powered Convair 580s began to appear on-line in 1965. This was followed by the introduction of another jet-prop, the Fairchild F-27J, later that same year. The two new types of aircraft allowed for retirement of the remaining Martins

1965 saw the introduction of the Fairchild F-27J into the Allegheny fleet. N2705J, c/n 116, joined the fleet in November of 1965 and remained with Allegheny until 1974. (Photo from the Tim Williams collection)

America's Local Service Airlines

Allegheny leased this Douglas DC-9-14, N6140A, msn 47049, in 1966 while waiting delivery of DC-9-30s that would begin to enter the fleet the following year. (Photo from the Tim Williams collection)

from passenger service but the company retained three of the 202s to continue operating the all-cargo flights.

In 1966, Allegheny truly entered the jet age as the company leased a single Douglas DC-9-14. The 'short' -14 was a temporary member of the fleet as the airline awaited delivery of the six stretched DC-9-30s that it had on order. The larger DC-9s began to enter service the following year.

1967 also saw the last of the Convair 440s converted to 580 standard, leaving Allegheny with an all-turbine powered fleet (the Martin 202 *Cargoliners* had been retired).

Management continued on its innovative path in 1967 with introduction of the first Allegheny Commuter operation, service to a smaller station subcontracted to a scheduled air taxi operator. In keeping with Les Barnes's pronouncement from three years prior, the Locals were now morphing into regional airlines, which in Allegheny's leadership role as an innovator meant turning over the responsibility of operating into some small stations (the reason for the Locals' existence in the first place) to yet a 'third level' of air carrier.

On March 1, 1968, Allegheny spread its wings south to Nashville and Memphis, expanding beyond its traditional service area. But this move was overshadowed by Allegheny's next big step, the acquisition of Lake Central Airlines, the local service carrier operating in the territory immediately adjacent and generally to the west of Allegheny's system.

The shakeout of the Locals had begun the previous year with the merger of Frontier Airlines and Central Airlines, from which Frontier had emerged as the surviving carrier. Central was the first of the 13 Locals, permanently certificated back in 1955, to disappear. Out west, a three-way merger of local service carriers Bonanza, Pacific, and West Coast in 1968 reduced the count even further. As for Lake Central, that carrier had struggled for a couple of years with a new aircraft type, the Nord 262, that it had banked on to be the elusive DC-3 replacement. After the Nords were temporarily grounded in order to fix a troubling engine problem, the carrier suffered a devastating Convair 580 crash, which was not Lake Central's fault, yet it was one more blow to the airline's reputation. The merger of Lake Central into Allegheny, which was effective July 1, 1968, took Allegheny as far west as Chicago and St. Louis, bringing the carrier's service to more than 100 cities in 17 states, the District of Columbia and Ontario.

Once Allegheny absorbed Lake Central, the airline's marketing department put special effort into improving the reputation of the French-built Nord 262s that it had inherited. Painting them in a purple and gold livery replete with *fleur de lys* on the tail, Allegheny gave the individual

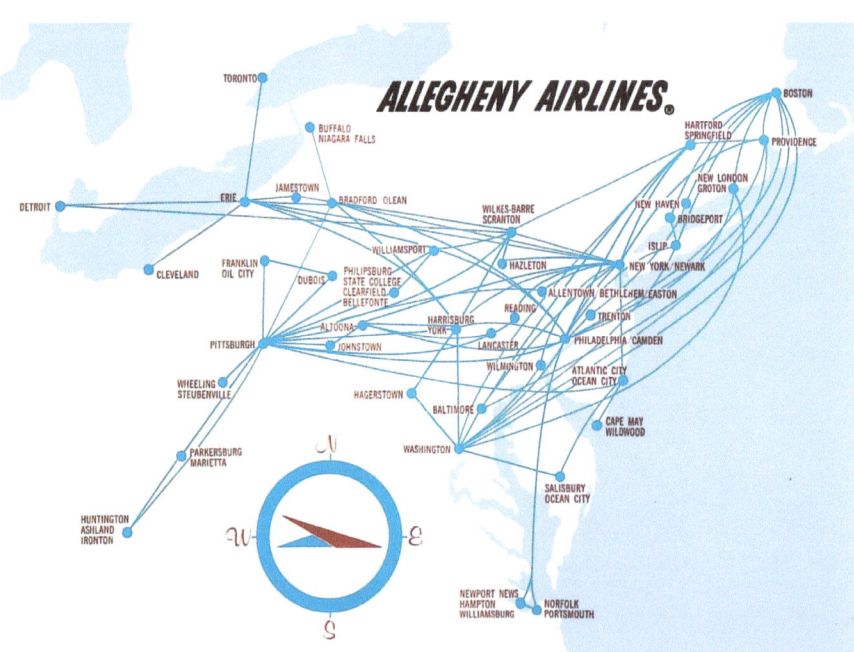

Allegheny's route system as of autumn 1967. (From the author's collection)

Nord 262s Nicole *(N26203),* Celeste *(N26208) and* Brigette *(N26211) d' Allegheny sporting their purple and gold paint livery in an attempt by Allegheny to improve the plane's reputation. (Photo from the Tim Williams collection)*

Allegheny acquired a number of BAC 1-11s through the merger with Mohawk in 1972, and continued to operate them until the late 1970s. N1125J is seen at Detroit (Metro) on November 22, 1977. (Photo by Tim Williams)

aircraft female French names, e.g. Claudette d'Allegheny, Nicole d'Allehgeny, and Yvonne d'Allegheny. The interiors carried a Paris street scene painted on the forward bulkhead. Flight attendants assigned to work the Nords wore a split miniskirt, black net stockings, a striped jersey and a "jaunty beret." They served wine and cheese snacks in an effort to evoke a French theme, which must have presented a bewildering sight for customers boarding in Kalamazoo and Terre Haute.

The positive spirit of expansion and growth was dampened by tragedy with the freakish occurrence of two fatal accidents at the same airport in less than two weeks. On Christmas Eve 1968, an Allegheny Convair 580, operating as flight 736, crashed on approach to the Bradford Regional Airport in northwestern Pennsylvania during an evening snow storm, killing 20 of the 47 aboard. Thirteen days later, on January 6, 1969, another Allegheny Convair 580, operating as flight 737, crashed under the same conditions at the same time of day on approach to Bradford. Eleven people were killed in that accident. Both aircraft were on approach to the same runway but from different directions. Each struck treetops on descent.

Allegheny's growth continued. The airline added Boeing 727-200s to its fleet in 1970, but sold them the following year.

As the era of the Locals was transitioning into the age of the regional airlines, Allegheny found itself growing larger once again from the acquisition of yet another of its local service neighbors. In 1972, Allegheny merged with Mohawk Airlines after that carrier had suffered financial setbacks followed by a lengthy pilot strike.

With that merger, the ranks of the 13 Locals were reduced to eight regional carriers. They all still served small and medium-sized cities but each was now flying jets and relying on the Civil Aeronautics Board to give them more liberal and expanded route authority that would help them put the expensive new airliners to their best use.

In 1978, the Airline Deregulation Act was signed into law and the Civil Aeronautics Board, which had created, nourished, and regulated the Locals every step of the way, was relegated to a slow death.

Allegheny managed to survive the turmoil of airline deregulation and continued to prosper after changing its name to US Air in 1979. Acquisition of yet another of its local service brethren, Piedmont Airlines, in the 1980s, along with the purchase of PSA (Pacific Southwest Airlines) kept US Air expanding.

The company was rebranded US Airways in the 1990s as the local service airline that had started out by picking up air mail pouches in the Appalachian Mountains was now flying passengers to Europe.

After ups and downs, including visits to bankruptcy court, US Airways merged with America West Airlines in 2006. The surviving company retained the US Airways name. The airline was the last direct descendent of one of the 13 permanently-certificated Local Service Carriers until it, too, succumbed to merger, with American Airlines in 2013. ✈

Convair 580s first entered the fleet in 1965, and the type continued to serve with Allegheny until the late 1970s. All of the company's Convair 440s were converted to 580s by 1967. (Photo from the Tim Williams collection)

CHAPTER 3

BONANZA AIR LINES

Edmund Converse saw a need in Nevada for air service between Las Vegas and Reno, so he decided to fill it. Operating totally within one state, an airline did not have to deal with the Civil Aeronautics Board (CAB) but only with the licensing authority of that state. Such intrastate operations were the training grounds for several of the companies that would eventually apply to the CAB for feeder certificates. Bonanza Air Lines, an outgrowth of Converse's Bonanza Air Service, which performed charters and pilot training, began offering scheduled service between Las Vegas and Reno on August 6, 1946.

In the Additional California-Nevada Service Case, decided by the Civil Aeronautics Board on June 15, 1949, Bonanza was awarded a certificate to operate as a feeder carrier between Reno, Las Vegas and Phoenix via intermediate points. The award was contingent upon transfer of TWA's Phoenix – Las Vegas route to Bonanza, which was finalized in November of that year. Bonanza began service as a certificated local service carrier with Douglas DC-3s on December 19, 1949.

Operations along the somewhat straight line from Reno to Phoenix via Carson City / Minden, Hawthorne, Tonopah, Las Vegas, Kingman and Prescott continued for more than two years as Bonanza's one-and-only route until 1952, when the next award was made by the CAB, this time in the awkwardly-titled Reopened Additional California-Nevada Service Case.

Western Airlines had been serving El Centro, Calif., and Yuma, Ariz., from San Diego, providing less-than-adequate service, and the CAB had tentatively awarded a transfer of that route to Southwest Airways, a feeder carrier operating mostly within California. The route was more suited for a local service operation like Southwest or Bonanza than it was for a trunk carrier like Western. But not only would the transfer put El Centro and Yuma on Southwest's map; it would also extend Southwest's network eastward beyond Yuma to Phoenix.

In the above-mentioned case, the CAB rescinded the transfer to Southwest Airways and gave the extension to Bonanza instead, in an effort to shore up that carrier's system. In contrast with some other local service airlines that served industrialized and heavily-populated parts of the country, Bonanza hopped across the desert. Dubbed "Route of the Gold Strikes", the little airline did serve Reno, Las Vegas and Phoenix, but none of those cities, particularly the latter two, were as bustling and popular as they are today.

The new route extended Bonanza's network westward from Phoenix to Ajo, Blythe, Yuma, El Centro and San Diego. In their wisdom, the members of the CAB allowed the route extension to continue up the Pacific Coast from San Diego to Oceanside, Santa Ana / Laguna Beach and Los Angeles, offering much greater potential for local and interline traffic. Things were looking up for Bonanza.

At the same time that the CAB was bestowing this new prize upon the company, it was also investigating the possibility of a merger between Bonanza and Southwest with an eye toward strengthening the local service network and reducing federal subsidy payments. Neither Bonanza nor Southwest wanted to merge at the time and the matter was eventually dropped, only to be revisited 16 years later.

Bonanza started service over the new route to Los Angeles in June of 1952. Also that summer, with the CAB's blessing, the

DC-3 N493 (c/n 3251) is seen here at San Diego's Lindbergh Field in Bonanza's early-1950s livery. (Bob Archer photo from the Jon Proctor collection)

LEFT: For its first two and a half years as a Local Service carrier, Bonanza operated over a route stretching from Reno to Phoenix via Las Vegas and intermediate points. This timetable from April 4, 1950, clearly shows Bonanza's original route system. It was not until July 15, 1952, that the first big addition to the system took place with the inauguration of service westward from Phoenix into southwestern Arizona and Southern California. **MIDDLE:** The February 1, 1957, timetable cover touts the 11th year of scheduled service, obviously including the years 1946-49, when Bonanza operated intrastate schedules before beginning certificated service. **RIGHT:** The January 3, 1958, timetable introduces service over the newest extension of Bonanza's system: northward from Phoenix to Salt Lake City. Bonanza would be serving several intermediate points on the route but the company was also given nonstop authority between PHX and SLC, ostensibly a trunk route, and a very long haul in 1958 for a DC-3! But the shape of things to come is shown on the cover of the timetable with a small sketch of an F-27 propjet appearing below the company name. It would be another year before the F-27s came on-line to take over some of the more lucrative routes from the DC-3s. (From the author's collection)

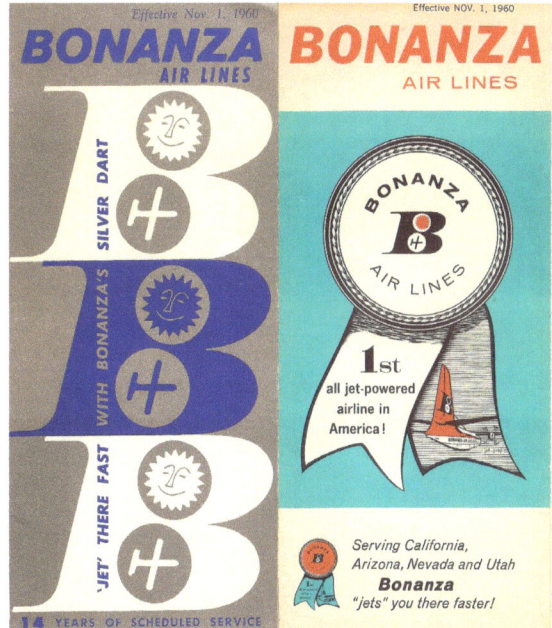

LEFT: On November 1, 1960, Bonanza issued its timetable with the silver (gray in this scan), royal blue and white cover, now showing a scheduled network operated entirely with F-27s. The DC-3 had been phased out of the fleet. **RIGHT**: Someone must have quickly realized that this could be a public relations 'bonanza' for Bonanza because the airline issued the same timetable with a different cover, this one stating that Bonanza was now the "first all jet-powered airline in America," a bit of a stretch but a slogan that was used for several years. (From the author's collection)

company offered a non-stop nighttime coach service between Phoenix and Las Vegas, an unusual prize for a Local to be able to offer non-stop service between two large cities. But there was no competition on the route. A few years later Bonanza would also be operating CAB-authorized non-stop service from Las Vegas to Reno, a two hour, 30 minute flight aboard a DC-3.

In 1955, Indio / Palm Springs (served through the Thermal Airport) and Ontario / Riverside, California (served through Ontario) were added to the route map. Riverside received service through its own airport in late 1956, and in December of 1957, Palm Springs / Indio service was transferred to the Palm Springs Airport.

Converse was on top of things in the search for new equipment to replace Bonanza's unpressurized and un-air conditioned DC-3s, which flew across the hot desert serving a growing populace. In 1956, the CAB announced that funding would be made available to the Locals, via subsidy, to assist with the purchase of new equipment. With this promise of financial aid, the company announced an order for three brand new Fairchild F-27 'prop-jets,' with options for three more. First deliveries were expected to take place in 1958.

1957 saw a new route award that was bound to play a crucial role for Bonanza in the years ahead. A segment between Los Angeles and Las Vegas, via Ontario or Riverside and Apple Valley, Calif., was authorized. For the time being Bonanza's DC-3s would have to make two landings between Los Angeles and Las Vegas in order to serve the residents of the intermediate points but that restriction would be lifted in a few years.

On January 3, 1958, Bonanza's system was further strengthened with the introduction of service between Phoenix and Salt Lake City, both non-stop and with several intermediate

Fairchild F-27s began to join Bonanza's fleet in 1959. By November 1960, they had taken over all services from the venerable DC-3s, which were phased out. N754L, c/n 91, was originally registered N154L, having joined Bonanza's fleet in 1962. (Photo from the Tim Williams collection)

landings. This time Bonanza wound up with the longest scheduled DC-3 flight in the Continental U.S. - three hours and 20 minutes non-stop from Salt Lake to Phoenix. Again, there was no competition on the route.

The F-27s finally arrived in 1959, and Bonanza christened them 'Silver Darts.' As more of the prop jets came on-line, the company began retiring its DC-3s until the last Douglas service, Flight 65 from Salt Lake City to Phoenix via Cedar City, Page, Grand Canyon, Flagstaff and Prescott, was operated on October 31, 1960.

A new timetable with a nice blue, white and silver cover was issued effective November 1, 1960. Someone within the company must have realized the significance of having an all F-27 fleet and another timetable with the same effective date was quickly issued. This one proclaimed on its cover: "First all jet-powered airline in America," a bit of a stretch since the aircraft were not turbojets but turboprops, yet it was a coup for the little local service airline snatching a probable future advertising catchphrase from a trunk carrier. This became Bonanza's slogan for the next few years.

In 1962, Bonanza was granted authority to fly non-stop between Los Angeles International Airport and Las Vegas in direct competition with trunk carriers also serving the route. The CAB was attempting to strengthen the networks of the subsidy-dependent local service carriers and allowing entry into competitive markets was a big step. The company had been serving the route with intermediate stops for several years but now Bonanza's F-27s were up against Western's four-engine Lockheed Electras shuttling vacationers on gambling junkets non-stop between the two cities. Both TWA and United also served the route but not on a turnaround basis. Las Vegas was an intermediate stop on through flights for those two carriers, which had more interest in capturing the long-distance traveler from Las Vegas. Bonanza introduced a reduced-rate excursion fare on the route and quickly captured 30 percent of the market.

The local airline had grown up with Las Vegas, which had transformed into a major tourist destination, and Bonanza was now the hometown airline.

Anticipating the need for larger aircraft to keep pace with the times and with traffic demand, Bonanza management boldly decided to purchase the British Aircraft Corporation BAC 1-11 twin-jet. The decision did not sit well with the CAB, which would have to guarantee a loan for the aircraft purchase. Politicians in Washington were becoming anxious to see the subsidy requirements lessen for this breed of air carrier and now a subsidized airline wanted taxpayers to pledge security for the purchase of foreign-made jets. The Board denied Bonanza's request, thus pointing the carrier in the direction of U.S. manufacturers. In 1963, Bonanza announced the purchase of three Douglas DC-9s, for delivery in 1966.

The first DC-9s entered scheduled service with Bonanza on March 1, 1966, and, in another one of those marketing moments, the company took the term 'DC-9 Fanjet' and christened its own DC-9s as *FunJets*. The new jets served the most heavily-travelled routes on the system while the F-27s continued to serve shorter local segments.

Bonanza had long served

The airline had originally looked at purchasing the BAC 1-11, but was persuaded to go with the Douglas DC-9. The March 1, 1966, timetable introduced Bonanza's DC-9 service. (From the author's collection)

Douglas DC-9-11, N945L, c/n 45728, was the first DC-9 delivered to Bonanza, arriving in December 1965. It would help inaugurate pure jet service on Bonanza routes in early 1966. (Photo from the Tim Williams collection)

both Grand Canyon Airport and the city of Page, Ariz., home of the Glen Canyon Dam project and gateway to Lake Powell, as intermediate points on its Phoenix – Salt Lake City route. In 1966, the company was given authority to serve Grand Canyon non-stop from both Las Vegas and Phoenix, greatly expanding the potential for tourist travel to the sight.

The city of Phoenix, which was second only to Las Vegas in importance on Bonanza's system, offered the company a deal on a new headquarters building and larger hangar facilities necessary for the jet aircraft. The company took the city up on its offer and relocated its general offices to Bonanza Way in Phoenix during the summer of 1966.

More DC-9s were ordered as Bonanza's management looked toward spreading the airline's wings south to Mexico. In significant CAB decisions, Bonanza was awarded authority to serve Tucson, Ariz., non-stop from several major cities on its network, and the company was approved for an international route south from Tucson to Guaymas, La Paz, Mazatlan and Puerto Vallarta.

After the CAB's first attempt to force a merger between Bonanza Air Lines and its neighboring local service carrier, Southwest Airways, back in the early 1950s, Edmund Converse had tried a couple of times to purchase that company, which was renamed Pacific Air Lines in 1958. His attempts failed. Nic Bez, the founder and president of West Coast Airlines, yet another local service carrier which operated in the Pacific Northwest, tried to purchase Pacific through stock acquisition but the takeover was thwarted by the CAB. It was not the first attempt at merger for those two carriers either. Finally, in the late 1960s, the three airlines reached an agreement to merge together into one large regional airline. Converse was not particularly happy with the deal but strength through merger appeared to be the next logical step for these three Locals. On April 30, 1968, Bonanza introduced its service to Mexico, officially becoming an international carrier while it was still independent. Two months later, on July 1, 1968, the three westernmost local service airlines operating in the United States officially became one airline known as Air West.

Howard Hughes purchased the company in 1970, and the name of the airline was changed to Hughes Airwest. ✈

The last two timetables issued by Bonanza. It is 1968, and the 3-way merger involving Bonanza, Pacific and West Coast is on the near horizon. That must have been a bit frustrating for the folks at Bonanza because the company is just starting to grow into some potentially-profitable new markets. **LEFT**: Service to Tucson is added with the April 1, 1968, timetable, offering nonstop DC-9s from that southern Arizona city to Los Angeles, San Diego, Las Vegas and Phoenix. RIGHT: With the April 28, 1968, timetable, Bonanza becomes an international carrier, introducing service to Mexico. Notice is also posted that the company is "Soon to become Air West." (From the author's collection)

Americas Local Service Airlines

CHAPTER 4

CENTRAL AIRLINES

In the summer of 1944, when the Civil Aeronautics Board (CAB) announced that it would consider applications for feeder airline operations throughout the country, Keith Kahle was ready. He had incorporated his company, Central Airlines, Inc., in March of that year with the purpose of applying for a certificate to operate routes radiating from his hometown, Oklahoma City.

Kahle was an aviation writer for the *The Daily Oklahoman* newspaper and, with a degree in engineering, had helped to build air installations during World War II. An avid aviation promoter and enthusiast, he had previously been involved with two proposed airline projects, one called Trans-Southern, the other named Southwest Feeder Airlines. Neither of those early efforts proved successful but his application for Central's certificate held promise. The CAB was preparing to open the Texas-Oklahoma Case, a forum to examine the need for more air service in the region, and feeder petitions would be considered along with other route requests.

To understand how coveted the CAB's new feeder certificates were, a look at the Texas-Oklahoma Case will give some insight. Twenty-seven applicants applied to establish local service in the states of Texas, Oklahoma and New Mexico. The applications encompassed 367 cities that these outfits suggested that they could serve. 328 of those communities were proposed to receive service for the first time. Among the 27 candidates were enterprises calling themselves Texas Central Airways, Great Plains Airways, Gulf Airlines and Oklahoma Airways.

Also vying for a certificate was a company called Spartan Airlines, controlled by oil baron J. Paul Getty, and another called Skylines, Inc., backed by Phillips Petroleum. Union Bus Lines and Texas Bus Lines both submitted applications to operate feeder service in the region as did Eagle Airlines, a subsidiary of the Missouri Pacific and the Texas & Pacific Railways. Not to be left out was Oliver Parks, whose Parks Air Transport was already busy trying to acquire certificates in three other CAB route cases.

Then there was Central Airlines that had no ties to oil companies or to other transportation businesses. Kahle had secured a loan guarantee from the First National Bank and Trust Company of Oklahoma City and he had access to the deep pockets of businessman Guy O. Marchant, and his son, W.C. Marchant, two of his first investors. The CAB noted that Central's management "presented an extensive study of the travel habits, the needs, and requirements of the area. The key figure of Central who made the study (Kahle) has long been associated with aviation activities in the state and is thoroughly familiar with the local transportation problems of the area."

Among all of the applicants, only one petitioner was selected to provide feeder service focused on Texas, an outfit called Aviation Enterprises, which would soon change its name to Trans-Texas Airways. In the Oklahoma area, the choice was down to two contenders: Skylines and Central Airlines.

Central had proposed a system that would serve dozens of cities and towns in Oklahoma, Texas, Kansas, and reach into Arkansas, Louisiana, and Colorado (the Colorado part of the proposal was deleted from hearings in the Texas-Oklahoma Case). This projected network would span 2,991 miles and was planned to be operated with 14 Beechcraft model 18s. The Twin Beech was the 'feeder-liner' of choice suggested by many of the early applicants.

In the end, the members of the CAB selected Central over Skylines because they wanted a company without any ties to other businesses, one whose management would concentrate solely on running an airline. The CAB declared that "it is apparent from a comparison... of the two applicants that Central has evidenced more interest in the development of local transportation, has given more study, and has better planned the details necessary to the inauguration of... local service... needed in the state." The CAB also noted that "the financial resources of Central appear adequate and its management clearly has sufficient comprehension of the undertaking and is prepared to devote its entire energies to that undertaking." Keith Kahle had done his homework and the CAB found Central Airlines fit, willing, and able to become the region's local service carrier. The first hurdle had been overcome.

Central's Certificate of Public Convenience and Necessity was issued by the CAB on November 14, 1946. The company was expected to become 'airborne' by March 14, 1947, and the certificate would expire on March 14, 1950. The whole concept of feeder airlines was experimental and each of the new certificates was issued for a period of just three years. After that time a company would be evaluated to see if it deserved to continue operating for another three years, or longer, or less, or have its certificate revoked or allowed to expire. There were no guarantees other than the desire of the CAB to see the scheme work, and the fact that government subsidy would be paid to each feeder airline to cover losses from operating the service. Subsidy was to be paid through the United States Post Office for carrying the mail by air.

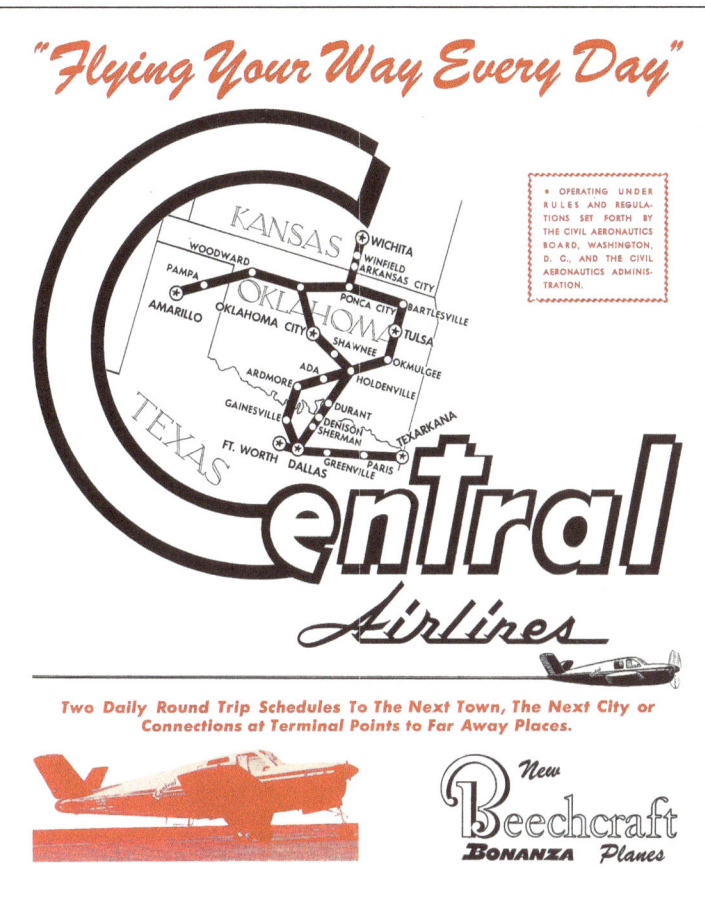

ABOVE: *Central Airlines A-35 Bonaza.* LEFT: *The center spread from a very early Central Airlines timetable (Jan. 28, 1950). Central first got airborne with a fleet of Beechcraft Bonanzas, which turned out to be an impractical choice for scheduled service. This timetable ad shows Central's original route map. (From the author's collection)*

The certificate issued was for a much smaller system than the one that Central had initially proposed. That in itself was probably a blessing. Instead of 2,991 miles, Central's network would cover 1,355 miles and span five routes: Oklahoma City to Wichita; Oklahoma City to Dallas and Ft. Worth; Amarillo to Tulsa; Dallas to Tulsa, and Dallas to Texarkana. Of course each route included intermediate points, small cities in between the bigger stations, which was the whole purpose of the feeder experiment.

The process of getting an airline into operation presented formidable problems to many of the newly-certificated feeders. Despite all of the graphs, charts and research presented to the CAB about expenses and how they would be covered, the reality of establishing facilities, hiring and training personnel, purchasing aircraft and putting a whole airline into operation became a Herculean task. It was another hurdle that some of the new feeder companies never did surmount. Central was not spared. Despite Keith Kahle's preliminary work behind the scenes, a lot of money was necessary and banks and investors didn't want to put their capital into a venture unless others were also willing to invest. Financing was hard to find for the new carriers in the late 1940s, with no guarantees that an airline hopping between small communities would make any money at all.

Kahle did not make the March 1947 deadline to get Central off the ground. Then Guy O. Marchant and his son apparently became disillusioned and wanted to sell their shares. Meanwhile the clock was ticking.

Stepping in to save the day financially were F. Kirk Johnson, an oilman from Fort Worth, Tex., and Deane Gill. Following their lead was the Fort Worth National Bank. With the airline's new financial backing coming from Fort Worth, it made sense to relocate the company's headquarters to that city. Kahle had also established a fixed-base operation (FBO), Keith Kahle Aviation, at Oklahoma City, leading the CAB to initiate an investigation into the propriety of interlocking relationships between Kahle's

Central's Beechcraft Bonanzas on the ramp at Meacham Field, Fort Worth, Texas. (From the author's collection)

America's Local Service Airlines

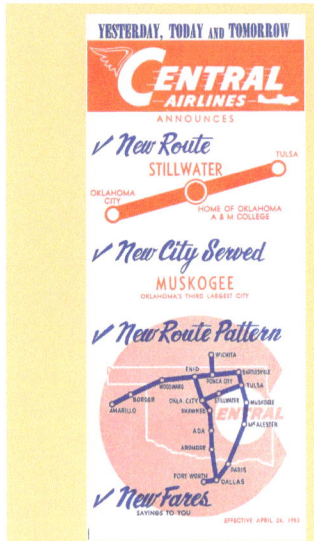

LEFT: *April 26, 1953, timetable cover. By this time the entire fleet of Bonanzas had been replaced with DC-3s.* RIGHT: *In December 1952, Central replaced its male pursers with female flight attendants. Here, on the cover of the February 15, 1954, timetable, is a photo of one of Central's hostesses standing on the steps of a DC-3. (From the author's collection)*

The CAB nurtured the Locals by bestowing new routes onto their network maps judiciously. A lot of study and debate went into the route award process. Here are two timetable covers from 1956 (Feb. 1 and Dec. 3) announcing new services for Central: entry into the lucrative major market of St. Louis and the award of a new route into Colorado via Liberal, Kansas, terminating at another major city - Denver. (From the author's collection)

two companies. Having the airline headquartered in Fort Worth while the FBO was in Oklahoma City helped placate the Board's apprehensiveness.

Finally came the question of aircraft. It was now 1949 and several of the feeder carriers that had been certificated in the previous three years, including Central, had yet to put their routes into operation. This was frustrating not only for the CAB, but also for the cities and towns that had fought for and won the privilege to be included in the nation's air transportation system. Part of the problem was that some of the cities did not have airports yet capable of handling aircraft as large as Douglas DC-3s, which had become the aircraft of choice as large numbers of used *Threes* were becoming available from trunk carriers disposing of the 'tail draggers' from their fleets. The other issue was money, of course, and a very small, brand new airplane would be cheaper to purchase and easier to resell than a DC-3 if the airline was not successful. On June 8, 1949, the CAB issued a press release stating that it would approve

"the use of single-engine aircraft in scheduled air transportation of passengers limited to day VFR conditions and over areas whose topography is favorable to single-engine operation and relatively short trips." They had to do something to give Central and the others a push. The CAB had issued a directive to Central on March 24, 1949, instructing Kahle to get his airline flying

A Central DC-3, N19937, at Denver Stapleton in the 1950s. (Photographer unkonwn)

 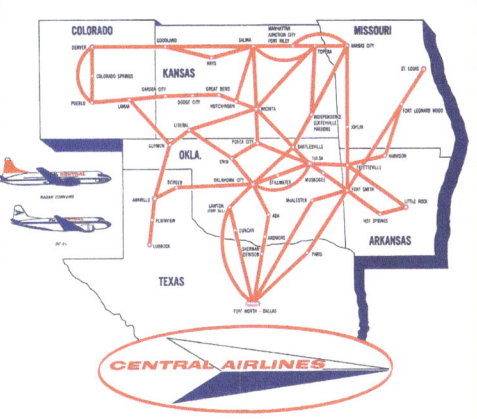 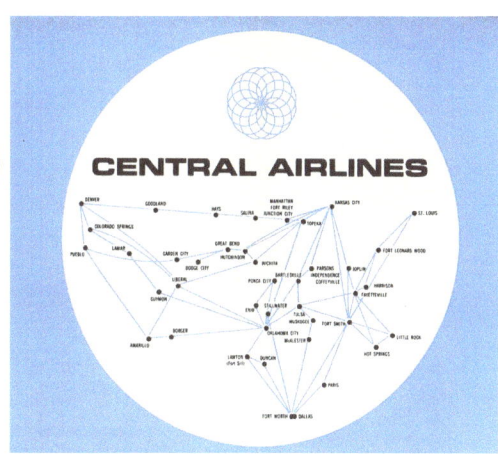

LEFT: *The route map from the Feb. 15, 1957, timetable. Central was proudly serving its territory with a fleet of 12 DC-3s at this point. A 13th "Gooney Bird," purchased from Northwest Airlines, would be added to the fleet in July 1957.* CENTER: *1961 was a big year for Central. Convair 240s, purchased from American Airlines, were introduced into the fleet and awards made in the Kansas-Oklahoma Case brought several new stations onto Central's system, some of them transferred from Continental Air Lines.* RIGHT: *Route map from Central's timetable effective September 1, 1967. The map shows Central's system at the end of the company's existence as an independent carrier. The jets never came to pass and Central was headed for a merger with Frontier Airlines the following month. Central would become the first of the 13 Locals permanently certificated in 1955 to lose its identity through merger. (From the author's collection)*

by July 1. The unwritten threat was that the carrier's certificate would be revoked if service was not inaugurated.

With the CAB's single-engine ruling, Kahle and company considered three basic types for possible use: the Cessna 190 or 195, the Ryan Navion, and the Beechcraft A-35 Bonanza. Kahle filed a request on June 30, 1949, to extend the date by which time he had to start operations because the CAB was still deliberating the interlocking relationship issue and the transfer of stock from the Marchants to Johnson and Deane.

A deal was struck with Beech Aircraft for the purchase of 11 Bonanzas. The final hurdle had been surmounted and Keith Kahle was ready to put his little airline into operation with a fleet of 'airliners,' each of which could carry exactly three passengers. Central Airlines inaugurated service on September 15, 1949.

The Bonanzas linked the 25 airports on the initial system, flying at low altitude with pilots using such archaic navigation methods as following railroad tracks. But Central's management played it to the hilt. As with passenger trains, individual flight numbers were given names: Flight 1, which operated between Ft. Worth and Wichita with 10 stops in between, was called "The Oklahoman." Flight 37 from Tulsa to Amarillo was dubbed "The Harvester," and Flight 32 from Tulsa to Ft. Worth was named "The Gusher."

Obviously Central wasn't going to make money operating a flight with 10 stops and only three seats to sell. But the Bonanzas bought Kahle and his company a little time. In 1950, DC-3s were procured and these 24-passenger, twin-engine aircraft, which became the backbone of every successful Local Service fleet, were introduced onto Central's system in November of that year. Over the course of the next few months the DC-3s operated alongside the Bonanzas, gradually replacing them on all routes until the transition was complete by June 1951.

From the start it was obvious that Central's system was weak. The majority of cities on the original network had populations of less than 20,000 (1950 census). The CAB allowed small adjustments to the airline's route map, making the first major changes when the company's certificate came up for renewal. Even when the new route pattern went into effect on April 26, 1953, Central was basically an Oklahoma airline with extensions into Texas and Kansas.

The first true strengthening of Central's system came in May 1954 with the inaugural of service to Ft. Smith, Ark., home of the U.S. Army's Camp Chaffee (later renamed Ft. Chaffee), then in December of that year to Joplin and Kansas City, Mo., and to Fayetteville, Hot Springs and Little Rock, Arkansas. Fayetteville would soon prove itself to be the most productive station served exclusively by Central.

As with all of the Locals, Central could breathe a sigh of relief with the announcement of permanent certification in 1955. No longer would the company be scrutinized by the CAB every three to five years in an effort to determine if the airline should continue to live or be put out of business. Permanent certification made the company more attractive to investors. Central Airlines was here to stay.

The airline issued its first formal Annual Report covering the year 1955. It was noted that, at the end of the year, Central was operating a fleet of nine DC-3s, now standardized to a basic 21-seat configuration. Just as interesting as the summary of the company's accomplishments presented in the report was the appearance of a celebrity name on the company's board of

The reliable Douglas DC-3 served in Central's fleet from 1950 until the merger with Frontier. At the time of the merger, eight of the 19 aircraft in Central's fleet were DC-3s. (Photo from the Tim Williams collection)

directors. Actor Jimmy Stewart, who was an aviation enthusiast and a friend of Keith Kahle's, served on Central's board for the duration of Kahle's presidency.

Lambert Field in St. Louis became a Central Airlines station in February 1956, while Denver and Colorado Springs, Colo., and Liberal, Kan., came on-line in December.

The following year saw Guymon, Okla.; Harrison, Ark.; and Lamar, Colo. added to the network. Topeka, Kan., was put on the route map in 1958, while Plainview and Lubbock, Tex., were added to the system in 1959.

But Central's system was still deficient. It lacked the industrial cities and resort locations served by other Locals. Aside from facilities established by the oil industry, much of Central's territory was agricultural. One area in which the company did excel was in its service to the military. Central counted a fair share of army and air force installations among the cities on its route map.

When it came to statistics such as the number of passengers carried and average load factor per flight, Central usually found itself in last place among the 13 Locals. In his article, "Central's Cure for Last-Place Woes," which appeared in *American Aviation Magazine's* Oct. 6, 1958, issue, Eric Bramley wrote that of the 160 pairs of points served by locals that averaged over 200 passengers a month, Central claimed just two pair.

Bramley went on to state that, adding up all of the passengers boarded by Central at all of its leading cities in 1957, the total was only 78,811. By contrast, Pacific Air Lines boarded 74,000 out of San Francisco, its number one city, alone. Mohawk boarded 114,551 out of New York, and North Central boarded 205,593 out of Chicago.

In addition to $45,000 per year in service mail pay, an additional $2.5 million in subsidy was paid to Central at the time. This was all over-and-above the more than $1.5 million that Central collected in passenger revenue. Keeping Central going was an expensive proposition.

As a prescription to cure its last-place ranking, Bramley went on to write that Keith Kahle and Central's management had a four-point plan: 1) cut competition from trunk lines, 2) increase frequency of service, 3) liberalize operating authority, and 4) add some productive new routes while deleting certain unproductive stops. Of course Kahle and his crew could not implement any of these points without the cooperation of the CAB. It was more of a wish list than a plan.

Central celebrated its tenth anniversary in 1959 with the annual report stating that it was the airline's best year ever, with Central flying "more passengers, more plane miles, more revenue passenger miles, cargo and mail ton miles than in any previous year."

But *Flight Magazine's* review of the Local Service industry for 1959 showed the airline's status from a different perspective. Of the 50 leading cities (in terms of passengers boarded) served exclusively by local airlines, only one, Fayetteville, Ark., number 48 on the list, was a Central station. By the end of 1959, each of the 13 locals, except Central, had boarded more than one million passengers since starting operations years before. Both Allegheny and Piedmont had boarded well over 3 million, and North Central had carried over 4 million. Central boasted just 814,198. In terms of enplaned passengers and passenger revenue generated during 1959, Central was dead last among the 13 Locals.

The airline was operating a fleet of fifteen, 21-passenger, DC-3s at the end of 1959. Nine of the other local service carriers had already added aircraft larger than the *Three* to their fleets. Keith Kahle told Bramley from *American Aviation* that Central's management had looked at the F-27, the Convair, "and others," but the choice of a new craft was difficult. "A plane with double the capacity would have to carry double the loads to maintain the present load factor, and Central's question is:

The final Central timetable announcing the merger with Frontier Airlines. (From the author's collection)

Would the airplane generate this on its own?"

Kahle acknowledged in the annual report for 1959 that modern equipment would be necessary "to develop the fullest traffic potential of selected routes," and disclosed that management was "finalizing economic studies pertaining to... modern turbo-prop flight equipment for presentation to the Board of Directors, the Civil Aeronautics Board, and stockholders."

The company was also betting on the outcome of the CAB's Kansas-Oklahoma Case, expected for a final decision in 1960, to give Central the boost that it would need to exit its position in last place among the Locals. Things could only improve.

As the 1960s dawned, Central Airlines was entering its adolescence. The company turned 11-years old in September 1960 (measured from the date of its first flight) and was lagging in last place among the 13 local service carriers in most areas of comparative measurement. But one area in which Central excelled was in on-time performance. Kahle proudly reported in the 1960 annual report that "Your company has constantly been among the top three of the nation's local airlines in regard to on-time flying... This record is one of great pride with Central employees."

The best news for the new decade was that Central had come out a winner in the CAB's Kansas-Oklahoma Local Service Case. It was inevitable that Central would receive awards in this case since the carrier was the primary local service airline in both states. But the Board's decision gave Central Airlines a boost like it had never had before. Central's system was going to be extended to 11 more airports serving 15 cities.

Several of those new cities were transferred from Continental Air Lines, which had been providing what was essentially local service throughout the state of Kansas for years. Central was now going to be the only airline serving the state's capital city, Topeka. In fact, Central would serve every airport in Kansas certificated for commercial service and hold the distinction of being the only airline at each of those airports except Wichita. The company already served every airport in Oklahoma that was receiving scheduled airline service.

The award also brought Central service to Pueblo, Colo., and to Ft. Leonard Wood, Missouri. But perhaps more significant was slightly liberalized operating authority, granted by the CAB, which would allow Central to fly non-stop or one-stop between certain pairs of cities where before multiple landings had to be included enroute. This would allow the airline to offer better service between some high-density traffic centers. The CAB was employing this technique in an attempt to strengthen not only Central, but the other Locals as well.

New aircraft were needed to help put all of this additional route mileage into operation. Although Kahle had stated that the company was looking into modern, turbo-prop equipment, "after much study" the board of directors decided to buy used Convair 240s from American Airlines instead. While they were not brand new, these 40-passenger, pressurized airliners would be a step-up to bigger aircraft for Central, bringing it on par with other Locals that had opted for second-hand, piston-engined equipment instead of factory-fresh turbo-props. Initially Central purchased three Convairs from American with options for two more. The first of the type arrived in December 1960. The next two were delivered in February of the following year. Central eventually operated eight of the piston-engined 240s.

In addition to the Convairs, Central acquired three more DC-3s to help inaugurate its new routes. While other Locals had increased the capacity of their DC-3s to 24, 26, or 28 seats, Central had settled on the basic layout of 21 chairs – seven rows of two seats on one side of the aisle, and one on the other. The 1960 annual report noted that a new cabin modernization program for the Douglases had been established, decorating the cabin interiors in "three shades of brown blended with gold." Passenger reaction was reported to be "most favorable as to the beauty of the interior."

Service was inaugurated to eight of the new stations on March 13, 1961, and the first Convair went on-line a week later, on March 20, between Forth Worth, Dallas, Lawton/Fort Sill, and Oklahoma City.

Goodland, Kan., came "on-line" on April 3, 1961, Ft. Leonard Wood on April 14, and service was inaugurated at the last of the new stations, Hays, Kan., on May 8. Central now served 46 airports in six states, but the network was still nothing to brag about in terms of passenger-generating potential. Kansas and Oklahoma were blanketed while routes extended into Colorado, Texas, Arkansas and Missouri.

Now that the company's unduplicated route mileage had increased by 40 percent, and 11 new stations had been added to the system, Central Airlines settled down to a period of relative stability, doing what it was created to do: transporting passengers, mail and freight safely and dependably throughout its operating territory as one of the nation's local service air carriers.

Even though the company actively sought additional routes in other CAB cases, no more awards were forthcoming and the airline's map remained practically unchanged for the next few years. The CAB allowed Central to terminate service at five low-volume stations in 1963, and slight route adjustments allowed for more favorable traffic flow, but no more new cities joined the

America's Local Service Airlines

Convair 240s, purchased from American Airlines, entered service with Central on March 20, 1961. Pictured is N74854 (c/n 51), which was delivered to Central from American in 1962. (Photo by Robert Hufford from the AAHS archives, AAHS-33460)

Central system for the rest of the company's existence.

Things were not as stable behind the scenes as they were out on the line. Ozark Air Lines was the local service carrier operating in the territory generally to the east and northeast of Central. Ozark was blessed with a better route system than Central's, feeding passengers from Midwestern cities to both Chicago and St. Louis, and to Minneapolis/St. Paul and Kansas City. In the Kansas-Oklahoma Local Service Case, Central had been granted permission to take over American Airlines' authority to operate from Tulsa, Okla., to St. Louis via Joplin and Springfield, Mo.; a route that American was flying with its own Convair 240s and one that would strengthen Central's system. But Ozark had been serving Springfield and Joplin from St. Louis for many years and that company's management felt that their carrier was a better choice for the route. Ozark appealed the award claiming that Central's "principal executive officer" tried to influence a CAB board member's vote. Central countered that Ozark had conducted a campaign using the public, the news media, and even members of Congress in an attempt to coerce the CAB into reversing its decision. The CAB agreed to reopen the matter for further hearings but then it was disclosed that, despite accusations flying back and forth, discussions were taking place between Central's management and Ozark's management about the feasibility of merging the two carriers.

With the possibility of merger came the chance to make money. F. Kirk Johnson had been Central's savior back in 1949 when he invested in the little airline that had yet to get off of the ground. Since that time he had served as the chairman of the airline's board of directors. Now an investor from Minneapolis named Carl Pohlad came looking for an opportunity and Johnson was ready to sell. In 1962, F. Kirk Johnson divested himself of his controlling interest in Central by selling a large portion of his shares to Pohlad, who assumed control.

But the merger negotiations between Central and Ozark ended without an agreement. The two sides could not concur on the ratio for exchange of stock. The CAB then decided to award American's Tulsa – Joplin – Springfield – St. Louis authority to Ozark instead of Central.

After the prospect of joining the two airlines together was shelved, less than a year after purchasing his shares of Central, Pohlad was ready to sell. Since Central was Keith Kahle's baby, he asked Kahle if he could find a buyer. The person with the money this time around was Andrew A. (Jack) Bradford, a banker from Midland, Tex., and a long-time member of Central's board of directors. Pohlad sold the majority of his stock to Bradford, and a small amount to Kahle, in March 1963. Now Bradford became chairman of the board while Keith Kahle retained the title of president... for the time being.

Meanwhile, Central's need for subsidy escalated with the new Kansas routes. While the company's passenger revenue more than doubled between 1960 and 1962, the editors of *World Airline Record* estimated that in 1962 the government had to shell out more than $14.00 to Central for every $15.65 spent by the average passenger for his ticket. Bringing scheduled air service to small cities on the Great Plains was an expensive proposition.

Jack Bradford obviously wanted to shake things up. In late 1963 he engaged International Management Services, a consulting firm from New York, "to make a survey of the Company's operations and to submit recommendations for improvement in organizational and functional areas" to develop a profit oriented company, as reported in Central's 1963 annual report. According to the chairman's and the president's letter accompanying that report, written on March 16, 1964, "International Management's recommendations... were accepted and, with their assistance, are now being implemented."

By March of 1964, the board of directors had shrunk from 22 members to seven. Among those whose names were no longer on the list of directors was Jimmy Stewart. And Keith Kahle was no longer president. He now held the somewhat empty title of "vice chairman."

Replacing Kahle as president was L.E. Glasgow, whom Bradford had lured from American Airlines. Glasgow assumed the roles of president and chief executive officer of Central Airlines on January 16, 1964, when Kahle was "elected" to his new position.

Apparently the growing divide between Messrs. Bradford and Kahle reached a point beyond reconciliation. In 1964, Keith Kahle left Central Airlines, the company that he had taken, in 20 years, from an idea on paper to an airline operating 24 aircraft, serving 41 airports in six states, grossing over $10 million per annum.

L.E. Glasgow served Central for less than a year and a half. On May 1, 1965, M. Lamar Muse, formerly vice president of

Beginning in 1965, Central's Convair 240s were converted to Convair 600 jet-props with the installation of Rolls-Royce Dart engines. The conversion work was performed by Convair. (Photo by Robert Hufford from the AAHS archives, AAHS-33464)

finance with Southern Airways, assumed the title of president of Central Airlines. Muse had been with Trans-Texas Airways and American Airlines before joining Southern. Now he was in charge of his own airline and he did not waste any time making his presence known.

On May 20, 1965, Muse joined Bradford and other Central executives at Lindbergh Field in San Diego, Calif., to witness the first flight of Convair's model 600 (also referred to as the 240D), a Convair 240 that had been re-equipped with Rolls Royce R. Da. 10/1 Dart turbo-prop engines. Central had committed to upgrading its 240 fleet before Muse's arrival.

The modified Convair enabled a 50 mph increase in cruising speed and a smoother, quieter ride for passengers. The conversion was estimated to save 22 cents per mile in operating costs and to extend the competitive life of the aircraft for 15 years or more. Central purchased the prototype aircraft and signed on to become the world's first operator of the type. Central would refer to the refurbished aircraft in promotional material as the Dart 600.

Central needed a new image. Muse hired Ernest G. Mantz Associates, industrial designers, to take on 'Operation Turnabout,' a program to revitalize the company and to create a new corporate identity. The airline's makeover was timed to be introduced with the arrival of the first of the Convair 600s in the fall of 1965.

The industrial designers found that Central presented an "inconsistent, contradictive graphic image", with the company's logo written differently at almost every station on the system. As reported in Central's employee newspaper, *The Skywriter*, the airline needed a "strong, single corporate identity program creating visual unity [that] will make the advertising dollar work more effectively and will build confidence in the corporate name."

Mantz developed a distinctive new typeface for the company name, selected new corporate colors (two tones of executive metallic gray on white), designed a new corporate symbol (called the Aerograph), and unveiled the entire 'new look' package in October 1965.

The new image was applied to everything from timetables, ticket counters and boarding lounges to aircraft. The aircraft paint scheme, embracing the new corporate colors, gave a "long, sleek look" to Central's Convair 600s and DC-3s. 35 paint jobs were tried out, 11 of them using an actual Convair parked at Lindbergh Field, before the final livery was settled on. New colors ("Indian ceramic, masculine rust, and executive beige") were chosen for aircraft interiors and a modern flight attendant uniform was created to complement the new look.

The Convair 600 entered service with Central on November 30, 1965. The company converted all eight of its 240s to 600 standards and purchased an additional three.

Operation Turnabout encompassed more than just a corporate image and modernized aircraft. Muse was determined to turn Central into a profitable company and his efforts began to bear fruit. Quick response to military demand resulted in "extraordinary gains in charter revenues" for 1966, according to that year's annual report. Passenger response to the Convair 600 was reflected in traffic growth: Central boarded 545,950 passengers in 1966, 105,000 more than the company had boarded the previous year. Load factor rose from 39.9% to 45.9% in the same time frame. And the company posted a net profit of $405,000 for 1966, as opposed to a loss for 1965. Muse and Bradford noted that "1966 will be remembered at Central as the year we moved from our historic position at the bottom of the regional carrier list of revenue passenger miles flown." Things were looking up for Central Airlines.

Meanwhile, the Civil Aeronautics Board was examining

A Central DC-3, N91003, painted in the final color scheme, showing the Aerograph symbol. (Photographer unknown from the author's collection)

a new way to bring revenue to the Locals. The plan involved awarding routes extending from a group of smaller cities within a company's operating area to a large market outside of that traditional zone. Central applied for authority to pick up passengers in many of its exclusive stations and fly them non-stop to Chicago from Topeka and Joplin. The company also applied for extensions to New Orleans and Houston. Such routes were the kind of boost Central needed to expand its passenger base and to increase profits. These would also be perfect markets in which to show off new jets.

Among the short-to-medium range twin-jets available, the company studied Boeing's 737 and British Aircraft Corporation's BAC-111, but settled on the Douglas DC-9-10. A lease was signed with Douglas Aircraft for two of the model to enter service with Central in the fall of 1967. Muse noted in the *Skywriter* that "The acquisition of the DC-9s is the most significant step forward into the jet age for Central and Operation Turnabout."

All of this remaking of the company's image masked a behind-the-scenes attempt to find a merger partner. In September 1966, Ozark and Central once again engaged in negotiations to bring the two companies together with Ozark to be the surviving carrier. That company went so far as to publish a map to show employees how the merged airline's network would look. But talks broke off two months later when Tom Grace, Ozark's president, announced that "the money market… has been tight and we found it untimely to complete the merger."

One can only speculate that, after years of watching Central struggle in 'last place' among the Locals, Jack Bradford was the force behind the merger scheme. It's difficult to believe that Lamar Muse would have worked so hard to polish up Central's image and its bottom line only to make the company an attractive prospect for marriage.

But the polishing worked. Frontier Airlines, Central's neighboring regional carrier (the new term being applied to The Locals) to its west and north, expressed an interest in acquiring the turned-around airline. A deal was struck, the CAB approved, and on October 1, 1967, Central Airlines, which had been carrying passengers in scheduled service for 18 years, ceased to exist as it became part of Frontier Airlines, the surviving carrier. The DC-9s never made it into Central's fleet. At the time of the merger, 11 Convair 600s and eight Douglas DC-3s carried Central's logo.

Had Bradford and Muse kept Central independent, there might have been some shining years ahead if the carrier truly turned around and reduced its subsidy need by flying passengers aboard DC-9s from Fayetteville, Lawton, Topeka and Joplin to Chicago, New Orleans and Houston. But we will never know.

Just a year and a half after the merger, Frontier was operating jets non-stop from Dallas to Denver, Oklahoma City and Kansas City, in the former Central Airlines territory, not to mention non-stop between Denver and Kansas City. Had Central lasted long enough to benefit from this liberalized route authority, the company's prospects may have been a lot brighter.

In the fall of 1967, Central became the first of the 13 local service carriers certificated for permanent operation back in 1955, to disappear. Central lost its identity through merger. It would not be the last of the group to meet the same fate. A string of mergers would reduce the number of 'Regionals' to eight by 1972, as America's local service airlines continued to evolve. ✈

The September-October 1966 issue of the company's newsletter, Central Skywriter, *announced the acquisition of two DC-9-10s to be delivered in August and September of the following year. Instead, Central merged with Frontier in 1967, and the order was cancelled. (From the author's collection)*

CHAPTER 5

FRONTIER AIRLINES

Financing was difficult for many of the feeder airlines just getting off the ground in the late 1940s. The CAB's feeder Certificates of Public Convenience and Necessity were temporary, all of them valid for just three years to begin with. This short-term guarantee did not inspire a willingness on the part of banks or private investors to infuse funds into the companies' coffers. The only guaranteed income was the compensation paid by the government for operating the services, offered in the form of air mail subsidy.

To save money, the two feeders operating in the Rocky Mountain States area, Monarch Air Lines and Challenger Airlines, prudently took it upon themselves to share maintenance, sales and other departmental tasks from their individual headquarters in Denver. The next step seemed natural, to enter into a merger agreement.

Monarch was the brainchild of Ray Wilson, who had received his feeder certificate from the CAB under the moniker of Ray Wilson, Inc. After the certificate award was announced, Ray Wilson, Inc. changed its corporate title to Monarch Air Lines. Of the carriers created specifically for the purpose of starting a certificated feeder operation, Monarch held the distinction of being the first in the nation to get off the ground. Service was inaugurated on November 27, 1946, (another airline, Essair, which later became Pioneer Air Lines, had started service in 1945 with a CAB-issued feeder certificate, but that company was already in business at the time of its award and had previously operated as an intrastate carrier). Monarch operated in the area from Denver and Salt Lake City stretching south through Utah and Colorado into New Mexico with a terminus at Albuquerque.

Challenger's history was a little more convoluted. Summit Airways, organized by Charles Hirsig, won the CAB certificate for feeder service stretching north from Salt Lake City and Denver, via intermediate points in Colorado and Wyoming, to the terminal point of Billings, Montana. Hirsig was killed in an aircraft accident before the certificate was issued to Summit by the CAB in the Rocky Mountain States Area Case. Ownership of the company passed to Fred Manning of Denver.

In the same Rocky Mountain States Case, an airline operating Beechcraft D-18s in intrastate service within Utah had been denied a feeder certificate. That company, originally organized as Midwest Airways, was called Challenger Airlines, and it was owned by George Snyder, Jr., of Salt Lake City. After losing his bid for a feeder certificate, Snyder, with the backing of the Claude Neon Company of New York, purchased control of Summit Airways. Snyder then petitioned the Civil Aeronautics Board to change the name of his newly-acquired certificated carrier, Summit Airways, to Challenger Airlines Company. The CAB approved and Challenger took to the air on May 3, 1947.

Monarch Air Lines acquired this Douglas C-47-DL, msn 4424, in June 1949. It was transferred to Frontier a year later and remained with Frontier until the early 1960s. (Photo from the author's collection)

It was in March 1948 that Monarch and Challenger began combining traffic, sales, and station functions. The following month, maintenance, overhaul and engineering activities were consolidated and then, in May, advertising activities were coordinated with a joint timetable being issued by both carriers, effective July 1, 1948. Challenger moved its headquarters from the Felt Building in Salt Lake City to Stapleton Field in Denver, home of Monarch.

In 1946, another airline began operations wholly within the State of Arizona. As an intrastate carrier, Arizona Airways was under the jurisdiction of the state government and did not need a federally-issued CAB certificate to conduct business. Using three Douglas C-47s converted to DC-3 standards, the airline began service on March 17. With the initial backing of Bob Goldwater, from one of the state's most influential families, and professional golfer, Johnny Bulla, Arizona Airways managed to operate for just less than two years, losing money every step of the way. Without a contract to carry the mail, which would come with a federal certificate, the intrastate carrier was totally dependent on whatever passenger and freight traffic it could solicit. But the point of conducting an intrastate operation was to gain experience and to illustrate the organization's ability to run an airline, an important factor for the CAB to consider when determining which company was fit, willing and able to operate a certificated feeder service.

While the intrastate service ceased operations in 1948, the CAB did award Arizona Airways its coveted Certificate of Public Convenience and Necessity on June 29 of that year. In its petition to the CAB, Arizona Airways had proposed using 14-passenger Lockheed Saturn aircraft, a type that never made

Frontier would continue to maintain a fleet of DC-3s well into the late 1960s. These 3 were photographed at Denver in 1968, wearing their final livery. (Photo from the Tim Williams collection)

it into full-scale production. Instead, Arizona's management stated that the airline could inaugurate service over its newly-certificated feeder routes with its three converted war-surplus DC-3s, which it had used in intrastate service.

Unfortunately for the company, it had lost so much money that finding funds to finance the start-up of the feeder operation became an insurmountable problem. In 1949, the management of Monarch Air Lines proposed acquisition of Arizona Airways through merger and Arizona's board of directors accepted the offer.

Next, the merger of Monarch and Challenger seemed a natural combination, made more inevitable by the sale of Challenger's majority shareholding by the Claude Neon Company to Hal S. Darr, then Monarch's president and primary backer.

Civil Aeronautics Board approval was needed for this combination of a trio of feeder carriers and, after the requisite hearings, the certificates of the three individual companies were reissued as a single certificate for the newly amalgamated company, to be called Frontier Airlines.

Operations began under the title of Frontier Airlines on June 1, 1950, with a system stretching from Billings to Albuquerque, Challenger's and Monarch's former systems, and now extending into Arizona and southwestern New Mexico with a southern terminus at El Paso, Tex., thanks to the authority acquired through the acquisition of Arizona Airways. Frontier was now the nation's largest local service carrier, a term that had replaced the title 'feeder airline'.

Frontier's system underwent minor tweaks manipulated by the CAB in its early years, but the first major expansion came in 1954 when the airline was granted authority to serve the Williston Basin of Montana and North Dakota, an area rich in oil deposits.

The next increase in route mileage came in 1958, and it was significant.

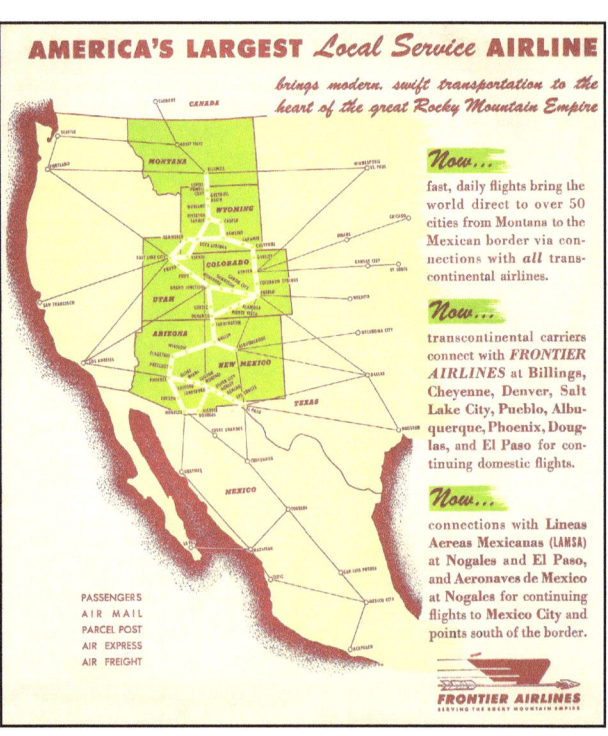

Frontier timetable with route map as of November 1, 1950, five months after the three-way merger took effect. (From the author's collection)

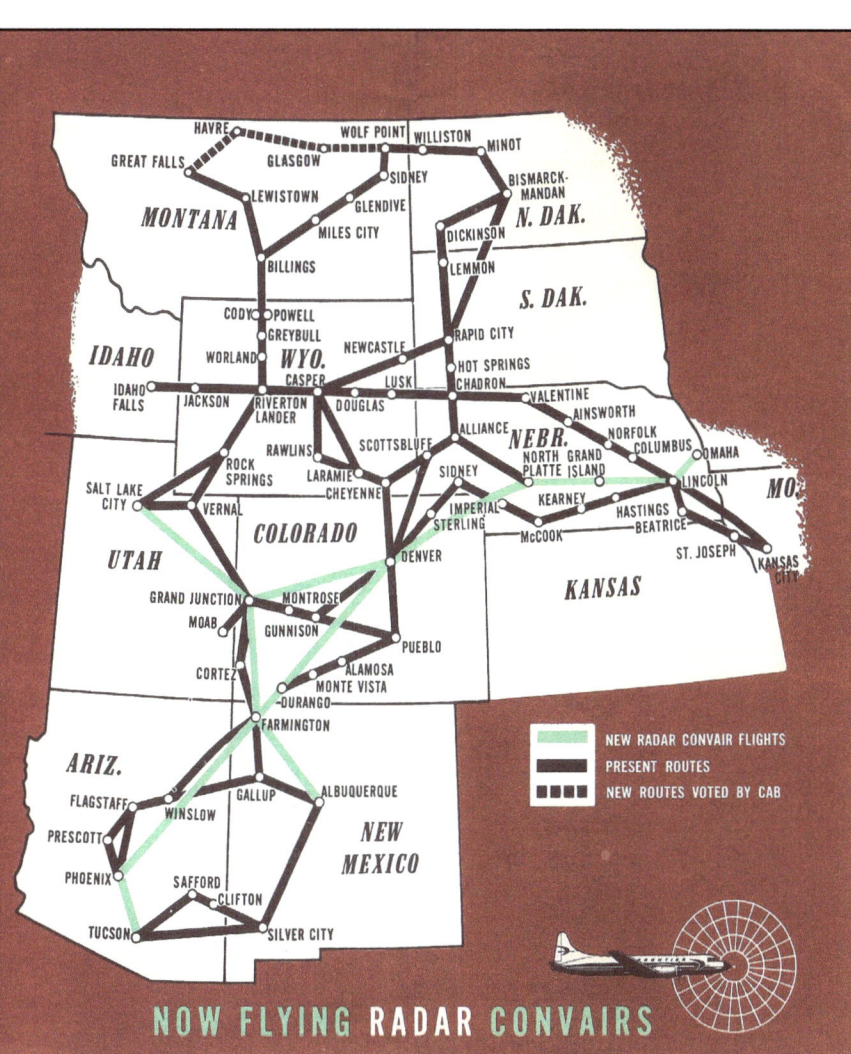

1958 and 1959 saw expansion into Nebraska and North and South Dakota, necessitating the addition of more DC-3s, along with new equipment in the form of Convair 340s. This is reflected in the 1959 route map and schedules featuring the DC-3s and promoting the Convair service. (From the author's collection)

Back in 1946, when the CAB first issued its award to Monarch, the route authority included some cities that could be described as remote or isolated. At the time the CAB stated: *"We believe that the establishment of an air service (to certain isolated communities) will result in a transportation facility so greatly superior to that now available that the patronage will exceed that which could be developed at even larger cities not so greatly isolated."* In 1958, the CAB continued to follow this philosophy when it awarded 27 new cities to Frontier, many of them falling into the category of remote or isolated. This was a result of the Seven States Area Case, a landmark CAB undertaking that transferred numerous small stations from trunk carriers to locals and also tested the truth of the remote city philosophy.

Some of the cities granted air service for the first time were very small. Lemmon, South Dakota's, population (in the 1960 census) was 2,412. Valentine, Neb., had 2,875 residents, while Ainsworth, Neb., boasted 1,982 citizens and Lusk, Wyo., 1,890. As small as they were, all of these cities, and others of similar size, were put onto Frontier's route map in the 1958 award. Service to these communities would have to be heavily subsidized but the hope was that, in time, the service would become indispensable and well-patronized, thus reducing the amount of financial support required. Because of the geography of the West, these communities were trading centers for their surrounding areas and, thus, their importance could be equal to that of cities with 10 times their population back East.

The airline was more than doubling its size and Frontier's own promotional material advised the public that *"communities once isolated by mountains or other geographical barriers, by inadequate surface transportation, or by sheer remoteness have now been brought within minutes of each other and their major trading centers."*

As a safeguard against putting an undue burden on the airlines required to serve small cities, in the same case the CAB put a requirement on the populace of the communities involved to patronize the new air service. Called the *Use It or Lose It* policy, the cities affected were given six months for their citizenry to become acquainted with the new transportation being offered. For the following 12 months, each community would be expected to enplane an average of five passengers per day (1,825 per year) or risk losing certificated air service. Thereafter, the five-passengers per day minimum would have to be sustained *"in the absence of unusual or compelling circumstances"*.

In the same year that the CAB awarded all of these small new stations to Frontier, the company was welcoming a new owner who had purchased majority control and established himself as the new president and chairman of the board. Lewis B. "Bud" Maytag, Jr., was the heir to a washing machine manufacturing fortune. He wanted to run an airline. Maytag's vision for his company was profitable routes among major markets,

America's Local Service Airlines

LEFT: *Timetable effective July 1, 1962, by which time Frontier had eliminated many of the small cities added to its system a few years prior.* MIDDLE: *Lew Dymond would oversee the transformation of piston-engine Convairs to jet-prop 580 standards (April 26, 1964 timetable).* RIGHT: *Dymond would also bring turbojets into the fleet with the addition of Boeing 727s in 1966, as featured on the cover of this July 7, 1969 issue. (From the author's collection)*

not reliance upon government subsidy and, thus, restrictive government control. He apparently had little regard for local service requirements, the basis for Frontier's existence.

In order to meet the needs of its rapidly-expanding network, Frontier scrambled to find additional airplanes. Nine DC-3s were purchased from Trans-Canada Air Lines and refurbished to Frontier's standards. The company had studied and almost purchased new Fairchild F-27 turboprops, but settled instead on second-hand Convair 340s, bought from United Air Lines. The Convair had better operating characteristics for the mountainous region served by Frontier.

The airline's new routes blanketed the state of Nebraska, bringing service to 17 airports in that state alone. The state had expended a lot of money and effort, working with the communities involved, to upgrade airports and establish navigation aids. Service was inaugurated and soon the complaints started. Schedules that were initially convenient for the public were reworked to make same-day return travel impossible and connections impractical. Flights operated late and there were complaints about everything from lost luggage to lack of heating aboard the DC-3s. Maytag was even accused of "sabotaging the service" to make it unattractive to customers, thus preventing it from achieving the *Use It or Lose It* minimums, resulting in a goal of having the CAB eliminate the heavily-subsidized stations from Frontier's network. Whether the accusations were true or not, there were lawsuits filed and injunctions issued. Several of the isolated cities, in which so much promise was seen, were eliminated from Frontier's network before Maytag sold Frontier in 1962 and purchased National Airlines, a company whose size and characteristics more closely matched his aspirations.

Maytag's replacement in the president's office at Frontier was Lew Dymond, who immediately went about the task of "mending fences" with the state of Nebraska and salvaging the service that remained. Ironically, Dymond was recruited from the

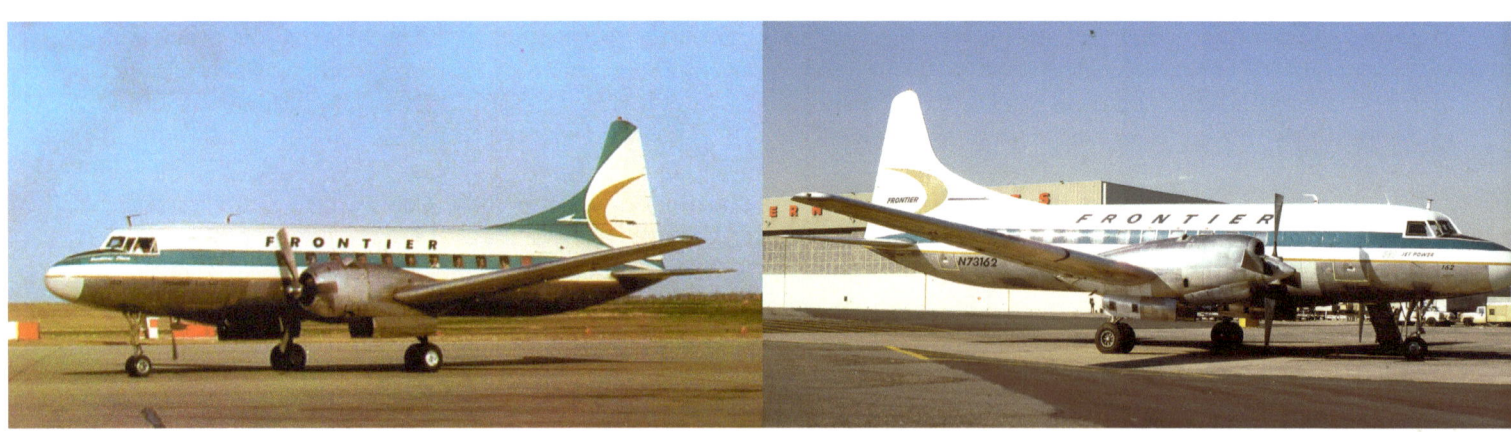

In 1959, Frontier began acquiring second-hand Convair 340s from United Air Lines. The 340 was selected over the Fairchild F-27 because it was better suited for the mountainous region served by Frontier. (Postcard photo from the Bill Thompson collection)

Frontier began upgrading Convair 340s with the installation of Allison turboprop engines. Dubbed the Convair 580, Frontier became the first airline to place this type in service. (Photo from the Tim Williams collection)

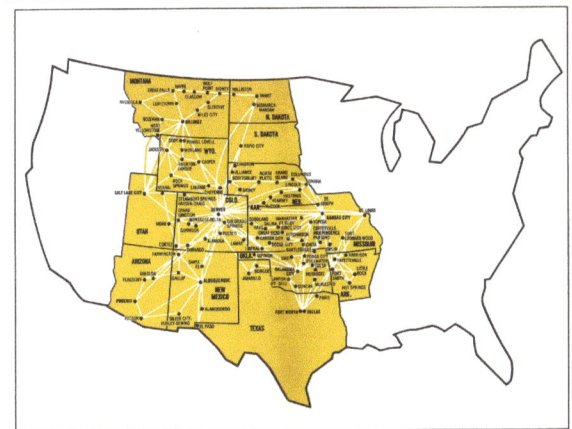

The 1967 merger of Frontier and Central Airlines led to the combined airline serving 114 cities across 14 states. (From the author's collection)

management team at National Airlines.

Under Dymond's leadership, Frontier joined the ranks of local service carriers operating "jet-prop" aircraft when the company contracted to install Allison turboprop engines on its Convair 340s. The resulting conversion was dubbed the Convair 580, and in 1964, Frontier became the first airline in the world to operate the type.

Lew Dymond truly brought Frontier into the jet age in 1966 with the purchase of Boeing 727-100 "Arrowjets." At first deployed on military charters and on scheduled runs between Denver and Grand Junction, and Denver – Lincoln – Kansas City, the 727s were an investment in the company's plans for unsubsidized long-haul service. The CAB was considering looser restrictions on local airline operations between major points on their systems. Frontier would be ready. The company also ordered the stretched -200 series of Boeing's famous tri-jet.

The next major event in Frontier's growth took place in the fall of 1967, and it was a dramatic step. Frontier absorbed, through merger, its neighboring local service carrier, Central Airlines. This was the first merger involving any of the Locals since the 1955 acquisition of Pioneer Air Lines by Continental, and certification of the "permanent" 13 carriers, which took place that year.

The acquisition of Central brought dozens of new stations, hundreds of new employees, and more DC-3s onto Frontier's system just as the airline was trying to reduce the number of DC-3s needed to operate its schedules. The merger also brought the Rolls-Royce Dart-powered Convair 600, a jet-prop conversion of the Convair 240, into the Frontier fleet. Frontier Airlines now served 114 cities in 14 states.

Throughout its history, the majority of Frontier's stock was

Neighboring local service carrier, Central Airlines, was absorbed through merger in the fall of 1967. The natural fit of these two local service airlines is captured in this photo of Frontier DC-3 N65276 and an unidentified Central DC-3 on the ramp at Kansas City (MKC) in June 1962. (Bob Woodling post card photo from the author's collection)

America's Local Service Airlines

  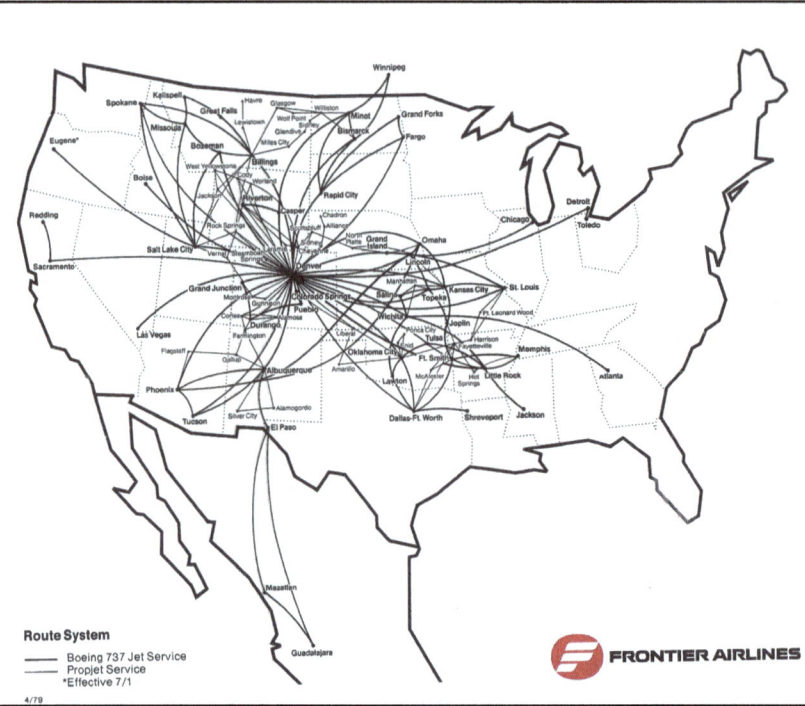

The 1970s saw the "good-times roll" for Frontier, up until deregulation in 1978. Then, like many airlines, Frontier attempted to rapidly expand as seen in the system timetable from May 1979 (middle) and the route map from the same period. (From the author's collection)

bought and sold by different parties. Each change of ownership was usually followed by a change in management, thus Frontier went through several corporate visions during its existence. Lew Dymond left the company in 1968.

After Boeing introduced the 737 twin-jet, Frontier's 727s were gradually withdrawn from service and over the course of the next few years the fleet was trimmed down to two primary types, the Convair 580 and the Boeing 737-200, with 16-passenger deHavilland Twin Otters handling service into a few small stations for several years. The CAB had eased up on Frontier's non-stop and skip-stop restrictions, awarding the airline some major subsidy-free, competitive routes, including Denver – Kansas City, Denver – St. Louis, Denver – Dallas, Denver – Las Vegas and Dallas – Kansas City.

During the 1970s, Frontier's in-flight meal service was enhanced and became noted in the industry. Under the guidance of CEO, Al Feldman, the company enjoyed several years of profitable operation. Then 1978 brought deregulation to the airline industry in the U.S., and Frontier's wild ride began.

Some in the company were looking forward to unfettered skies that lack of a regulating agency would bring. But the reality of deregulation took twists and turns that most in the industry could not foresee. Some airlines, most notably Braniff, expanded recklessly, entering new markets with unrestrained growth. Others began cutting fares dramatically, forcing competing carriers to do likewise.

Frontier entered its own share of new cities, eventually expanding its network from Atlanta to Vancouver, and added the Douglas DC-9 Super 80 (MD-80) to its fleet.

On May 31, 1982, Frontier became an all-turbojet carrier as the last Convair 580 was retired from service. Frontier had experimented with turning over service at some small stations to contract third-level carriers before, but now Combs Airways took over the remaining small stations, operating as Frontier Commuter. Like some other former local service carriers now operating in a deregulated environment, Frontier abandoned its initial reason for being in favor of a chance to compete for passengers travelling long distances, enticing them to connect via the company's Denver hub. Unfortunately, almost every other airline was vying for the same passengers, hoping to route them via their own hubs.

Boeing 737-200s were brought in to replace Frontier's 727s in the late 1960s. These, along with the Convair 580s and deHavilland Twin Otters comprised the fleet for most of the 1970s. (Photo from the AAHS archives)

LEFT: *In an attempt to compete with low-cost, non-union carriers, Frontier Holdings, parent company of Frontier Airlines, created Frontier Horizon. This precipitated a backlash from the unionized employees of Frontier. (From the author's collection)*

RIGHT: *Frontier's Sept. 4, 1985 timetable. One year later the airline would be out of business. (From the author's collection)*

But Frontier was being squeezed at its own hub airport by Continental Airlines, which had been reinvented as a low-cost carrier after it was absorbed by Frank Lorenzo's Texas Air Corporation. In a desperate move, Frontier Holdings, parent company of Frontier Airlines, fought back by launching a low-fare, non-union subsidiary called Frontier Horizon. The result was an internal war when unionized Frontier employees, who had already taken pay cuts themselves, picketed against their low-wage non-union sibling company, Frontier Horizon.

United Air Lines also operated a hub in Denver, so now that Frontier was playing in the big leagues, the competition was coming from two sides. Gone were the days when Frontier "fed" its trunk carrier neighbors. The game had changed entirely and now, thanks to deregulation, it was a fight for survival.

There was talk of merger with Western Airlines. There was dramatic downsizing and the threat of a takeover by Lorenzo's Texas Air. Finally, Frontier was acquired by People Express, a large discount carrier that itself was a product of deregulation. People Express tried remaking Frontier in its own mold by charging passengers for checking their luggage, by selling soft drinks and by eliminating hot meals. But People Express itself was losing money and soon began looking for someone else to sell Frontier to. A deal with United Air Lines fell through and Frontier declared bankruptcy, ceasing operations on August 24, 1986.

Later that year, Lorenzo's Texas Air Corporation (Continental Airlines) purchased the remaining assets of Frontier and absorbed many of Frontier's former employees into Continental's workforce. ✈

With deregulation, Frontier, like many of its competitors, rapidly expanded its route system. The company acquired Douglas MD-80s, like DC-9-82, N9801F, to service many of these routes. (Photo from the AAHS archives, AAHS-P004584)

America's Local Service Airlines

CHAPTER 6

LAKE CENTRAL AIRLINES

Like Amelia Earhart and Jimmy Doolittle, in the 1930s Roscoe Turner was an aviation celebrity. He won numerous air racing trophies, his face graced the cover of *Time Magazine*, and he dressed the part of a dashing pilot, always wearing a powder blue military jacket accessorized with a cap, scarf, boots, and a diamond-studded set of wings. For a final touch to his appearance and reputation, Roscoe Turner traveled with Gilmore, his pet lion cub, named after the Gilmore Oil Co., for whom he did publicity work.

Turner settled in Indianapolis, Ind., where he established a fixed-base operation (FBO) in a building and hangar erected for him by the city at Indianapolis Municipal Airport (renamed Weir-Cook Airport in 1944). The building was dedicated on May 29, 1941, and Roscoe Turner Aeronautical Corp. (RTAC) began offering flying lessons while it also sold, serviced and chartered aircraft.

When the United States entered World War II, Turner's company began training pilots for the military via the Civilian Pilot Training Program and later through the War Training Service Program. RTAC graduated 3,500 new fliers for the armed forces by 1944.

Turner had some airline experience under his belt. In 1929, he had been the manager of operations for an outfit called Nevada Air Lines that operated Reno – Bishop – Los Angeles and Reno – Tonopah – Las Vegas. Then, for a couple of months in 1944, RTAC had maintained a non-scheduled 'charter' service between Detroit and Memphis via intermediate points until the Civil Aeronautics Board (CAB) shut the unauthorized operation down. But Roscoe Turner's brief forays into the airline business, his pilot-training contribution to the war effort and, perhaps most of all, his reputation impressed the CAB when he applied for a feeder airline certificate.

Turner wanted to establish a system of air routes to smaller communities in the same manner that the interurban railroads had fanned out from the city in previous decades. From the 1910s through the 1930s, Indianapolis had been famous for being the heart of an electric railway network that spread out across the state of Indiana from the city's big downtown Traction Terminal. RTAC applied to the CAB for nine routes that would serve 94 cities, 73 of which would be receiving service for the first time. The proposed network would span 2,463 miles and was planned for operation with a fleet of 14 Beech D-18S aircraft flying under visual flight rules (VFR). All aircraft would be serviced in the RTAC shops at Weir-Cook Airport.

When the CAB handed down its ruling in the Great Lakes Area Service Case on September 3, 1947, it was Roscoe Turner Aeronautical Corporation that was selected over other applicants to provide feeder service from its base at Indianapolis. The award was for a much smaller network than the one originally envisioned by Turner: two routes intersecting at Indianapolis that would have terminal points at Chicago and Louisville, Grand Rapids and Cincinnati. Both routes would serve several intermediate points in addition to Indianapolis.

It was a good thing that Turner's award was for a smaller system than the one he applied for. Finding financing for a new, experimental airline concept was not an easy task. The CAB issued RTAC's feeder certificate in February 1948, and, like all of the other feeder certificates being issued for airlines around the country, it was temporary, valid for just three years, after which time the entire operation would be scrutinized before the CAB decided

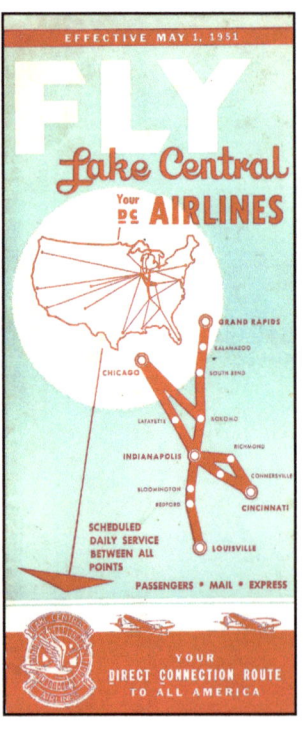

LEFT: *Turner Airlines, with Roscoe Turner as president, inaugurated service in November 1949, but by early 1950 was already beginning to promote its system as the "Lake Central Route"* RIGHT: *Turner Airlines officially became Lake Central Airlines in November 1950, operating along the routes shown on the cover of this May 1, 1951 timetable. (From the author's collection)*

Like all of the other permanently-certificated local service airlines, Lake Central operated Douglas DC-3s. N12716 is seen here in the company's early livery. (From the AAHS archives, AAHS-P006030)

whether or not the certificate should be renewed.

The availability of war surplus C-47s, converted to 21-passenger Douglas DC-3 standards, made that aircraft the favored choice of most of the new Feeders as the local service concept was evolving. The need to accommodate several passengers boarding at each intermediate point made aircraft with fewer than 10 seats look less desirable. Unfortunately for Turner, some of the airports on his new "system" were not yet able to accommodate aircraft as large as the DC-3.

Several other new Feeders were also struggling with financing and aircraft issues. Reacting to the problem, the CAB issued an order on June 8, 1949, stating that single-engine aircraft would be approved for scheduled service on relatively short trips "where the topography of the area is favorable to their operation." This was a stopgap measure intended to help the new airlines get into operation, with larger aircraft to be purchased when airport facilities and financial arrangements had improved. But a single-engine Beech Bonanza or Cessna 190 accommodating only three or four passengers was not an appropriate aircraft for scheduled service. Still, the ruling would allow Turner to serve the smaller airports on his system until they had been sufficiently improved to allow DC-3 operations.

Now that the aircraft issue was settled, at least temporarily, financing still had to be dealt with. Roscoe Turner found his financial saviors in the form of a couple of brothers named Weesner. Roscoe Paul Weesner ("Paul") was a lieutenant commander in the U.S. Naval Reserve and the president of Nationwide Air Transport Service (NATS), a non-scheduled airline also known as a large irregular carrier. John Verlin Weesner ("John") had been a captain in the U.S. Army Air Force and was the president of Nationwide Airlines, a scheduled intrastate carrier operating in Michigan.

Large Irregular Carriers did not carry Certificates of Public Convenience and Necessity issued by the CAB and they were prohibited from participating in regularly scheduled operations except in circumstances with severe restrictions. They were relegated to the sphere of charter operations, and some in the ranks of the certificated airlines derided them as "fly-by-nights" or "non-skeds". However, Paul Weesner had built NATS into an impressive operation flying mostly cargo in a fleet that consisted of 14 DC-3s by 1949. NATS also owned two subsidiary companies that performed aircraft overhaul and maintenance. Paul had expressed his displeasure with the CAB before, during testimony at CAB hearings. He felt that the CAB was too restrictive when it came to oversight of the irregular carriers.

Intrastate airlines generally operate without CAB certificates and, thus, without air mail contracts since their service area is totally within the boundaries of a single state. Therefore, they are under the supervision of the state's regulatory agency. Nationwide Airlines operated scheduled flights connecting Detroit City Airport with cities on the Upper Peninsula (U.P.) of Michigan, via Lansing.

Roscoe Turner had the coveted Certificate of Public Convenience and Necessity and the guarantee of federal air mail subsidy that came with it, while the Weesner brothers had money and airplanes. Together they formed a new company called

Lake Central introduced this modern red-white-blue livery in the late 1950s. Pictured is DC-3 N18667. (From the author's collection)

Turner Airlines, with RTAC holding 25 percent interest and the Weesners owning the balance. The CAB transferred RTAC's certificate to Turner Airlines on the condition that Paul divest himself of control of NATS within six months, eliminating the possibility of any common control of both Turner Airlines and NATS. The newly certificated feeder airlines were governed and nurtured every step of the way by the CAB. The CAB did not want any shady mingling of the non-sked's resources and the feeder's finances.

Of the 14 NATS DC-3s, four of those, plus spares and radio and communication equipment, were to be made available to Turner Airlines. The new company had Roscoe Turner as its president, now mainly just a figurehead, with Paul Weesner running the show as executive vice president. John Weesner was also a vice president.

Turner Airlines inaugurated service on November 12, 1949, with two daily round-trips between Indianapolis and Grand Rapids via Kokomo, South Bend and Kalamazoo. This was the only segment on which every airport could handle the "big" DC-3s.

Service from Chicago to Louisville via Lafayette, Indianapolis and Bloomington, using single-engine Beechcraft Bonanzas, was inaugurated on January 30, 1950. The airports at Lafayette and Bloomington could not yet accommodate the Douglases. The remaining segment between Indianapolis and Cincinnati via Connersville, Ind., was put into operation with Bonanzas in February. Bloomington's and Lafayette's airports were upgraded for DC-3s during the year leaving Connersville and, thus, the Indianapolis – Connersville – Cincinnati segment the only one still requiring the Bonanzas. The type would remain in the fleet to service that route until August 1952.

In November 1950, the company officially changed its name to Lake Central Airlines (LCA). Even before the official name change, the airline had begun using the slogan, the "Lake Central Route," painting the words above the window band on its DC-3s. Roscoe Turner's association with the airline that he founded would end completely when he sold his share of the company to the Weesners.

In October 1950, the airline leased a Curtiss C-46 to join two of its DC-3s in a military Commercial Air Movement (CAM) operation. The contract required the transportation of personnel among various air force bases and airports. This was a charter commission from the United States government that brought a significant amount of revenue into LCA's coffers. Two DC-3s and the C-46 were assigned to the operation and the company stationed two of its personnel in San Antonio, Tex., to handle the large number of flights into and out of that city as part of the movement. Unfortunately, the C-46 in question was leased from Nationwide Air Transport Service (NATS).

It appeared that the CAB had been justified in its concern about interlocking activity. When the CAB examined Lake Central's books, they found that depreciation of the C-46's modification costs had been improperly charged to Lake Central's account for the CAM operation. But that was the tip of the iceberg. Both of the aircraft overhaul companies owned by NATS had performed engine maintenance for Lake Central or had billed LCA for parts and service. Bookkeeping adjustments had to be made by the CAB for thousands of dollars worth of transactions incorrectly charged to Lake Central's accounts. The feeder carriers were tightly regulated and were subsidized with public funds. An air carrier with a Certificate of Public Convenience and Necessity could not be as cavalier about its bookkeeping practices as could a non-scheduled airline.

Then there was the relationship between John Weesner's intrastate carrier, Nationwide Airlines, and Lake Central. The CAB found that Nationwide Airlines had leased DC-3s to LCA. In the CAB's Michigan-Wisconsin Service Case, both Lake Central Airlines and Nationwide Airlines submitted identical applications for authority to operate between Detroit and the U.P. via Lansing and Grand Rapids, Mich., and Green Bay, Wisconsin. If either carrier won the authority, the Weesners would be in charge. As it turned out, the route was given to Wisconsin Central Airlines.

Even after the books had been straightened out Lake Central was bleeding red ink. Furthermore, the casual transactions among all of the Weesner companies and the flagrant violation of the CAB's edict requiring separation of LCA and NATS interests caused the CAB to question the competence of Lake Central's management and their ability to keep the airline operating. The Civil Aeronautics Board issued a directive: If the Weesners could find a buyer for Lake Central and would step down from management, the company might be given a reprieve and authority to expand. But Lake Central was on life support and, as if to add insult to injury, one of the Bonanzas (N8765A) crashed at Indianapolis on August 1, 1952, when the small airplane was caught in the wake turbulence of a Constellation. Fortunately, all three aboard survived.

Paul Weesner sold Nationwide Air Transport Service (NATS) to Resort Airlines, a carrier that offered all-inclusive tours to passengers aboard C-46s, then took an executive position with Resort. Having Paul and NATS removed from Lake Central's sphere of influence should have made the CAB happy, but Paul's brother, John, was now in charge of Lake Central.

By 1954, Lake Central was serving 26 cities and the airline had adopted a new slogan: "Serving the Industrial Heart of the Nation." (From the author's collection)

In early 1957, Lake Central added Detroit, Mich., Buffalo, N.Y., and Toledo, Ohio, to its route system and the all-DC-3 fleet was increased to 10 aircraft. (From the author's collection)

To appease the CAB, on November 18, 1952, the Weesners entered into a trust agreement with Harry V. Wade, president of Standard Life Insurance Co. of Indianapolis. Mr. Wade would hold, as trustee, the vast majority of Lake Central's stock, most of it still owned by the Weesners, and manage reorganization of the company. All officers and directors of Lake Central submitted their resignations and Mr. Wade rebuilt the company's board of directors.

Dr. Robert B. Stewart, vice-president and treasurer of Purdue University, was one of the people who joined LCA's new board. Purdue, with its world-renowned School of Aeronautics, had tried to purchase Mid-West Airlines, a failing feeder carrier based in Des Moines, Iowa, in order to rehabilitate that company and use it as "a live laboratory to study airline transportation and its various ramifications." But the CAB saw Mid-West as a lost cause and did not renew the carrier's certificate.

Next, the university offered its assistance to Wisconsin Central Airlines, another struggling feeder that had recently transitioned from Lockheed L-10A Electras to DC-3s, and had undergone a rapid route expansion, taking on a lot of debt in the process. Dr. Stewart wound up on that airline's board after Purdue agreed to sell nine DC-3s to Wisconsin Central and take up the balance of an insurance company loan. With its expanded network and growing fleet of DC-3s, Wisconsin Central changed its name to North Central Airlines.

Dr. Stewart was now serving on the boards of both North Central and Lake Central, so it was no surprise that the next announcement was an offer by North Central to buy Lake Central, with the intent of merging the two Purdue-influenced companies together. North Central would be the surviving carrier.

But the CAB was watching Lake Central's rehabilitation. The CAB transferred several small stations in Ohio and Indiana from TWA to LCA, and gave the airline entry into the industrial markets of Pittsburgh, Cleveland, and Youngstown. The CAB renewed Lake Central's certificate only through December 31, 1954, but it was a show of reserved confidence that the airline could turn itself around.

Lake Central began its expansion and adopted a new slogan, "Serving the Industrial Heart of the Nation." The little airline was now serving some cities of substance with dynamic smaller stations in between presenting a perfect example of the local airline model. The company had its share of problems but Lake Central's revenue passenger load continued to climb.

The management and staff of Lake Central worked hard to build the airline's reputation and offer the best service they could. But, with all of the stock tied up in a trust fund waiting for North Central to purchase it, the airline was stymied. Meanwhile, North Central Airlines was having its own problems with losses exceeding $100,000 in 1953, for the second year in a row. On June 25, 1954, after waiting over a year and a half for North Central to act, the employees of Lake Central entered into an agreement with the trust holding LCA's stock. Asserting that North Central had breached its contract by not following through on its promise to purchase LCA, the Lake Central Employee Stock Purchase Group was formed. The group's intent was to buy 80,954 shares, the vast majority, of Lake Central's common

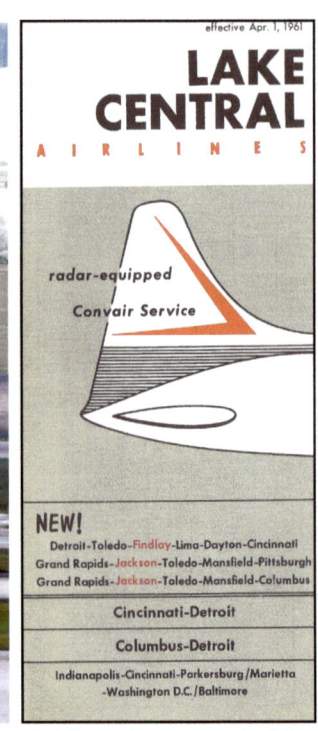

LEFT: *In 1960, Lake Central adopted a new corporate logo.* CENTER: *(Top) The search for a DC-3 replacement led the company to bet its future on the French-built Nord 262, introduced into service on Halloween Day 1965. (Bottom) The company's Convair 340s were upgraded to jet-prop 580 standards, starting in 1966.* RIGHT: *1961 brought the greatest expansion in the company's history as 14 new stations came on-line, employee ranks doubled, and Convair 340s were added to the fleet. (Schedules from the author's collection, photos from the Tim Williams collection)*

stock from the Weesners, via the trustee, at the price of $1 per share to be paid for through payroll deduction. North Central countered that its acquisition agreement was senior to the employee stock purchase plan and was legally enforceable. But talk was cheap as long as North Central didn't put up any money to back its offer. North Central would continue to challenge the employee group and the trust in court for its "right" to purchase Lake Central for several more years, but the employees began purchasing their company's stock and, in 1955, a new slogan, "America's Only Employee-Owned Airline," began to grace timetables and advertising materials.

Back at North Central, Purdue's Dr. Stewart left the board of directors. However, he would remain on Lake Central's board for several years to come.

Then, on May 19, 1955, President Dwight D. Eisenhower signed legislation granting permanent certification to America's "grandfathered" Local Service (Feeder) Carriers. Thirteen airlines qualified for a permanent Certificate of Convenience and Necessity, including Lake Central. LCA was now an established entity with a permanent certificate guaranteeing financiers that the airline was here to stay. Investors still couldn't touch the stock while it was tied up in the trust, challenged by North Central and being purchased by Lake Central's own employees, but now there was hope that the company and its employees would soon be able to generate cash for fleet and route expansion. After the formal CAB process, the company's permanent status became effective as of January 24, 1956.

Without outside investors putting money into the company, with litigation constantly hanging over its head from North Central, and with the CAB controlling the company's growth based on LCA's ability to function under such conditions, the airline slowly added more stations to its route system. The important terminals of Buffalo, N.Y., and Detroit, Mich., were added in 1957. Lake Central leased two DC-3s from the Navy in the summer of 1957, increasing the company's all-DC-3 fleet to a total of 10 aircraft.

The airline saved money any way possible, performing its own airframe and accessory overhaul and printing all company material, including timetables, in its own print shop. LCA raised what money it could by offering 'convertible subordinated debentures' for sale. These were financial instruments that would be converted to common stock at $3 per share, if and when Lake Central won its court battle against North Central.

In 1959, the court ruled in favor of Lake Central and its employees for the final time. The threat of a North Central takeover was removed and the voting trust that had been established back in 1952 was dissolved on January 7, 1960. The employees of Lake Central Airlines could now do what they wanted with what were truly their own shares of LCA stock and the company could finally generate revenue by offering more shares to the public. Lake Central was one of the smallest of the 13 Local Service Carriers, operating a fleet of just 12 Douglas DC-3s at the beginning of 1960, but things were about to change.

An evolution of marketing messages is portrayed in these three timetables, from "We pamper passengers throughout Mid-Central U.S.A." to "The airline with a heart." LEFT to RIGHT: January 5, 1964 timetable; September 1, 1965 timetable; January 3, 1968 timetable. Note the subtle change to the logo between 1965 and 1968. (From the author's collection)

The Civil Aeronautics Board was ready to help Lake Central live up to its potential. With awards that transferred routes and stations from trunk carriers to LCA, and with further authority to serve more new stations, Lake Central embarked on its 1961 expansion, the largest in the company's history. The airline added seven new airports in West Virginia alone as its system was extended eastward to Washington (National) and Baltimore (Friendship). New north-south authority to operate Buffalo – Erie – Pittsburgh and Detroit – Toledo – Columbus – Cincinnati was granted. Evansville, in southernmost Indiana, was added to the network as was a route from Grand Rapids to Pittsburgh via intermediate points. Every city certificated for airline service in the state of Ohio, and all but two in Indiana, would now be on Lake Central's route map. LCA's system mileage doubled from 2,175 to 4,309 with the addition of 14 new stations.

A new issue of stock was offered and loans were secured from Indiana banks. The company doubled its employee ranks, from 450 to 900, and bought eight additional, second-hand DC-3s. For its more heavily-travelled routes, the airline was ready to purchase Convairs. Initially the plan was for Lake Central to be one of two carriers to introduce the 52-passenger Allison prop-jet Convair (later called the Convair 580, a turboprop conversion of the Convair 340) to the world. But problems arose and the Allison order was cancelled. LCA purchased five traditional piston-engine Convair 340s from United Air Lines.

The expansion officially began on January 1, 1961. The Convair 340s were introduced into the timetable on March 1, and the expansion was completed on October 29, with the introduction of service to Martinsburg, West Virginia.

The airline spent the next few years dutifully serving its role as one of America's local service airlines. Instead of jumping into the race for jets, Lake Central continued to look for the elusive DC-3 replacement, a modern aircraft with capacity comparable to the aging *Gooney Bird*, but with better passenger amenities and lower operating costs.

Lloyd Hartman, LCA's president in the mid-1960s, thought he had found the perfect design in the French-built Nord 262, an upgrade of the 260 Super Broussard design powered by two Turbomeca Bastan 6-C1 turboprop engines driving Ratier-Figeac three-blade, variable pitch propellers. The 262 could carry 27 passengers in pressurized, air-conditioned comfort with such amenities as built-in tray tables and pull-down window shades. The aircraft had only a 500-mile range but its airport runway requirement was a short 3,770 feet at maximum gross takeoff weight at sea level with standard temperature. Takeoff performance was enhanced by a water-methanol mixture injected into the engines. Hartman had such faith in the type that he signed for exclusive sales rights in North America, purchasing several examples for the airline's own use. He was betting Lake Central's future on the new aircraft.

Company publicity spoke of the "grand old lady" (the DC-3) being replaced by a new French model. Unfortunately, the new French model would turn out to be a very temperamental lady, and the publicity for Lake Central would be mostly of the unwanted kind.

The Nord 262 received its FAA type certificate for operation in the U.S. on March 15, 1965. Lake Central's initial order was for eight, with financing in place for a total of 13 262s. The plan was for the Nords to totally replace LCA's DC-3 fleet by mid-1966. Fanfare accompanied the arrival of the first 262 in Indianapolis and, after training and familiarization, Lake Central introduced its new bird into scheduled service on October 31, 1965, Halloween Day - appropriate timing for the nightmare that lay ahead.

As with many new aircraft, the Nords experienced maintenance teething problems resulting in delays and cancellations. Then, much more serious issues with the Turbomeca Bastan power plants started to surface as catastrophic engine failures began to occur in flight. The last two engine explosions happened a week apart in August 1966, one near Morgantown, the other near Martinsburg, West Virginia. Parts of the engine penetrated

New slogans and a heart logo were not enough to stem the red ink. Lake Central succumbed to merger with Allegheny in July 1968. (From the author's collection)

One of Lake Central's Nord 262s displays the heart logo on its tail. (From the Tim Williams collection)

the fuselage and entered the cabin in both instances, seriously injuring two passengers in the Morgantown incident. Safe landings followed each episode but the entire Nord fleet had to be grounded until the source of the trouble was identified. The reliable DC-3s were pressed back into service.

Corrosion caused by the water-methanol injection system was the culprit in the Nord engine failures and the aircraft remained grounded for several months while Nord engineers resolved the problem. The French planes were returned to service in February 1967 carrying the new moniker, Nord IIs. But the damage had been done to the type's image and the Nords never caught on as a viable DC-3 replacement in the U.S. market.

While the Nords were grounded, Lake Central began conversion of its Convair 340s to Allison jet-prop Convair 580 standards. The company focused its advertising on the renovated Convairs, attempting to downplay the Nord issue. The public's attention was now being directed to the company's 580s, advertised on timetable covers with an image of their distinctive propeller blades and Lake Central's logo in the center of the prop hub. Sadly, it would be those distinctive blades and prop hub that would write the next chapter in Lake Central's history.

On March 5, 1967, Convair 580 registration number N73130, operating as flight 527 on a leg between Columbus, Ohio, and Toledo, disappeared from radar screens as it made its way through the evening sky in western Ohio. Thirty-eight people (35 passengers plus a crew of 3) lost their lives that night in Lake Central's first and only fatal accident. Reminiscent of the Nord in-flight engine failures, an improperly-machined propeller blade had failed on the right engine causing all four blades to separate from the hub, one of which caused catastrophic damage to the fuselage as it sliced through the cabin of the aircraft. A warning telegram from the FAA had been received by Lake Central and other operators of the 580 just two days prior: check propeller hydraulic fluid for signs of steel powder or filings. A problem with some of the 580 props had been reported to the agency by outside sources on March 2. The hydraulic fluid in N73130's right engine had passed inspection and, even though Lake Central was not at fault, the accident was another blow to the company's reputation.

Between September 1965 and March 1967, Perry R. Bass of Ft. Worth, Tex., and his associates had acquired approximately 25 percent of Lake Central's outstanding common stock. The Bass interests also owned 6.6 percent of the common stock of Allegheny Airlines (121,000 shares) with warrants to purchase 41,000 additional shares. Lloyd Hartman, who had led Lake Central since 1962, was replaced as president by L. Thomas Ferguson, recruited from the executive ranks of Allegheny. But before being ousted as president, Hartman had negotiated with Boeing Aircraft to truly bring Lake Central into the jet age. He signed an agreement to purchase three Boeing 737-200s with the intent of putting them into service on LCA's most heavily-traveled routes. The order was cancelled as events unfolded.

In the fall of 1967, a new advertising campaign was introduced as Lake Central became "the airline with a heart." As part of the campaign, the company began painting the vertical fins of the 580s and the Nords bright red with a white heart emblem in the center.

But catchy phrases and airplanes with hearts on their tails were not enough to stop the financial losses or to prevent what appeared to be inevitable. On October 18, 1967, Lake Central and Allegheny filed a joint application with the Civil Aeronautics Board requesting permission to merge. Allegheny would be the surviving carrier. The Bass interests had two members sitting on Lake Central's board of directors. Leslie O. Barnes, the president of Allegheny, testified before the CAB that, even though Mr. Bass and his associates would own about 14 percent of the common stock of the surviving company, this investment would not constitute control of Allegheny "by any stretch of the imagination".

The stockholders of both airlines overwhelmingly approved the merger on March 14, 1968. Mr. Ferguson, LCA's president, would find himself returning to be among the familiar faces in Allegheny's executive offices once again.

On July 1, Lake Central's identity was lost as Allegheny issued the first timetable of the merged companies. The "airline with a heart" was now just a memory as its system was incorporated into Allegheny's route map above the advertising copy: "People in a hurry fly Allegheny." ✈

CHAPTER 7

MOHAWK AIRLINES

Several of the local service carriers were the result of a single man's vision, the founder of the company, who was usually the same person that remained at the helm for most of the airline's existence. Mohawk's story is the tale of two men: the founder, Cecil S. Robinson (who went by his initials, C.S.), and the person who took over from him, Robert E. Peach.

Robinson was a civil engineer and an aerial photographer from Ithaca, N.Y., the hometown of Cornell University. When taking photographs while airborne he became frustrated by the fact that the rubber base on which his camera was mounted would freeze and stiffen at high altitudes causing the camera to shake along with the vibration of the airplane. He designed a base made out of spun steel to absorb the movement of the airplane allowing his camera to remain steady. Robinson obtained a patent for the apparatus, which he called *Vibrashock*, and his invention quickly caught the government's attention as a product that could be used to stabilize instruments aboard military aircraft.

He created the Robinson Aviation Company, based in Ithaca, and established a factory in northern New Jersey, across the Hudson River from New York City, to manufacture his Vibrashock product. Robinson's need to commute between his two locations prompted the purchase of, first, one Fairchild F-24, then a second. Businessmen from Ithaca soon began to request space aboard his flights between Ithaca and Teterboro, the airport he used in the New York metropolitan area that was closest to his New Jersey factory. The next logical step in Robinson's view was to establish a scheduled service.

Robinson Aviation applied for a feeder certificate from the Civil Aeronautics Board (CAB) in 1945 in order to operate under federal jurisdiction with the desire for routes extending outside the State of New York and with the possibility of receiving an air mail contract. Until the CAB acted on Robinson's application, passengers could be transported between Ithaca and New York City solely as an intrastate operation with licensing from the State of New York.

To function as an intrastate carrier, Robinson's scheduled flights would utilize Roosevelt Field (now the site of a shopping mall of the same name) as their New York City airport. The field was located on Long Island and, thus, within the State of New York. Service between Ithaca and Roosevelt Field began on April 6, 1945. In the fall of that year, two twin-engine Cessna T-50s were acquired to augment the Fairchilds.

One of the first pilots hired by Robinson was a 25-year old law student from Cornell University named Robert E. (Bob) Peach. Peach had received his pilot training in the Navy during World War II, and he was joining this new airline venture at its very beginning. He would stay with it almost until the end of its existence.

Four brand new Beechcraft D-18s, which carried two pilots and could accommodate seven passengers, were acquired to upgrade the fleet in the spring of 1946. Trading now as Robinson Airlines, the company paid homage to the Native American history of the region it served by christening itself the "Route of the Air Chiefs".

At first a big part of Robinson's financial backing came from Cornell University and from Ithaca's Grange League Federation. As the airline grew and filled the air transport needs of the nearby Triple Cities: Binghamton, Endicott, and Johnson City, N.Y., the major businesses of those cities (Link Aviation Devices, manufacturers of the Link Trainer; International Business Machines – IBM; and the Endicott-Johnson Shoe Company) all invested in Robinson's service.

Robinson carried 12,000 passengers in 1946 and 22,000 in 1947, transporting them from Binghamton and Ithaca to New York City, Buffalo, and Albany. The part of New York State that C.S. Robinson's airline served was obviously ready for air transportation, as demonstrated by the fact that while 2,100 people took advantage of Robinson's service during May 1947, another 1,500 potential customers had to be turned away that month because of insufficient space.

Robinson purchased three 21-passenger Douglas DC-3s from Pan American-Grace Airways (PANAGRA), in 1947 to help cope with the demand.

The following year, impressed with the little airline's stunning operation, the CAB chose Robinson in the Middle Atlantic Area Case to

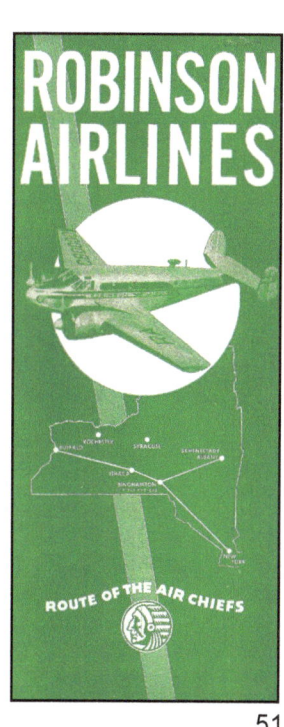

Robinson Airlines operated initially as an intrastate carrier within the confines of New York State. This is the company's timetable effective April 27, 1947. (From the author's collection)

America's Local Service Airlines

LEFT: *The August 30, 1950 timetable announces the addition of Utica / Rome, N.Y. to Robinson's system.* MIDDLE / RIGHT: *In 1954, Mohawk acquired a Sikorsky S-55 helicopter that was used for three months operating between Newark Airport and Jennie Grossinger Air Field in Liberty, N.Y. (From the author's collection)*

operate feeder routes throughout New York State, adding such important stations as Syracuse, Rochester, and Elmira/Corning to the little airline's network. Robinson was now a certificated feeder, or 'local service', air carrier.

The technicality of transferring the airline's new certificate from Robinson Aviation, the applicant, to Robinson Airlines, the operating company, took place on November 9, 1948. With the certificate came the responsibility of carrying the mail and the coveted guarantee of federal air mail subsidy. Robinson transferred New York City service from Roosevelt Field to Teterboro and provided limousine service for its passengers between that airport and Manhattan. The company also held a permit as a federally-approved messenger service to transport the mail between Teterboro Airport and the New York City Post Office.

C.S. Robinson traded his title of company president for a new position as chairman of the board. He then resigned from the airline that he had founded after what was described as a "result of disagreement with established policy" of the board of directors. Day-to-day operation of Robinson Airlines had been turned over to Bob Peach, described as young and energetic. Peach's title was executive vice president and general manager.

In 1950, Robinson moved its New York City operations from Teterboro to Newark Airport, finally allowing for direct interline connections to and from the carriers serving that major airport.

On August 30, 1950, a new station was added to the Robinson network, one that would play a big role in the company's future. Utica / Rome, N.Y., served through Oneida County Airport, was another market with great potential just waiting for air service to connect it with New York City. Robinson Airlines was selected to fill that need.

Unlike some of the other young feeder carriers, Robinson had no problem growing its customer base. The densely-populated territory served by Robinson was home to many diverse industries. Carefully prepared schedules offered a perfect local airline experience. Residents of the upstate communities could fly to New York in the morning, spend the day, then return home in late afternoon or early evening. New York City businessmen could experience the same pattern in reverse. The company increased seating capacity aboard its DC-3s from 21 to 24 and added self-contained 'airstair' doors that would become standard equipment on the type for all local service operators. The fleet was increased to nine DC-3s in 1951.

After C.S. Robinson's departure from the airline, it made sense to seek a new name for the company. The top three choices, selected by employees, were Atlantic Airlines, Yankee Airlines, and Mohawk Airlines. In keeping with the "Air Chief" theme of its aircraft, the Native American name was chosen and submitted to the CAB. Effective August 23, 1952, the CAB officially recognized the certificate holder as Mohawk Airlines, Inc.

In 1953, Mohawk's system finally left the states of New York and New Jersey when authority was given to serve Bradford, Penn., from Newark via Binghamton / Endicott / Johnson City and Elmira / Corning, New York.

Mohawk also benefited from the demise of EW Wiggins Airways, the feeder carrier originally certificated to serve

LEFT: *With the addition of Convair 440s in 1959, Mohawk adopted an aircraft paint scheme incorporating new corporate colors of black-and-gold, seen here on September 1959 and June 1960 timetables.* ABOVE: *Mohawk began phasing out DC-3s in the late 1950s, but retained two, which the company decked out in a Gay Nineties "Gas Light Service" livery. (From the author's collection)*

Massachusetts, which the CAB put out of business by not renewing its certificate. Mohawk began operating in the former Wiggins territory between Albany, N.Y., and Boston, Mass., on August 1, 1953. By now the company's DC-3 interiors had once again been refurbished, this time with seating for 26 passengers.

Robert Peach officially assumed the presidency of Mohawk in 1954, a year in which the airline embarked upon a novel experiment. The company had been authorized to serve Middletown, N.Y., since 1948, but the airport at Middletown had never been made adequate for DC-3 operations. Mohawk requested to have the Middletown authorization transferred to Liberty / Monticello, N.Y., which was closer to the heart of the Catskill Mountains resort area. The request was granted but the Sullivan County Airport, serving Liberty and Monticello, was not ready for DC-3s either. Mohawk purchased a single Sikorsky S-55 helicopter, originally intended for military operation, equipped it with eight passenger seats, and put it to work shuttling passengers between Newark Airport and the airfield at Jennie Grossinger's Catskill Resort in Liberty from June 7, 1954. The flight was scheduled for 59 minutes ("less than an hour", in Mohawk's publicity), and the S-55 put in a total of 198 hours operating the schedule for three months, until Labor Day. Only 341 passengers were carried all summer with an average load factor of 25.83 percent. It was the end of Mohawk's experiment with scheduled helicopter service.

The helicopter operation aside, Mohawk served a strong market area with the highest load factor among the Locals. An opportunity presented itself in 1955, and Robert Peach grabbed it. Six 40-passenger, pressurized Convair 240s that had been destined for Central Air Transport, a mainland Chinese airline, had been flown to Hong Kong before the Communist takeover in 1949. After a court battle, ownership was transferred to Civil Air Transport (CAT) of Taiwan, Chiang Kai-shek's Nationalist Chinese airline formed by Gen. Claire Chennault. By the time the legal battles subsided, Chennault was ready to dispose of the planes and Mohawk purchased three of them. These like-new aircraft, which had accrued very little flight time, were introduced on *The Route of the Air Chiefs* in the summer of 1955. They became the first pressurized airliners to be flown by a local service carrier in the United States.

Eleven Convair 240s eventually served in the Mohawk fleet. Peach converted seven of them to a 46-passenger layout by taking advantage of unneeded galley and cargo space. Capacity aboard the DC-3s was increased once again, this time with 28 seats. Peach wanted to make sure that he could meet as much of the demand for passenger space aboard his flights as possible.

Mohawk spread its wings westward to Erie and Detroit in

Mohawk introduced Convair 240s in 1955. They were the first pressurized aircraft to serve in a local service fleet. (Photo from the AAHS archives, AAHS-35537)

One of the 11 Convair 240s that would serve with Mohawk. The company converted seven of these to a 46-seat configuration by using unnecessary galley and cargo space. The other four were eventually sold to raise funds for the purchase of Convair 440s. (Photo from the Bill Thompson collection))

1956, adding the Motor City as a strong connecting point and source of origin and destination traffic.

A significant event that would have repercussions throughout the local service industry took place on March 27, 1957. On that day, the CAB authorized Mohawk to operate non-stop between Syracuse and New York City (Newark) in direct competition with American Airlines. This was a pivotal award by the CAB because it pitted a local service carrier against a trunk airline in a major market. It had become obvious that the Locals needed to serve some strong markets in order to offset the requirement for subsidy in weaker ones and the Syracuse to New York route could support two carriers. Since Mohawk already had a strong presence in the area and was serving the route via intermediate points, the CAB decided to reverse its previous pledge to keep the Locals from competing directly with trunks and see how the non-stop arrangement would work out. Mohawk instituted its new non-stops between the two cities in June 1957. Both airlines employed the same equipment on the route (Convair 240s) but Mohawk operated its flights on turnaround service, meaning every seat on the aircraft was available for Syracuse – Newark passengers, while American's services were through-flights continuing on beyond Syracuse to Rochester or Buffalo and other points, thus limiting the number of seats available for Syracuse customers. The service was a success and joined Mohawk's two other most-popular non-stops: Binghamton (Triple Cities) to New York (Newark) and Utica / Rome to New York (Newark). The CAB slowly began to loosen the reins at other local service carriers allowing non-stop competition with trunks on certain routes.

Bob Peach's desire to keep Mohawk ahead of the pack was evidenced once again as Mohawk scored another first, this one an important social advancement. In 1957, Mohawk became the first U.S. carrier to employ an African-American flight attendant after TWA apparently found the move forward too controversial. When the larger airline refused to hire a black applicant as a stewardess, Mohawk announced that it was actively seeking minority candidates for flight attendant positions. Several hundred women applied and Ruth Carol Taylor was hired by Mohawk in December 1957. On February 11, 1958, she became the first African-American cabin attendant to crew a flight in the United States when she worked her first segment between Ithaca and Newark. Mohawk received publicity for "opening the door" and the trunk carriers followed suit with TWA hiring Margaret Grant to become that company's first black flight attendant in 1958.

Mohawk's need for a new headquarters building and hangars offering more space was met by Oneida County, N.Y., which built Mohawk a $3 million complex at the Oneida County Airport serving Utica and Rome. Mohawk moved its general offices 78 miles, from the airline's birthplace in Ithaca to its new home at Utica in 1957, occupying the brand new 'headquarters plant' in 1958, "one of the finest, most complete facilities in the scheduled airline industry today," according to the company's own public relations.

More capacity was needed and, once again, Mohawk upstaged its fellow local service compatriots by acquiring the most advanced model of the piston-engine Convair Twin series, the 440 Metropolitan, brand new from the manufacturer instead of second-hand from another airline. The examples purchased by Mohawk in 1959 had been ordered by LACSA of Costa Rica and by SAS (Scandinavian Airlines), but those carriers cancelled their orders leaving the ships available for purchase by Mohawk. Bob Peach's financing for the transaction included funds obtained from the sale of Mohawk's four Convair 240s that had not been converted to the 46-passenger layout.

With the introduction of the Metropolitans into the

With the transfer of stations in Upstate New York and Vermont from Eastern Air Lines in 1961, Mohawk acquired 15 of Eastern's Martin 404s. (Photo from the AAHS archives, AAHS-35566)

This advertisement from 1965 touts Mohawk's position as the first "Regional" airline to put pure jets into service. The company no longer wanted to be known as a Local airline. (From the author's collection)

Fairchild FH-227s were introduced into Mohawk's fleet in 1966, eventually replacing all of the Convairs. (Photo from the AAHS archives, AAHS-P005875)

company's fleet, Mohawk adopted a rich black-and-gold corporate branding scheme and aircraft livery, designating Convair 440 flights as "Golden Metropolitan Service".

Also in 1959, Mohawk occupied space in the new Terminal One (known as the Eastern Air Lines Terminal) at New York International Airport (Idlewild). Concurrent with its inauguration of service to the airport that would later be known as JFK, Mohawk occupied a ticket counter in Manhattan's East Side Airlines Terminal where passengers could check in for their flights before boarding a bus for Idlewild. The company ended 1959 with a fleet of five Convair 440 Metropolitans, seven Convair 240s (christened "Cosmopolitans"), and eight Douglas DC-3s.

Mohawk entered two more strong markets in 1960 with the inauguration of flights to Cleveland, Ohio, and Providence, Rhode Island. In keeping with its local service mission to bring air service to smaller cities, both Olean, N.Y., and Jamestown, N.Y., were also added to Mohawk's network that year.

Pittsburgh, another good interline point, joined the system in 1961, which was the year in which Mohawk got its biggest single route mile boost to date. Eastern Air Lines had inherited several stations in upstate New York and Vermont through its merger with Colonial Airlines in 1956. Like most of the other small cities still on Eastern's route map, the company had served these points with its Martin 404 Silver Falcons, 60 of which had been purchased brand new and put into service between 1951 and 1953. Now, with the advent of the jet age, Eastern and the other trunk carriers were trying to shed themselves of their remaining smaller cities to concentrate on major markets. The CAB approved the transfer of these stations from Eastern to Mohawk, along with non-stop service between New York and Albany, another prized New York State market. To handle the transferred service, Mohawk acquired 15 of Eastern's Martin 404s (14 for flying; 1 for spares). Eight of the type went into service in September 1961, and Mohawk designated them "Cosmopolitans," the same designation given to its Convair 240s.

Meanwhile, Mohawk was phasing out the last of its Douglas DC-3s, but wanted to keep a few of them around as long as possible to provide extra lift and generate revenue. In the most novel marketing ploy to make the old birds as attractive as possible, the company painted them in a Gay Nineties theme and christened them "Gas Light Service" aircraft. The interiors of the planes featured brocade curtains and carriage lamps while the flight attendants assigned to the service wore dresses styled in 1890s fashion. Beer, pretzels, cheese and cigars were offered on board and, at first, the flights were restricted to men only, another marketing ploy to make businessmen feel like they were enjoying an exclusive 'private club' type of service. The 'men only' restriction was soon dropped. The Gas Light Service concept received lots of favorable publicity and proved to be a popular concept. The company finally retired its last DC-3 in 1962.

Mohawk's strong presence at its New York State stations was enhanced by the company's frequent commuter service from each major point to New York City. By making flights available

Despite worsening financial problems, the company began applying an updated paint scheme, referred to as the Buckskin livery, to its BAC 1-11's. The original black-and-gold livery can be seen on the aircraft taxiing in the background in this January 1972 photo taken at Newark. Across the Hudson River, the new World Trade Center Twin Towers are nearing completion. (Photo by George Hamlin)

throughout the day, more customers found it convenient to rely on Mohawk as their way 'out of town.' Instead of offering the typical schedule of a local airline with either two or three flights per weekday in each direction, Mohawk in 1962 offered 12 weekday departures from Albany to New York, seven each from Binghamton and Syracuse and four non-stops from Utica/Rome along with two one-stops.

Mohawk was riding high. In 1963, Toronto joined the airline's system officially making it an international carrier. Mohawk was the largest of the 13 local service airlines in terms of passenger miles flown and the company had placed the first order among the Locals for pure jets, British Aircraft Corporation BAC 1-11s, to be delivered starting in 1965. The jets would take the Locals to a whole new level. Mohawk was already referring to itself as a regional instead of a local, and, of all the Locals, Mohawk had the densest population base to draw passengers from and put them aboard those jets, which would compete with American Airlines in some markets.

The jets started to arrive in 1965. More and more of them were purchased. Twenty-four BAC 1-11s would eventually join the Mohawk fleet. Meanwhile, the entire piston-engine fleet was being replaced by brand new Fairchild-Hiller FH-227s. The Martin 404s had already been traded with Ozark Air Lines for that company's handful of Convair 240s, reducing the number of different aircraft types in Mohawk's fleet. Now all of the Convairs, 240s and 440s, were to be replaced by the factory-fresh Fairchilds. Mohawk had entered a whole new world of economics.

A new training center was built in Utica, and service was inaugurated to Washington, D.C., and to Philadelphia in 1966. But in 1966, Mohawk ended the year with less net income than it had the year before. Reduction in subsidy and a strike against Mohawk by the IAM were listed as part of the blame.

Then, in 1967, passenger load factor declined and the cost of the re-equipment program made itself felt. Also in 1967, one of the BACs was lost in an accident. The plane crashed 13 minutes after takeoff from Elmira / Corning, claiming the lives of all 34 aboard. Malfunction of a part in the auxiliary power unit was blamed. Mohawk lost money that year, certainly an anomaly.

But, economically, 1968 was worse than 1967, and 1969 was worse than 1968. The airline lost $4.3 million in 1968 and $4.9 million in 1969.

1970 would prove to be no better as the country suffered through a recession. Mohawk's huge outlay on turbine-powered aircraft was just one of the factors adding to Mohawk's losses. A 1968 work 'slowdown' by the Professional Air Traffic Controllers Organization had greatly disrupted Mohawk's New York City-centric operation. Government subsidy payments were being drastically reduced as Mohawk was relying more and more on subsidy-ineligible services between its larger cities.

Despite the bad financial news, Mohawk continued to grow. CAB authority was received in 1967 permitting non-stop flights between Detroit and five major cities in upstate New York. Montreal was added to the network and, in 1969, Mohawk announced an order for three Boeing 727-200s. Minneapolis/St. Paul and Chicago were added to the system in 1970 and 1971, respectively.

Problems within the company escalated. Robert Peach had moved from president to chairman of the board and CEO, but he was removed from office and replaced by Russell Stephenson, who acted as both president and CEO.

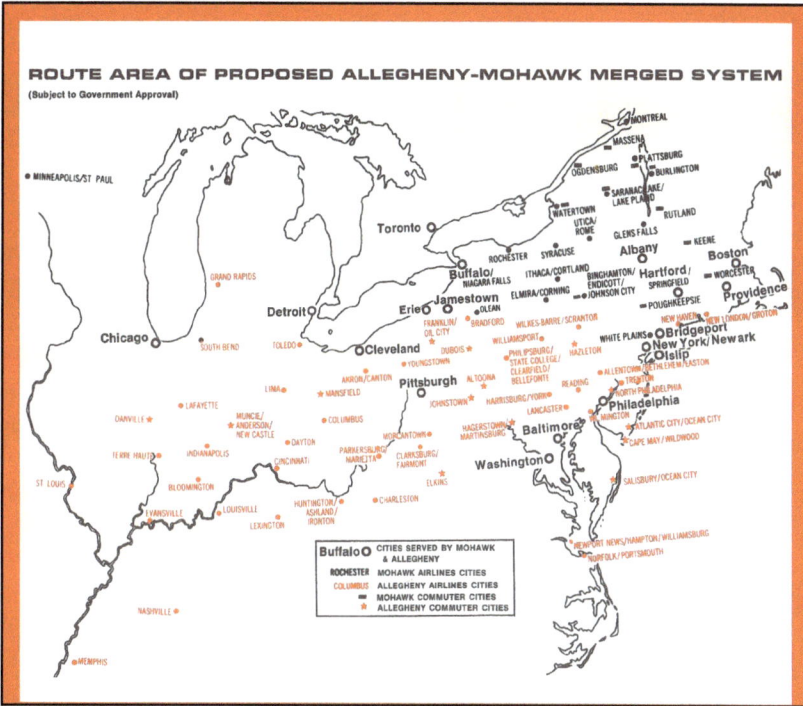

Mohawk continued to expand, adding Montreal to its network in 1969, Minneapolis / St. Paul in 1970, and Chicago in 1971. The company placed an order for Boeing 727-200s to handle capacity on high density routes, but the order was cancelled. Worsening financial condition, exasperated by a 154-day pilot strike, forced Mohawk into a merger with Allegheny Airlines in 1972. The territory covered by the merged system is illustrated in the map on the right. (From the author's collection)

Then, on November 19, 1969, a Mohawk FH-227 crashed on approach to Glens Falls, N.Y., killing all 14 aboard.

Peach had not been a fan of organized labor and during the 1960s Mohawk had suffered two strikes: the first, an 18-day action by flight attendants in 1960, then the 53-day IAM strike during the holiday season in 1966. On November 12, 1970, Mohawk's pilots walked out over the issue of transferring some of Mohawk's flying into smaller stations to contracted commuter carriers. The strike lasted 154 days, with the pilots returning to work on April 14, 1971.

The shutdown had been too much for the company and the damage was done. Mohawk was now a dying airline and negotiations were entered into with Allegheny, its local service neighbor. Mohawk would lose its identity as it merged into the Allegheny Airlines system but, before that happened, two more sad events would play out in the Mohawk story.

On April 20, 1971, Robert E. Peach, the man who had overseen Mohawk from its inception through to the jet age, was found dead in his home of an apparent self-inflicted gunshot wound.

Then, on March 3, 1972, another Mohawk FH-227, this one on approach for landing at Albany, NY, crashed into a house 3.5 miles short of the runway. Seventeen people were killed.

On April 12, 1972, Mohawk officially became part of the Allegheny Airlines system, an inglorious end to what had been, at one time, among the most successful of the thirteen permanently certificated local service carriers. ✈

Mohawk's final system timetable, effective April 1, 1972, illustrates the company's aircraft legacy. One more timetable, with a cover announcing "Mohawk Again", was issued with effective dates of April 14-24, but the merger with Allegheny was officially consummated on April 12. (From the author's collection)

America's Local Service Airlines

CHAPTER 8

NORTH CENTRAL AIRLINES

Like Mohawk, North Central owes its birth to the needs of one small city and the desire for air transportation to connect it to the outside world. Clintonville, Wis., was home to the Four Wheel Drive (FWD) Auto Company. As early as 1939, FWD had purchased a Waco biplane to transport company executives to meetings outside of Clintonville. The primary destination for these excursions was Chicago and, as in Robinson's case, local businessmen from other firms in Clintonville began to request space on flights to the Windy City.

With the Civil Aeronautics Board's (CAB) institution of its feeder airline policy in 1944, FWD decided to incorporate its flight service subsidiary and apply for a feeder airline certificate. Dubbed Wisconsin Central Airlines, the new company officially came into being on May 15, 1944, with Francis M. Higgins, advertising manager of FWD, as its president. The airline filed its application with the CAB and waited for the hearing and examination process to run its course.

While waiting for the CAB to rule on its application for a federal certificate, Wisconsin Central decided to get experience by operating a scheduled intrastate service, which only required authorization from the State of Wisconsin. Two Cessna T-50s (UC-78s) were acquired in the postwar marketplace and service was inaugurated on April 4, 1946, to six airports on a route stretching from Madison and Milwaukee to Superior. Of course Clintonville was at the center of the 'system.' The operation lasted until November of that year when the undertaking, which had lost money, was shut down.

But good news came the following month when the CAB announced its awards in the North Central Case. Wisconsin Central Airlines was selected to operate over five routes serving 34 airports in a network stretching from Chicago on the southern end to Hibbing, Minn., and Hancock, Mich., in the north. The award was "subject to a further showing as to the adequacy of airport facilities and that Four Wheel Drive Auto Company has divested itself of control of Wisconsin Central Airlines." The CAB was very thorough in its vetting of potential feeder certificate holders. Any suspicion that interlocking relationships might prevent the company from totally devoting itself to the public good, as opposed to serving private interests, was met with a mandate for dissolution of the association.

FWD divested itself of its investment in Wisconsin Central and Francis Higgins went searching for someone who knew something about running an airline to help him get the company off the ground. He found that person in 25-year old Hal Carr, an analyst in route development working for TWA. Carr accepted the offer to become Wisconsin Central's Vice President-Traffic, and thus began the long career of a man who would be instrumental in the company's development and growth. He would also be the airline's savior several years later.

Initial financing was a problem for the start-up, as it was for most of the new feeders. With the help of a stock issue put together by a Milwaukee investment firm, the company accrued enough capital to purchase two used Lockheed 10-A Electras from Pioneer Air Lines, another feeder, which had upgraded to DC-3s. The twin-engine Lockheeds had accommodation for 10 passengers but Wisconsin Central had to remove the tenth seat to make room for radio equipment, thus reducing customer capacity to nine. A third 10-A Electra was acquired before the start of service.

Wisconsin Central inaugurated scheduled operations on February 24, 1948. By that time the company's headquarters had been established in Madison, Wisconsin. It took until December 1949 for service to be introduced over all of the initially-awarded segments and, by the end of 1950, the young airline's route map was set for awhile. Some stations had been eliminated (Racine / Kenosha and Baraboo / Portage, Wis.) due to poor airport conditions, and Beloit / Janesville, Wis., which was not part of the original award, was added to the system. Some of the originally certificated stations would never receive service from the airline due to a lack of proper facilities. *Whiskey Central*, as it was affectionately called, had settled in to serving 22 airports in four states, including Land O' Lakes, Wis., the smallest city in the continental United States with certificated air service (1950 pop.: 548), which was served on a seasonal basis (summer) when tourist traffic to the area mushroomed.

Calling itself "The Route of the Northliners," the airline eventually assembled a fleet of six aging Lockheed 10-A Electras. But it was obvious that larger aircraft, namely Douglas DC-3s, would be needed to handle expanding passenger demand. In late 1950, six DC-3s were purchased from TWA. They entered service early in 1951, and by May of that year the Electras were gone from Wisconsin Central's fleet. With the introduction of the DC-3s came a new member of the crew, a steward, to tend to the needs of passengers in a 21-seat cabin.

But the transition to larger aircraft came with costs: for the planes themselves plus spare parts, for staff training, and for conversion of the aircraft to Wisconsin Central standards. The company's financial position began to deteriorate and Hal Carr advocated improving the airline's service, spending money to make money. The majority of the board of directors was in disagreement with Carr's policies and Hal Carr resigned from the company in December 1951.

The CAB renewed Wisconsin Central's certificate for another five years and awarded more new stations and routes

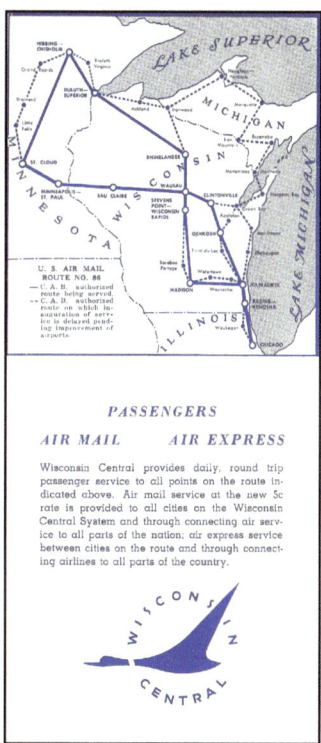

This timetable from Wisconsin Central's first year of certificated operation shows the route system served by the company's Lockheed 10-A Electras. (From the author's collection)

By May of 1951, all of the Lockheeds were gone, replaced by DC-3s, one of which is seen here in Wisconsin Central's livery. (Photo from the Tim Williams colleciton)

to the feeder carrier. Service over two new segments reaching westward from Minneapolis/St. Paul, to Fargo and Grand Forks, N.D., via intermediate stops, was inaugurated in 1952, as well as service to LaCrosse, Wis., and Winona, Minnesota. More DC-3s were purchased and leased to handle the expansion and the financial situation continued to deteriorate.

In the fall of 1952, several important events occurred in the airline's development. Despite the fact that the company was in the red, more DC-3s were needed and a source was found in Purdue University, which, with its School of Aeronautics and Purdue Research Foundation, agreed to sell nine DC-3s to Wisconsin Central and take over the balance of an insurance company loan to the airline in exchange for a vice-presidency within the company and a seat on the board of directors. Wisconsin Central agreed and Purdue University's Grove Webster became a Wisconsin Central vice-president while the university's Dr. Robert Stewart joined the board.

Then, in the CAB's Michigan-Wisconsin Service Case, decided October 17, 1952, the airline was awarded a route to Grand Rapids, Lansing, and Detroit, Mich., from Hancock / Houghton and other points on the Upper Peninsula of Michigan, via Green Bay, Wisconsin. In the same decision, the CAB approved the company's requested name change, from Wisconsin Central to the more appropriate North Central Airlines.

In the midst of all of these developments, the airline moved its headquarters from Madison to Minneapolis.

Purdue's Dr. Stewart had also invaded the board room of another feeder carrier, Lake Central Airlines, which itself had struggled through financial mismanagement, and on January 1, 1953, he was appointed president of that airline. Purdue's next announcement was an offer for North Central to purchase Lake Central, with the goal of merging the two together to form one large local service airline. North Central was to be the surviving carrier.

All of these grand plans, new headquarters, new routes, additional airplanes, and the new name could not prevent another disastrous financial year in 1953, the second in a row in which net loss topped $100,000. Francis Higgins had resigned, there was bickering in the boardroom and the reaction to the company's financial situation was to retrench and cut back on service, which is never the best solution. North Central faced the possibility of being the first certificated air carrier in the United States to declare bankruptcy.

Finally, the board of directors made an offer to Hal Carr, asking him to please come back and take over. He accepted and returned to North Central Airlines as the youngest airline president in the country, on April 7, 1954. Then things began to turn around. Improved scheduling, emphasis on service and customer relations, cost reduction, the addition of more seats to each DC-3 interior, and negotiation for a permanent air mail rate (subsidy) were just a few of the tactics undertaken to recover from the downward spiral.

1954 also saw the first female cabin attendants added to North Central's payroll.

The gents from Purdue packed up and left, but North Central tenaciously held on to their legacy of an attempted acquisition of Lake Central for several more years. Despite defeats in the court room and a decision by the CAB that the merger would not be in the public interest, North Central continued to push for a merger with Lake Central. North Central was finally defeated in its bid for the other carrier in 1959.

In the meantime, *The Route of the Northliners* continued to grow methodically through the CAB's tightly-controlled process. 1955 saw the transfer of a route between Chicago and Detroit, via

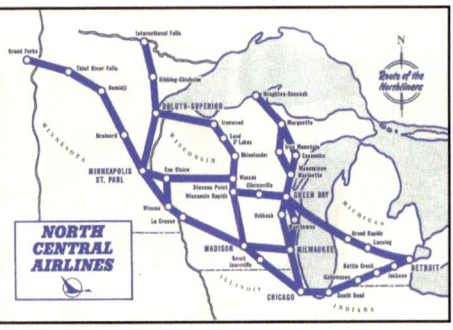

The mid-1950s saw additional routes and the first female flight attendants. (From the author's collection)

By 1959, North Central was operating a fleet of 32 Douglas DC-3s emblazoned with this 'feather' livery. (Photo from the Tim Williams collection)

several important intermediate points, from American to North Central. This would become a very profitable "bread-and-butter" route for the airline.

In 1957, the CAB transferred stations from Braniff to North Central on a route extending southward from Grand Forks, North Dakota, to Omaha, Nebraska. On December 1 of that year, DC-3 Northliners began operating non-stop over the 404-mile segment between Duluth / Superior and Chicago.

1958 brought the extension of North Central's system to Sault Ste. Marie, Mich., and 1959 saw the addition of 15 new stations to the *Route of the Northliners* as a result of the CAB's Seven States Area Case. By this time North Central was operating a fleet of 32 DC-3s, and was the leader among all 13 of the Locals in number of passengers, pounds of mail and pounds of cargo carried. Hal Carr's airline had come a long way since its death spiral in 1953.

In 1959, North Central entered the ranks of local service carriers operating equipment larger than DC-3s when five Convair 340s were acquired from Continental Air Lines. These 44-passenger, pressurized airliners were placed into service on high-density and 'long haul' segments starting April 1.

The route system continued to grow in 1960, as service was established at 10 more airports in Michigan and at Port Arthur / Fort William (Thunder Bay), Ontario, the company's first international destination.

During 1960, North Central boarded more than one million passengers making it the first local service airline to do so in a single year. The company was now referring to itself as "America's Leading Local Airline."

Cleveland, Ohio, became a North Central station in February 1961, with a lucrative route non-stop across Lake Erie to Detroit. Regina, Saskatchewan became a Northliner city on May 1, 1961, with a non-stop DC-3 flight to Minot, N.D., continuing to points beyond, but the service was discontinued early in 1963.

The airline's operating territory was affected by harsh winter weather every year. Personnel and equipment faced sub-zero temperatures, freezing rain, and snow, sometimes in the form of blizzards, for periods of up to six months. The company instituted a program called Operation Cold Front that covered every aspect of necessary planning and preparation for complete winterization of the airline by mid-October of each year.

North Central was now a healthy, profitable carrier at, or near, the top in rank among the Locals in almost every category. By 1962, with a fleet of 18 Convairs and 29 DC-3s, the slogan in the annual report had been adjusted slightly to read, "America's Leading Regional Airline."

In 1963, the airline was selected by the U.S. Agency for International Development (AID) to help rehabilitate Bolivia's national airline, Lloyd Aereo Boliviano (LAB). The project lasted two years, during which time North Central personnel from various departments lived in Bolivia offering technical and managerial assistance to the staff of the South American carrier.

Carr led his airline through "The Sixties," the most dynamic decade for all of the Locals. By late 1961, all 13 of the local service carriers had added equipment larger than DC-3s to their fleets, and one, Bonanza, had already disposed of all of its *Gooney Birds* in favor of the larger ships (in Bonanza's case, F-27s). North Central continued to add Convair 340s and the advanced 440s to its fleet, upgrading the 340s to 440 standards. The next step seemed a logical progression but it would also prove to be the catalyst for transformation of the Locals into something other than what they were designed to be. In the 1960s, all 13 of America's local service airlines signed contracts to buy or lease jets. North Central investigated the models that were scheduled to become available, finding favor with the DC-9 but not satisfied with its passenger capacity. When Douglas Aircraft announced the -30 stretched version of the aircraft, which would accommodate 100 customers, North Central signed on to purchase five of the pure jets, taking an option on five more.

The airline was ready for the jet age as net profits topped one million dollars in 1965, then repeated that achievement in 1966, and reached 1.5 million dollars for 1967. During 1966, for the first time, North Central's passenger boardings topped two million in a single year.

The first of the DC-9-30s arrived in 1967, going into service on September 8. But before the turbojets arrived the company had introduced turbine power in the form of jet-prop Convair 580s, which went into service on April 1, 1967. The 580s were the company's own 440s upgraded with Allison turboprop engines.

LEFT: *North Central's DC-3s were given a new livery in the early 1960s. N8854 is seen here at Omaha, Nebraska in 1965.*
RIGHT: *The company re-powered its piston-engine Convairs with Allison turboprops, transitioning them to Convair 580s. Pictured is N2044. (DC-3 from the AAHS archives, AAHS-P006959)*

The jets brought North Central and the other Locals up to a new level of prestige and into a whole new world of economics. The planes and their parts were expensive. All of those seats had to be filled, and with passengers travelling a substantial distance - not just 60 miles, a typical hop for a local airline DC-3. The equipment transition continued as North Central operated its final DC-3 flight on February 7, 1969. For the year 1969, North Central lost money for the first time since 1953, even after carrying over three million passengers during the 12-month period.

The late 1960s brought a few new stations to North Central's system. Kansas City, Denver, and Toronto all joined the *Route of the Northliners*. Following North Central's lead, the Locals were calling themselves Regionals now and no more small, marginally-productive cities were being added to their route maps. Now the focus was on longer hauls, flights that could generate more revenue.

New York (La Guardia) came on-line in 1970, as did Columbus, Dayton, and Cincinnati, Ohio. Non-stop authority was granted in more markets, including Minneapolis / St. Paul – Chicago and Minneapolis / St. Paul – Omaha. The airline returned to profitability and stayed there.

As the prospect of airline deregulation loomed, North Central faced a tough decision about its future. The reality of deregulation would bring a free-for-all in the world of route expansion, and the strongest carriers with sensible growth strategies would be the survivors. One strategy for assuring strength and growth was to merge with another healthy carrier. Even before the Airline Deregulation Act was signed into law on October 24, 1978, North Central's upper management had been engaged in talks with the management of Southern Airways, another local-turned-regional, based in Atlanta and serving its traditional market in the Southeast. The two airlines agreed to merge and, on July 1, 1979, joined together to form Republic Airlines, a whole new carrier (technically, North Central was the surviving company) retaining North Central's famed logo, Herman, the blue goose.

The strategy proved successful as Republic became a national carrier, acquiring Hughes Airwest (itself formed from the merger of three local airlines) in 1980. Republic was purchased by Northwest Airlines in 1986, bringing an end to the story of the little airline formed in Clintonville, Wis., 42 years prior. ✈

North Central truly entered the jet age with the introduction of Douglas DC-9-30s on September 8, 1967. (Photo from the Tim Williams collection)

America's Local Service Airlines

CHAPTER 9

OZARK AIR LINES

Like several other Local Service Carriers, Ozark got its first experience operating an intrastate service. However, it was five years from the time that the intrastate operation in Missouri was shut down until Ozark Air Lines once again became airborne.

Ozark was the brainchild of Laddie Hamilton, who had transportation in his blood. Born June 28, 1910, Laddie's given name was Homer Dale Hamilton. His father worked for the St. Louis – San Francisco Railway (*The Frisco*). After operating his own automobile garage in Springfield, Mo., Laddie went to work for Floyd W. Jones, first as a bus driver, then, in 1936, as manager of the southern portion of Jones's Mo-Ark Coaches (later Mo-Ark Trailways). Floyd Jones and Laddie Hamilton developed a business relationship that would serve them both well for many years to come.

With Jones's help, in 1937 Hamilton purchased the bankrupt Dixie Coaches, a bus line operating in Alabama and Mississippi. He resuscitated the company, turning it into a financially-healthy enterprise, then sold it for a profit to Southeastern Greyhound Lines in 1942.

Laddie Hamilton had earned his pilot's license in 1928, so it was no surprise that his next move would be into the field of aviation. He was training pilots during the war working part-time for Oliver Parks's Alabama Institute of Aeronautics while

Ozark Air Lines Logo from the 1950s. (From the author's collection)

acting as regional manager for Southeastern Greyhound Lines in Tuscaloosa.

On a spring day in 1943, he met with his friend, Floyd Jones, and two other gentlemen, Barak T. Mattingly and Arthur Heyne, both attorneys, at Mattingly's office in the Title Guarantee Building on Chestnut Street in downtown St. Louis. The purpose of their meeting was to discuss forming an intrastate airline that would operate between Springfield, Mo., St. Louis, Kansas City and Columbia.

Articles of Incorporation were filed with the Missouri Secretary of State on August 26, 1943, and a charter was granted on September 1. Ozark Airlines was officially in business (note that "Airlines" was one word in the original incarnation of Ozark). Ozark's founders intended for the company to

Ozark DC-3 N141D at Chicago Midway Airport in 1959. (Photo from the Tim Williams collection)

eventually become one of the new "feeder" airlines that the Civil Aeronautics Board (CAB) was contemplating. Hamilton and his cohorts felt that the CAB would look more favorably upon a company that had intrastate operating experience when it came time to issue the Certificate of Public Convenience and Necessity, required for inter-state operation.

Ozark's initial experience was gained by offering charter service out of Springfield. Then, with three Beech Model F-17D Staggerwing aircraft, scheduled operations were inaugurated on January 10, 1945. A triangle route pattern was flown with one aircraft leaving Springfield for Kansas City via Clinton, Mo., and one departing for St. Louis via Rolla. From those terminals the aircraft would then proceed to Columbia, Mo., and then repeat the pattern back to Springfield. Warrensburg, Mo., was substituted for Clinton in April of 1945 due to poor airport conditions at Clinton.

Towards the end of summer 1945, Ozark replaced its fleet of Staggerwings with two Cessna C-78s, converted to T-50s. These were five-seat twin-engine aircraft. Columbia had been eliminated from the 'system' and Fort Leonard Wood was added as an intermediate point on the Springfield – St. Louis route. Although the service had gained in popularity, by November 1945 the company had yet to turn a profit and the owners decided to end the drain on their personal finances. The little airline was shut down. The intrastate version of Ozark had lasted just shy of 10 months.

Meanwhile, the Ozark executives had filed an application with the CAB for feeder authority. In the Mississippi Valley Case, decided in December 1947, Ozark applied for a route pattern in the shape of an 'X', with one line stretching from Kansas City to Montgomery, Ala., via nine intermediate points, the other running from St. Louis to Tulsa, Oklahoma, with four stops along the way. The two routes would intersect at Springfield, Mo. Also included in the application were three different routings from Kansas City to St. Louis via different sets of intermediate stations. Altogether, the requested network would have served 28 cities in six states.

Unfortunately, the application was not approved. Instead, the CAB selected Parks Air Transport as the carrier to be certificated for feeder routes reaching from St. Louis to Memphis and from St. Louis to Tulsa with an extension from Tulsa to Kansas City. Each route embraced several smaller intermediate cities, which was the purpose of the new feeder carriers. Parks Air Transport was another outfit owned by Oliver Parks.

Oliver L. Parks was a well-known man in aviation circles. He had formed his pilot training school in 1927 and, by the mid-1930s, he was operating a full-fledged aviation academy, Parks Air College, located at the Parks Metropolitan Airport, formerly the Curtiss-Parks Airport, in East St. Louis.

When the U.S. military required thousands of pilots during World War II, Parks trained flyers in several different locations. In addition to his "College" in East St. Louis, he operated four other schools: the Alabama Institute of Aeronautics, the Mississippi, the Missouri, and the Cape Institutes of Aeronautics. After the

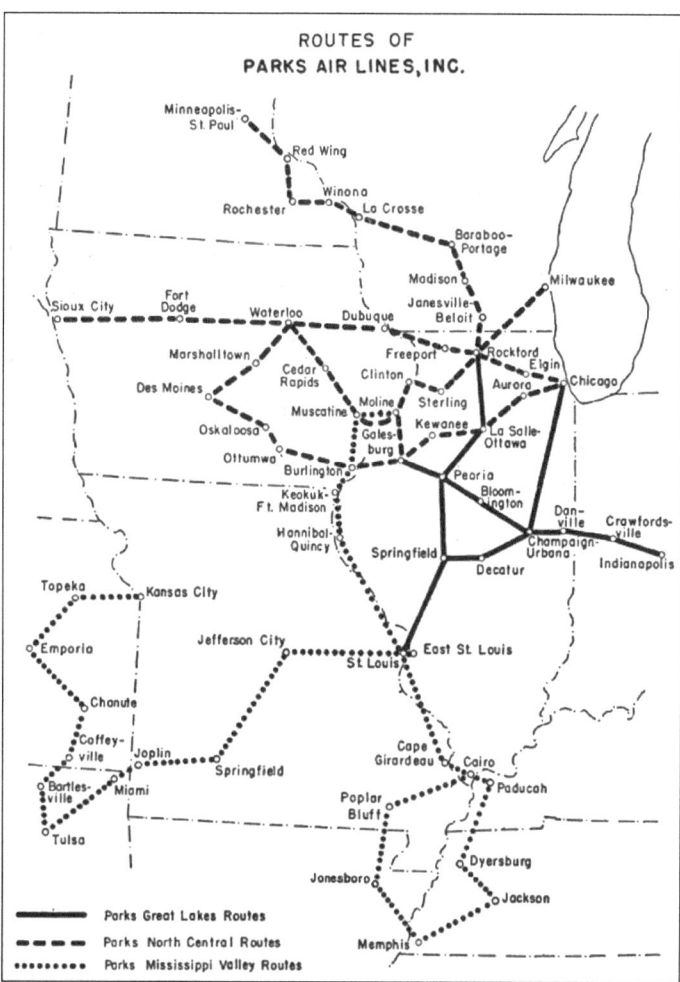

Parks Air Lines Route Map. (From the CAB via SFO Museum Aviation Library)

war he merged his assets into Parks Aircraft Sales and Service, Inc., which operated fixed-base services in various locations. By the time the CAB was holding hearings on new feeder routes after the war, Oliver Parks was a respected name that everyone in the realm of aviation recognized. He was just the type of experienced person that the CAB was looking for to bid on the new routes being proposed.

It was no surprise then, in December 1946, when Parks Air Transport won five of the feeder routes awarded in the CAB's North Central Case.

The CAB's confidence in Mr. Parks's ability did not stop there. The Great Lakes Area Case was decided on September 3, 1947, with the CAB noting that "Mr. Oliver L. Parks has a wide background of experience in the field of aviation." Parks Air Transport was officially selected to operate three feeder routes in that proceeding.

Finally came the Mississippi Valley Case, in which Parks beat out Ozark and other applicants. Parks was selected over Ozark Air Lines (now separating "Air Lines" into two words) as the feeder air carrier certificated for this region partly because of Parks's "long and varied experience in aviation."

In a final gesture, as an adjunct to the Great Lakes Area

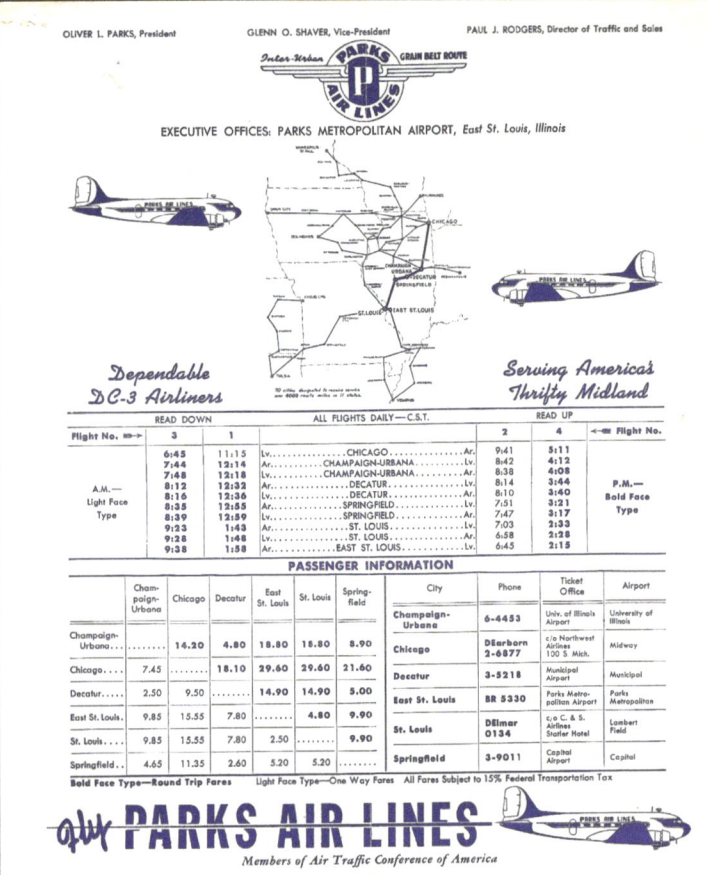

Parks Air Lines timetable effective Aug. 1, 1950. The company had just had its certificate revoked. (From the author's collection)

Case, on February 4, 1948, the CAB announced that all of Parks's awards would be placed under one certificate and two of the previously-awarded routes were connected permitting through-service between St. Louis and Chicago. The CAB found Parks "fit, willing and able." The selection of Parks in three different cases, to serve such a large area, "will demonstrate the effectiveness of increased size of local operations in meeting the problems of operating costs, equipment, equipment utilization and financing." The CAB members would come to regret their decision.

For a year the Parks system remained dormant. While feeder airlines in other parts of the country were starting operations under their newly-issued certificates, no service was inaugurated by Parks. This was particularly disturbing because Parks had been awarded such a large network. The cities and towns that had lobbied for this new air service were expecting it. When Parks Air Transport, now calling itself Parks Air Lines, had not inaugurated service over any of its routes by March 1949, the CAB decreed that the company would have a 102-day period in which to get its act together. The CAB stated that service over the certificated routes should be inaugurated by July 1, 1949.

Oliver Parks and his executive team had faced problems raising the capital required to start operations. More specifically, it appears that they had been unwilling to risk much of their own money on this new feeder operation. When Mr. Parks applied to the Reconstruction Finance Corporation (RFC) for a loan to help get his airline off the ground, he was refused because of a lack of sufficient equity capital. With the latest edict from the CAB, Parks and his associates quickly came up with a new plan. They approached the board of Mid-Continent Airlines, a certificated trunk carrier whose route system, which stretched from Minot, North Dakota, to New Orleans, looked more like large local airline. Mid-Continent was a financially healthy, conservative company that still operated an all-DC-3 fleet. The plan was for Mid-Continent to acquire Parks by exchanging 13,496 shares of Mid-Continent stock for 32,392 shares, the total outstanding Parks stock. This would, of course, put money into the pockets of Mr. Parks and his cohorts. Mid-Continent would operate Parks Air Lines as a wholly-owned subsidiary. The Mid-Continent Board of Directors authorized this agreement at their annual meeting. Of course the plan required CAB approval and a public hearing before the Board in Washington, D.C., was set for September 28, 1949.

After examining the text of the hearings that ensued, it does not appear to be an exaggeration to say that the CAB was livid. The Parks Investigation Case, which presented the prospect of revocation of Parks's certificate by the CAB, was initiated. The Parks team contended at the hearing that circumstances beyond its control prevented it from obtaining the necessary financing for inaugurating service as an independent company prior to the expiration of the designated period, that its acquisition by Mid-Continent should be approved and, if not, that it should be permitted to retain its certificate and conduct operations as an independent company with small, single-engine aircraft.

The CAB was not satisfied with Oliver Parks and his associates. The CAB stated: "We feel that the record warrants a conclusion that Mr. Parks and his associates could long ago have taken steps that would have resulted in the start of service over a substantial part, or perhaps over all, of the routes if they had been willing to risk their own capital in the manner that the CAB had a right to expect in the light of the presentation made on behalf of Parks at the original hearings." When the awards were first made, Oliver Parks had stated that he, his directors and the companies he controlled would provide approximately $650,000 of equity capital. Only $81,000 had been contributed by 1950.

In denying the request to have Mid-Continent "acquire" Parks Air Lines, the CAB stated that approval of the acquisition would not only condone the unreasonable delay in inaugurating service but would also permit Oliver Parks and his associates to profit from their inaction.

Then, during the hearings, on May 17, 1950, Mr. Parks announced that he had found "new capital" and could activate the routes with twin-engine aircraft. The sudden change of fortune had come from the 'merger' of a struggling non-scheduled carrier, Twentieth Century Airlines of Charlotte, N.C., into the Parks organization. With Twentieth Century came DC-3s and two founders of that airline now willing to throw their lot in with Oliver Parks: The Rev. Chris A. Bachman, an

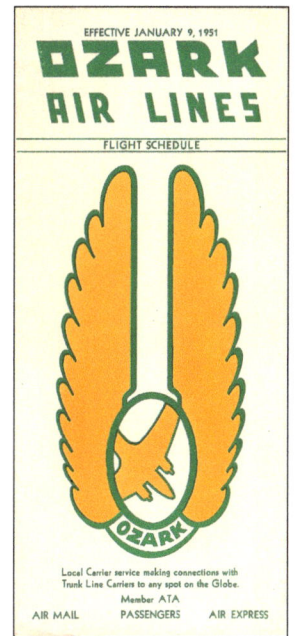   

Timetable cover and route map from 1951, plus timetable covers from 1952 and 1953. (From the author's collection)

ordained minister and president of Twentieth Century, and Glenn O. Shaver, the company's general manager and a pilot. But the CAB told Oliver Parks that it was too late. "There must come a time when administrative proceedings of this nature are brought to a close." The CAB was ready to give all of the Parks routes to some other applicant.

First consideration was to be given to feeder airlines or, rather, "carriers that did not operate trunk line or regional services." The companies that wanted Parks's routes were: Central Airlines, Keith Kahle's new feeder operation based in Fort Worth; Turner Airlines, the company associated with famed flyer, Roscoe Turner, which would soon change its name to Lake Central Airlines; Continental Southern Lines, owned by the Trailways Bus Company of Dallas; Wisconsin Central Airlines, which would eventually change its name to North Central Airlines; and the company that had run an intrastate operation five years earlier, Ozark Air Lines.

But Oliver L. Parks would not go down without a fight. On June 21, 1950, Parks Air Lines inaugurated service over the St. Louis to Chicago route with intermediate stops in Springfield, Decatur and Champaign/Urbana, Illinois. Parks stated that he intended to commence service over the other routes, activating his entire system, by November 6, 1950. He said that he now had the organization and the financing to accomplish this. But the CAB would have none of it. On July 28, 1950, the decision was announced: Parks Air Lines' certificate had been nullified by the CAB.

Arthur G. Heyne, the attorney who had been part of Ozark's team of founding executives, received a telephone call in late July of 1950 from his friend, Clyde Brayton, of Brayton Flying Service. Brayton was also an instructor at Parks Air College. Retelling the story, printed in the Aug.-Sep. 1965 issue of the *Ozark Air Lines News* on the occasion of the company's 15th anniversary, Mr. Heyne recalled that Brayton told him

"Congratulations!"

"For what?" Heyne replied.

"I see you just got a certificate from the CAB!"

"Aw, you're pullin' my leg. It's been seven years. Are you sure it's us?" Heyne asked.

On August 1, 1950, the official telegram arrived. Ozark Air Lines had, indeed, been awarded all of Parks's routes from the Great Lakes and the Mississippi Valley cases. The only other beneficiary was Mid-Continent Airlines, which was given routes into Chicago and Milwaukee originally awarded to Parks in the North Central Case.

Ozark was selected over the other applicants for several reasons. It was most familiar with the area to be served. Ozark would be headquartered in St. Louis, as was Parks, from where the system would radiate, and Ozark's financial plan was sound although the examiner did express some doubt that the company had the finances to start both the Great Lakes and the Mississippi Valley routes.

A meeting was held at Floyd W. Jones' estate, called Riverdale, near Springfield, Missouri. The Korean War had just started and the United States government put a freeze on available aircraft. "All those World War II surplus DC-3s and C-47s vanished," according to Heyne. Something had to be done to get a very big feeder airline up and operating quickly.

Oliver Parks was invited to Riverdale and Glenn O. Shaver flew him there in a Parks Air Lines DC-3. Parks had filed lawsuits in conjunction with the CAB's actions. Ozark wanted what Parks could offer: DC-3s, pilots and other personnel. It took some convincing but a deal was struck to exchange Ozark Air Lines stock for Parks Air Lines stock, which required having the lawsuits dismissed. That involved a trip to Washington where the Parks fight was laid to rest. According to Arthur Heyne,

Ozark's 1950s DC-3 livery is captured in this typical winter scene as passengers board N144D. (From the author's collection)

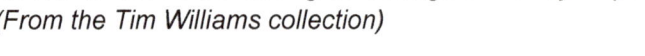

N147D is seen here taxiing at Chicago's Midway Airport. (From the Tim Williams collection)

"Ozark, in essence, merged Parks Air Lines into its organization – the only solution since each badly needed one another."

Ozark became the last, and thus, the youngest, of the air carriers that would develop into the 13 permanently certificated Local Service Airlines of the 1950s. The certificate for operation of Ozark's new route system became effective on September 26, 1950. On the evening of September 25, the Ozark group gathered at the Statler Hotel in downtown St. Louis and waited for the strike of midnight. At 12:01a.m., the founders of Ozark signed the paperwork officially accepting the certificate and the airline was in business. At 6:58 that morning, Ozark's first flight took off from St. Louis's Lambert Field bound for Springfield, Ill.; Champaign/Urbana and Chicago... with one passenger on board. That would be the first in a history of flights that lasted for 36 years.

Ozark's initial fleet consisted of four Douglas DC-3s inherited from Parks Air Lines. The story goes that the "P" and the "S" were removed from the Parks name on the planes and an "OZ" was added ahead of the "ARK." The initial fleet was a mismatched lot of *Gooney Birds* and it would not be until 1951 that all of Ozark's DC-3s were standardized with the same equipment and interiors.

With all of Parks's, and thus, Ozark's maintenance facilities located at Parks Metropolitan Airport in East St. Louis, Ozark's flights were scheduled to originate and terminate in East St. Louis, with Lambert Field being the first stop outbound and the last stop inbound on all flights. East St. Louis was dropped from the schedules in January 1951, but the routine of ferrying airplanes back and forth across the river for servicing continued until the company had its own facilities at Lambert Field.

By August 8, 1951, less than one year from the date of its first flight, Ozark had inaugurated service to 29 stations covering all of the routes awarded to the company as a result of the Parks Investigation Case. Of course, this could not have been accomplished without the manpower, the expertise and the equipment provided by the Parks team. Many former Parks Air Lines employees went on to enjoy long careers with Ozark.

Laddie Hamilton's dream was now a firmly established reality. In June 1951, St. Louis became the first Ozark station to board over 1,000 passengers in a single month and for the first calendar year of operation, January – December 1951, 49,507 passengers flew Ozark.

The airline grew steadily, adding new stations and deleting unproductive points as allowed by the CAB. Ozark worked with the cities it served to establish navigation aids and equipment for instrument flying and night operations. This project, completed by September 1953, allowed Ozark to operate into every airport on its system by instruments, both day and night.

In 1954, Ozark's original three-year temporary Certificate of Public Convenience and Necessity was renewed for another five years. With the renewal came a tweaking of the airline's route system by the CAB. Service to Memphis was discontinued and Nashville was authorized as the terminal point beyond Paducah, Kentucky. The route map was also redrawn west of St. Louis.

Ozark's redefined route system promised more revenue for the company but the real prize was received on May 19, 1955, when President Dwight D. Eisenhower signed the bill that gave permanent certification to Ozark and the nation's 12

Fairchild F-27s entered service on Ozark's scheduled routes in January 1960. N4301F is pictured. (From the R. Dean Denton collection via the author)

 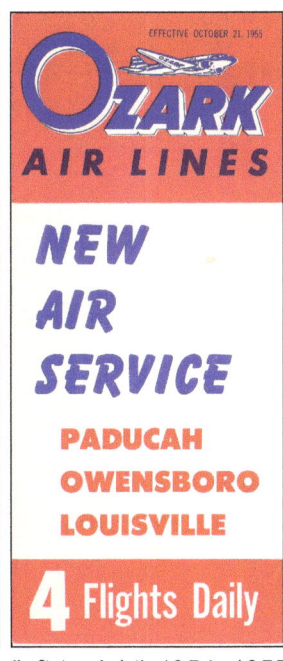   

Ozark timetables from (left to right) 1954, 1955, 1957, 1958 and, finally, the Dec. 15, 1958 issue announcing the company's order for F-27s. (From the author's collection)

other Local Service Airlines, as the Feeders were now called. This acknowledgement of a permanent place in the U.S. airline system made investors much more confident about betting their money on Ozark stock.

Also in 1955, the piece of the Parks Air Lines network that had been awarded to Mid-Continent, the route from Sioux City to Chicago, was transferred to Ozark from Braniff, which had acquired Mid-Continent. Ozark ended 1955 with 535 employees and 16 DC-3s.

In order to keep its aging fleet as competitive as possible, Ozark undertook a modification program for its DC-3s. Dubbed the 'Challenger 250' project, the goal was to upgrade the fleet to higher performance standards by installing wheel well doors, flush-type antennas, short exhaust stacks, wing fillets and aerodynamic oil coolers, turning Ozark's DC-3s into the most efficient in the industry. The program was completed by September 1957 when all aircraft had been standardized with the new equipment and each was configured with 27 passenger seats.

In December 1958, Ozark placed its initial order for three brand new Fairchild F-27s, which carried 40 passengers, capacity similar to that of the second-hand Martins and Convairs being purchased by other Locals. The F-27 employed modern turbine-propeller power, referred to as jet prop, with two engines set into a wing above the fuselage, giving every passenger an unobstructed view of the world below.

New aircraft would not be arriving a minute too soon. In 1957, Ozark began service over another route, this one to the Twin Cities of Minneapolis/St. Paul via Cedar Rapids, Iowa, and Rochester, Minnesota. Then, in 1958, the CAB concluded its Seven States Investigation Case awarding Ozark more new mileage and eight new cities to be served. In the summer of 1958,

Ozark bought four additional DC-3s from Northwest Airlines, upgrading them to Challenger 250 standards and bringing the fleet total to 24. In September 1958, it was announced that Ozark ranked first among all 13 local service carriers in load factor for the preceding 12 months.

Laddie Hamilton's health began to decline and in June 1959 he was granted an extended leave of absence from his positions as president and chairman of the board. On August 6, 1959, his old friend, Floyd W. Jones, was selected to fill out his term as board chair and Hamilton eventually resigned from both positions.

Joseph H. FitzGerald had been hired by Hamilton in 1958. FitzGerald had previously been with both the CAB and the FAA (then called the CAA, Civil Aeronautics Administration). On October 16, 1959, he was installed as president of the company.

F-27 service was set to begin on September 27, 1959, but there was a setback. The company's contract with its

Ozark added four Convair 240s in 1962, initially to handle expanded service at Peoria and Springfield, Illinois. (From the R. Dean Denton collection via the author)

   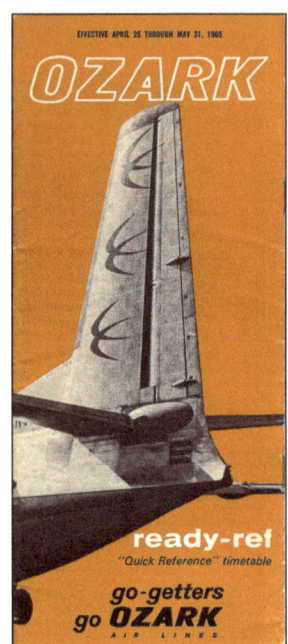

The March 1959 timetable announced seven new routes and continued to promote the F-27s that would enter service less than a year later. By 1961, the F-27s were firmly entrenched and the June 1964 route map shows operations throughout the Midwest. 1964 saw the introduction of the marketing program "Go-Getters Go Ozark," as reflected in this April 1965 timetable. (From the author's collection)

ALPA-represented pilots did not cover specific conditions related to flying the F-27. Negotiations addressing these issues had to be concluded before the aircraft entered scheduled service. In the meantime, Ozark's new airplanes spent their time touring the system and being used for promotional flights. Contract issues were settled with the pilots and the F-27s made their debut operating scheduled flights on January 4, 1960.

With the introduction of the F-27s, Ozark adopted a new logo: "Three sets of two overlapping elliptical curves arranged to suggest the graceful swept-back wings and deeply forked tail of the swallow." The *Three Swallows* symbol became so associated with Ozark Air Lines that its use was continued until the end of Ozark's existence.

After two years of CAB hearings, American Airlines terminated service at Peoria and at Springfield, Ill., on August 13, 1962. American's service at Joplin and Springfield, Mo., would end the following year. Ozark would now be the sole carrier at all four points. To accommodate the expanded schedule at these stations and to replicate American's level of service, FitzGerald's team purchased four 40-passenger Convair 240s, the same type of equipment that American had used on its service to these cities. Ozark increased its schedule and pretty soon the "little"

Ozark exchanged its four Convair 240s plus some cash for 14 Martin 404s from Mohawk Airlines. Martin N468M is seen at Chicago O'Hare in October 1965. (Photo Paul Kutta from the Tim Williams collection)

Ozark's DC-3s got an updated livery in the 1960s. Note the Three Swallows on the tail. N134D is pictured. (Photo from the Tim Williams collection)

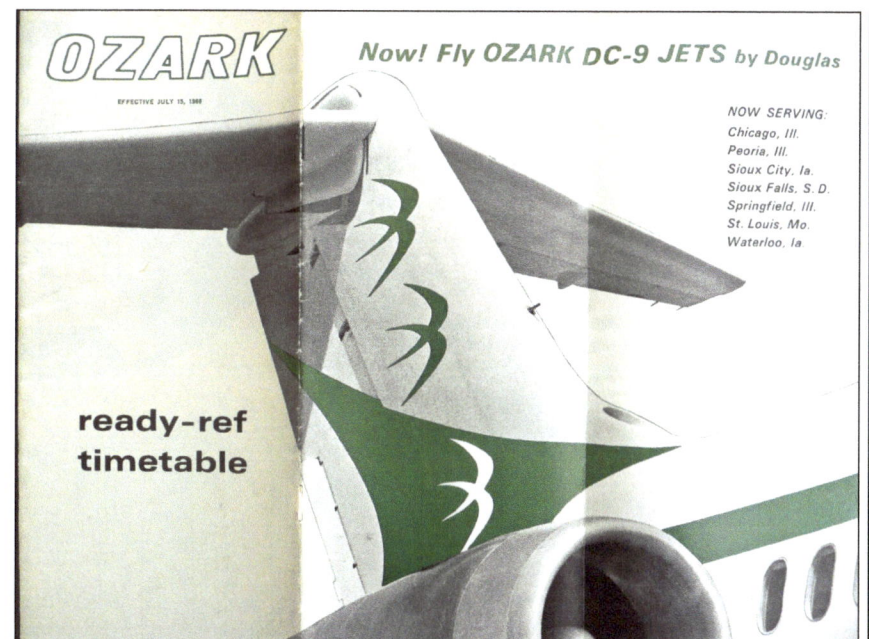

Ozark's July 15, 1966 timetable introduced the DC-9. In 1967, the company unveiled its advertising program known as the "Hostess Campaign." This was followed in 1968 by the "Go-Getter Bird" promotion. (From the author's collection)

airline with the green airplanes was carrying more total traffic out of all four stations than had ever been generated before.

Ozark maintained its slow and steady growth throughout the early 1960s while the search for more aircraft continued. The jet age was firmly in place and Ozark management knew that it would not be long before the Locals were expected to join the ranks of pure-jet operators. They looked at British Aircraft Corporation's BAC-111 twin-jet, designed for short-to-medium haul routes. While studying their jet options for the future, the need was growing for even more immediate capacity. By 1964, 12 Ozark stations were each boarding more than 20,000 passengers per year with Chicago at the top of the list enplaning almost a quarter of a million. The company introduced the slogan, "Go-Getters Go Ozark!"

Joseph H. FitzGerald resigned as Ozark's president at the end of July 1963 and Thomas L. Grace was recruited from Northeast Airlines to fill the vacancy. Grace was an airline man, having served as president of Slick Airways, an all-cargo line, before his tenure as Vice President of Operations at Northeast. He dove headlong into the issues facing Ozark, primarily aircraft acquisition, and he worked out a lease/trade agreement with Mohawk Airlines to take that company's 14 Martin 404s, another postwar twin-engine airliner handed down from the trunk carriers, in exchange for Ozark's Convair 240s, a type that Mohawk had been flying since 1955. The aircraft swap began with the first Martins going into service on Ozark's system on December 1, 1964.

But the big news came the following month, in January 1965, at the dedication of Ozark's new general office building and maintenance facility at Lambert Field, which was built by the city of St. Louis. At that ceremony, Thomas L. Grace announced that Ozark would be entering the ranks of pure-jet operators in early 1966 with the arrival of three Douglas DC-9-15s. Grace's plans did not stop there.

The Martin 404s had replaced the Convairs, and they were also intended to replace the DC-3s. Grace ordered yet another new aircraft type to replace both the Martins and the F-27s. The Fairchild-Hiller FH-227B was an enlarged and modernized version of the F-27. The new airplane would carry 48 passengers in the layout chosen by Ozark. It had a stronger Rolls Royce turbine engine than the F-27 and it carried its own Auxiliary Power Unit (APU) reducing the need for ground power units. The company placed an order for 21 FH-227Bs, scheduled to start coming on-line shortly after the first DC-9s arrived. Grace's goal was to turn Ozark into an all-turbine powered carrier by the end of 1967.

The first scheduled DC-9 service took to the skies on July 15, 1966, from St. Louis to Chicago via Peoria. On board that inaugural jet flight was Arthur B. Skinner of Kirkwood, Missouri. Mr. Skinner had been Ozark's very first passenger in September 1950 when a DC-3 taxied away from the gate in St. Louis with just one paying customer on board... himself!

The first scheduled FH-227B service took place on December 15, 1966, postponed from December 1 due to a system certification delay. With the FH-227Bs entering service, Ozark would spend the next several months operating five different aircraft types: DC-3, Martin 404, F-27, FH-227B and DC-9.

A merger between Ozark and neighboring local service carrier, Central Airlines, had been speculated upon for years.

The 1968 "Go-Getter Bird" campaign was followed in 1969 by the promotional message "Letting George Do It" featuring young comedian George Carlin. By 1972, Ozark was marketing itself as "Up there with the Biggest", while in 1975 the company celebrated its 25th year of operation. 1978 saw expansion to Philadelphia, followed by the onset of deregulation in October of that year. (From the author's collection)

On September 20, 1966, Floyd W. Jones, chairman of the board of Ozark, and Jack Bradley, chairman of the board of Central, announced that the two companies would merge, with Ozark to be the surviving carrier. Less than two months later the merger was called off. Tom Grace stated that "the money market... has been tight and we found it untimely to complete the merger."

Ozark did not need a merger to expand. Just three days after disclosing that it planned to merge with Central, Ozark announced a new route to Denver, awarded by the CAB. The flight to the Colorado capital non-stop from Sioux City would give Ozark a relatively long segment to use its DC-9s on.

The airline of the *Three Swallows* embarked on three memorable advertising campaigns in succession in the late 1960s. In 1967, the company introduced the "Hostess Campaign," which featured St. Louis model, Pat Christman, wearing an Ozark flight attendant uniform. Photos of her in different poses were presented along with two-line copy. "Have a sudden meeting in Chicago? We'll rise to the occasion," and "I can't bear to think of you driving all the way to Kansas City. No one to spoil you," are two examples of the ads from the award-winning series. The Hostess Campaign was followed in 1968 by "Go-Getter Bird." A cartoon bird dressed in an Ozark pilot's uniform, became the company *spokesperson*. Finally, in 1969, the airline introduced a campaign entitled "Letting George Do It." Ads featured a young comedian's face inside a somewhat rectangular "O," with advertising copy underneath. The young comedian was George Carlin, who had yet to achieve his great success.

Ozark retired its last Martin 404 from service on August 14, 1967. With the October 29, 1967 timetable the last F-27 was also removed from scheduled service. Three DC-3s continued to soldier on in the fleet as long as there were airports on Ozark's system that could not accommodate larger aircraft. But a year later, on October 27, 1968, Ozark finally met Tom Grace's goal of becoming an all-turbine powered airline. The last DC-3 flight was made the previous day into the only remaining station that could not handle larger aircraft – Columbia Municipal Airport in Missouri. On the 27th, Ozark flights began serving the new Columbia Regional Airport, with its 6,500 foot runway, located midway between Columbia and Jefferson City. FH-227B flights into the new airport replaced DC-3 service at the two individual city airports. Moberly and Kirksville, Mo., the two other stations served by the DC-3 flights, also received jet-prop service from October 27.

The difference between trunk carrier and local carrier blurred when the CAB began awarding non-stop authority between big-city pairs within the local's own network. Permission for Ozark to fly non-stop between Louisville and Indianapolis, and non-stop between St. Louis and Milwaukee was followed by an award that really put Ozark's status into a new perspective. On November 15, 1968, Ozark introduced non-stop DC-9 service between its two biggest stations, Chicago and St. Louis. This put Ozark in direct competition with American Airlines and with Delta. You could now board a jet offering both first class and coach accommodations non-stop between these cities on either a trunk carrier or a local carrier; there was no difference. Ozark had begun outfitting its DC-9s with a two-class configuration a few months before (the first class cabins would be removed in 1972).

Floyd W. Jones, the bus line owner who had financed Laddie Hamilton's plans for an airline, died on February 3, 1969, in

Springfield, Missouri. Jones, 79 years of age, was still serving as the chairman of Ozark's Board of Directors when he died. Hamilton, who had retired 10 years before due to failing health, outlived Jones by two years.

On April 27, 1969, service was introduced to Washington, D.C. (Dulles), and New York (LaGuardia) from Peoria and from Champaign/Urbana, Illinois. The award also allowed flights from Waterloo, Iowa, and Springfield, Ill., to the East Coast. The 956-mile Waterloo – New York authority was the longest segment awarded to a local service carrier up until that time.

One more new market, Dallas/Fort Worth, served through Love Field, was added to Ozark's system in 1969, and service was permitted non-stop from St. Louis to the Texas airport.

In 1971, with a modern fleet of DC-9s and FH-227Bs the airline introduced its new slogan, "Up there with the biggest!"

Thomas L. Grace, Ozark's president and chairman of the board, who had led the company into the jet age, passed away in July of 1971. Edward J. Crane, executive vice-president and treasurer of the airline and a company employee since 1951, took Grace's place as president of Ozark.

Ozark's system remained fairly stable during the early 1970s. On August 1, 1970, the airline inaugurated seasonal service to Lake of the Ozarks, Missouri. It would be the last of the typical, small Midwestern airports that Ozark would add to its network. As the decade progressed, the company sought permission to eliminate more and more of its smaller stations, which were the original reason for its existence. In 1974, when Ozark filed to terminate service at Clinton, Iowa, and Owensboro, Ky., the company complained that the stations were producing only 3.9 and 5.2 passengers *per departure* respectively. Those would have been considered exemplary boarding figures in the 1950s!

Innovations such as the internationally-themed *Flair* meal service and wine tasting flights brought attention to Ozark's cabin service.

In 1973, a strike by the company's mechanics, represented by the Air Line Mechanics Fraternal Association (AMFA), shut the airline down for 73 days. It would not be the last time that Ozark was grounded by a labor dispute. Shortly after the strike was settled, Ozark suffered its only accident that resulted in loss of life to passengers. On July 23, flight 809, an FH-227B operating between Nashville and St. Louis via Clarksville, Paducah, Cape Girardeau and Marion/Herrin, crashed while on final approach to St. Louis in a thunderstorm. Of the 44 aboard, 37 passengers and the flight attendant perished.

The company boarded its 30 millionth passenger on May 19, 1975. Then, just two and one-half years later, on December 16, 1977, the 40 millionth customer was welcomed aboard.

Ozark's management was vehemently opposed to the concept of deregulation. An editorial in the *Go-Getter News*, the company newspaper, warned that if deregulation became a reality, airlines would fly wherever they wanted and go after the larger markets while neglecting the smaller ones. The opinion piece forewarned that smaller and less-profitable markets would be abandoned, jobs would be lost and airlines would go under. As it turned out, many of those predictions would prove accurate.

The push to deregulate the nation's airlines became even stronger on Capitol Hill after a pro-deregulation economist from Cornell University named Alfred Kahn was appointed to head the CAB by President Jimmy Carter. Airline deregulation in the United States became a reality when President Carter signed the final bill into law on October 24, 1978.

Ozark's expansion after passage of the Airline Deregulation Act started out in an orderly fashion. Atlanta was added to the route map on December 1, 1978. The company also jumped into the Florida market, a natural destination for Midwest vacationers. Houston (Hobby) was welcomed to the system on April 1, 1979, followed by Little Rock and New Orleans. Following the new liberalities offered by deregulation, service to Little Rock was

Ozark began replacing Martin 404s and Fairchild F-27s with the enlarged and upgraded Fairchild F-227Bs in 1966. Ozark was on track to become an all-turbine airline by the end of 1968. (Photo by R. Dean Denton from the author's collection)

When deregulation became law, Ozark jumped into the Florida market. In early 1981, Ozark printed 20,000 "Emergency Timetables" in anticipation of a PATCO strike. When the air traffic controllers finally did walk out in August, the company was better prepared and the emergency timetables were not needed. The April 25, 1982 timetable advertises 90 flights a day to St. Louis, all of them operated with DC-9s, and the Oct. 1, 1985 timetable introduces Ozark Midwest, a commuter feed to Ozark's flights offered by Air Midwest. (From the author's collection)

quickly dropped after enplanements proved disappointing.

Unlike Braniff and other carriers, Ozark seemed to be meeting the challenges of the new environment by expanding in a conservative yet methodical and disciplined manner. Sadly, on the other side of the coin, smaller cities including Quincy, Bloomington, Mattoon/Charleston and Mt. Vernon, Ill.; Ft. Leonard Wood, Mo.; Ottumwa, Iowa; Clarksville, Tenn., and Paducah, Ky., all were abandoned by the *Three Swallows*. Local Service Airline was no longer a designation that appropriately described Ozark. The term Regional Airline had come into use as a more fitting characterization.

On Christmas Eve of 1978, Arthur G. Heyne, the last of Ozark's four founding fathers, passed away in St. Louis. He was 80 years old and had witnessed Ozark's growth from that very first day on Chestnut Street in 1943. Now Ozark was heading in a new direction, forced, some would say, by circumstances beyond its control. Ozark operated its last FH-227B flight on October 25, 1980, leaving the company with a fleet of 30 DC-9-30s, two DC-9-30LRs and seven DC-9-10s. Only airports with runways long enough to support DC-9 operations would be receiving Ozark service in the future.

In 1979, the Association of Flight Attendants shut the airline down with a 53-day strike. Shortly after recovering from that work stoppage, Ozark's operations were again brought to a halt in 1980 with a 38-day strike by mechanics. While the flight attendants were on strike, in order to generate cash, the company sold two factory-fresh Boeing 727-200s, having never put them into service.

Ozark was no longer in business to feed passengers to other carriers. Now its goal was to feed passengers to itself through the St. Louis hub. The marketplace had become a contest where each airline tried to attract the same passenger. By the end of 1982, Ozark had 102 daily departures scheduled from St. Louis. The company also pulled out of markets that were once synonymous with Ozark: Chicago to Peoria and Chicago to Springfield, Illinois. It seemed that President Crane was making his prediction about deregulation from several years before come true: smaller and less-profitable markets were being abandoned.

If a company could not survive after choosing to follow the same hub-and-spoke, abandon-smaller-markets path as most of its competitors, then the inevitable outcome was merger or bankruptcy. Ozark also had the disadvantage of competing with another strong player at its own hometown hub: Trans World Airlines (TWA). To have two airlines centering domestic operations in a market the size of St. Louis was a recipe for trouble.

The realignment of Ozark's system was reflected in the introduction of the Executive Express, an hourly non-stop service between Chicago's O'Hare Airport and Lambert Field. Non-stop service from Chicago to all other cities was eliminated; the Windy City was now just a spoke from St. Louis.

On July 28, 1983, Ozark placed an order with McDonnell Douglas for four new MD-80s (previously referred to as DC-9 Super 80s), each equipped with 152 passenger seats. Sanford N. McDonnell, CEO of McDonnell Douglas, noted at the time that Ozark was the largest exclusive operator of DC-9s in the world.

In 1984, Ozark Holdings was formed, a company intended to be an umbrella for corporate expansion opportunities.

Ozark became the largest exclusive operator of DC-9s in the world. The last of the company's turboprops was retired in 1980, leaving a fleet comprised entirely of DC-9 variants, which would eventually include the DC-9 Super 80, or MD-80, as it became known. MD-82 N950U is seen on approach to Washington's Ronald Reagan National Airport on May 1, 1985. (Photo by Aero Icarus)

Ozark Air Lines became a subsidiary of the holding company. Former baseball legend, Stan Musial, was elected to the board of directors.

Ozark inaugurated service to the state capitals of Lincoln, Neb., and Oklahoma City, Okla., on April 15, 1985. These would be the last two stations added to the Ozark route map.

When the new Southeast "D" Concourse at Lambert Field opened for business it gave Ozark a state-of-the-art airport complex for its hub operation. The concourse, along with Ozark's other facilities at Lambert, was dubbed AIRPLEX and the company now had 22 gates available for exchanging passengers among its flights. Ozark entered into an agreement with Air Midwest, a third level carrier, to provide feed from smaller stations to the company's St. Louis hub. Operating under the banner of Ozark Midwest, the operation, which started October 1, 1985, provided for Ozark the same type of feed that Ozark once provided for other carriers. In a striking example of changing times all service into Springfield, Ill., once an Ozark bastion, was now turned over to the commuter carrier.

In 1985, two things happened that would change everything for Ozark: Southwest Airlines, the low-cost carrier that did not follow the pack, entered St. Louis, going right into the St. Louis – Chicago market, among others. Then, through a hostile takeover, Carl Icahn gained control of TWA. Icahn went to work reducing labor costs at TWA and reducing passenger fares, making it a more formidable competitor. Ozark was forced to meet new challenges. Ozark had made money during the first half of 1985, but lost almost as much as it had made in the first half during the second half. Cash flow was critical and, in December, Mr. Crane approached the unions at Ozark proposing profit sharing and stock ownership in exchange for wage concessions. It was all happening a little too late in the game.

Edward J. Crane, the accountant, had abandoned Ozark's smaller stations and built the airline into a national player with routes radiating solely from St. Louis, which wound up being the corner that he painted himself and his company into. The Crane management team had produced a few profitable years for Ozark since deregulation but the clock was running out for the airline of the *Three Swallows*. It had not grown big enough to withstand major players, the way USAir had, and it was too late to totally change its game plan and become a low-fare point-to-point carrier like Southwest. When Carl Icahn made an offer to buy Ozark for $19 per share, he knew he had the upper hand. Ozark's board, its investment bankers and the company lawyers met at the St. Louis Airport Hilton, a property co-owned by Stan Musial, to consider the proposal. Although Crane insisted that "it was not a bang-bang decision," meaning that it had not been made in a hurry, the offer was accepted by the board and announced to the public in February 1986. Ozark employees certainly wondered why their company, which had been profitable for the past few years, should now be up for sale. Ozark management felt that TWA and the low cost carriers would crush Ozark if the company tried to remain independent so they took advantage of an offer that might not have been made a second time.

Icahn would merge Ozark into TWA and get rid of the *Three Swallows*, the green paint and the name of the company that had been associated with Midwestern states for so many years. The official merger date was October 27, 1986. On that day the eradication of Ozark began. Ozark Air Lines disappeared into Icahn's TWA, an airline that would meet the same fate when it merged with American Airlines 15 years later.

Ozark's successful rise from a four DC-3 operation to a national airline with a fleet of 50 jets was the result of the dedication and hard work of its loyal employees, proud to work for the great "little" airline that was "up there with the biggest." ✈

America's Local Service Airlines

CHAPTER 10

PACIFIC AIR LINES
(FORMERLY SOUTHWEST AIRWAYS)

Southwest Airways was born in Hollywood, or, more specifically, in Beverly Hills at Chasen's Restaurant. That's where Leland Hayward and Jack Connelly came up with the idea (*TIME Magazine*, Feb. 8, 1943). Hayward, Southwest's co-founder, was one of Hollywood's best-known theatrical agents and the husband of actress Margaret Sullavan. But his first love was flying. In 1940, he and Connelly, a test pilot and Civil Aeronautics Administration employee, formed Southwest with the intention of establishing a fixed-base operation and pilot training school. Their timing coincided with the military's need to teach thousands of prospective pilots how to fly in preparation for the United States involvement in World War II.

Unlike other aviation ventures trying to find financing, Southwest had no problem as Hayward's friends among the Hollywood elite, including Jimmy Stewart, Henry Fonda, Cary Grant and Hoagy Carmichael, purchased shares to help put the scheme into operation. The new company built an airport, Thunderbird Field, northwest of Phoenix, Arizona. Western artist, Millard Sheets, designed the complex to resemble a giant thunderbird from the air. The thunderbird was an Indian symbol that represented either thunder and lightning or flight, depending upon the tribe.

Southwest began churning out pilots, hundreds of them, at Thunderbird under contract to the military. The company soon built two more facilities, Thunderbird Field Number Two, and Falcon Field, both of which served as sites for Southwest Airways pilot training schools. After building the three airports complete with dormitories and classroom buildings, Southwest sold each facility to the government, then ran the operations and earned revenue for every flier they trained. By the end of the war Southwest Airways had minted more than 10,000 new pilots, and the company had earned a tidy profit.

As with other fixed-base operations that had served the government well during the war by training pilots, Southwest Airways was looked upon favorably when the company submitted an application to the Civil Aeronautics Board (CAB) for authority to operate scheduled service as a feeder airline. The company was selected to operate 1,153 miles of local service routes "radiating from San Francisco." The award included authority to operate between San Francisco and Los Angeles via eight intermediate points, and two routes northward from San Francisco to Medford, Oregon: one roughly along the coast, the other up through the Sacramento Valley. Like all of the other feeders, Southwest's initial certificate was valid for just three years.

Pacific Air Lines DC-3 N67588 stands ready for duty at San Francisco International in November 1959. (From the Tim Williams collection)

 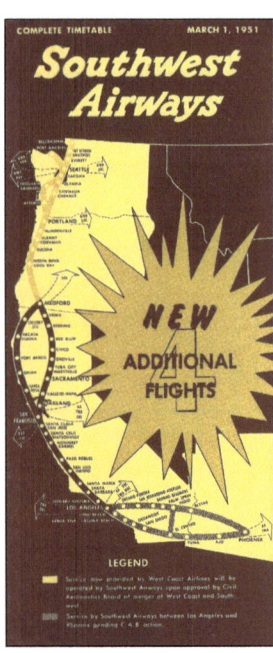

LEFT: *Southwest's route system extending from Los Angeles, Calif., to Medford, Ore., is illustrated on the cover of this 1949 timetable.* RIGHT: *Southwest received tentative approval from the CAB (later rescinded) to extend its system east to Phoenix. Meanwhile, the company was negotiating for merger with West Coast Airlines (which did not happen). Southwest printed a 1951 route map showing the envisioned system. (From the author's collection)*

America's Local Service Airlines

1. *Southwest Airways DC-3, N63107, seen at Los Angeles (LAX) in 1952. Note the airstair door that this airline pioneered and that greatly assisted in reducing turnaround time at a station. This innovation would be adopted by other feeder lines. (From the Tim Williams collection)* **2.** *Detail of airstair door. (From the Ed Coates Collection via PacificAirLinesPortfolio.com)* **3.** *Cartoonist Wiley Smith promoted Southwest's half-fare "Family Plan" in this comic advertisement. (From the author's collection)* **4.** *The Thunderbird logo for the airline incorporated into a baggage label. (From the author's collection)*

Again Southwest had no problem raising capital, which was far different from the experience of most of the new feeder carriers. Service was inaugurated on December 2, 1946, between San Francisco and Los Angeles while the two routes north from San Francisco were activated early the following year. By May of 1947, Southwest was serving 23 airports, 22 of which were in California. Southwest would have been the first of the airlines created from scratch as a feeder to become airborne but was beaten to that claim by Monarch Air Lines of Denver, which inaugurated service just five days earlier on November 27, 1946.

Southwest started out with a fleet of eight 21-passenger DC-3s, each aircraft adorned with the company's thunderbird logo. Hayward and his team put a lot of thought into the creation of their feeder airline. There were no guidelines to follow since it was an entirely new concept.

First of all, station stops at intermediate points would be scheduled for one minute with the right engine continuously running, unless there were no passengers to be boarded or deplaned, in which case both engines would be left running. Both engines would be shut down and ground time increased slightly to allow for fueling, when necessary. Pilots fueled their own aircraft. While this was an ambitious schedule, it was not practical. After a bit of experience, Southwest's management lengthened the time at intermediate stops to two minutes and, by the 1950s, the local airline norm would eventually become three minutes of ground time.

In order to facilitate the original one-minute schedule, stewards were hired, instead of stewardesses, to act as flying station agents. Referred to as pursers, their job included moving all cargo and baggage to be off-loaded at the next stop to the front of the bin, next to the baggage compartment door. This was accomplished by installing a door between the cabin and the aft cargo/baggage bin. When the aircraft came to a stop on the ramp, the purser assisted with loading and off-loading cargo and bags, as well as passengers. The presence of the purser allowed Southwest to save on the expense of an extra agent at each station.

Each intermediate point would require just one agent to

LEFT and MIDDLE: *Southwest's April 26, 1953 timetable cover advertises service to more California cities than any other scheduled airline, while the center spread advertises the local service experience: leave home in the morning, conduct business in a different city, then return home in the evening.* RIGHT: *This October 27, 1957 timetable center spread was alluding to the upcoming name change, which took place on March 6, 1958.*

assist the purser (and vice-versa) in loading and unloading, while also handling station duties. In order to facilitate this quick ground stop, it was decided that all boarding, deplaning and loading activity must take place at ground level. Therefore, the forward cargo door would not be used. Instead, the last row of seats in each aircraft was removed and reinstalled up front where the forward cargo area had been located. In the back of the plane in front of the door, in the area formerly occupied by the last row of seats, a baggage rack was installed allowing passengers to carry aboard their own items, if desired.

The most important innovation that allowed for this quick-stop service was the installation of boarding stairs on the inside of the boarding door, which was hinged at the bottom. This *airstair* design, which became standard equipment on all local service DC-3s, was first used in service by Southwest. The airstair door allowed the steward (purser) to lower the stairs from inside the cabin by using leather-covered chains installed on either side of the stairs, which also served as handrails. The self-contained airstairs eliminated the need for passenger loading stands to be rolled into place by an agent at each airport.

James G. Ray, a Southwest vice-president, applied for a patent for the self-contained airstairs, and that caused contention. Sam Solomon, former president of Northeast Airlines, had left his position at that carrier and applied for a certificate to operate a company he called Atlantic Airlines. Among the innovations planned for Atlantic were integral stairs inside the doors of DC-3s, using the same concept, but not exactly the same design, as that adopted by Southwest. Atlantic's steps-in-the-door design was created by an engineer named David Morrow and pre-dated Southwest's design. Sam Solomon displayed a scale model of the design before the CAB during testimony in the Middle Atlantic Case. James G. Ray was present in Washington, D.C., at the time and asked Solomon if he could study the design. Solomon consented. Atlantic Airlines was not chosen to receive a CAB certificate and, later, Southwest's Ray went on to receive a patent for the door without Solomon's permission. Though Southwest Airways claimed to be the innovators of the design, people who read the aviation press were well aware of who really originated the airstair concept.

Another Southwest Airways innovation was a buzzer system with which the purser could signal the cockpit to alert them that all loading and unloading had been completed.

As the airline gained experience some modifications were made to the original model of service. A second station agent was hired for each intermediate airport as the workload for a single agent, even with the assistance of the purser while an aircraft was on the ground, was sometimes too great. As mentioned above, the flight schedule was adjusted to allow ground time of two minutes at intermediate points instead of one.

Southwest had a good population base along its system and the company quickly rose in the ranks of the local service carriers (the more-appropriate term being applied to feeders). After 22 months of operation, at the end of September 1948, the company posted its first profitable quarter with a net of $47,118.00. Meanwhile, other locals were still struggling to make ends meet in their infancy.

In 1950, Southwest's management entered into discussions with Nick Bez, who controlled West Coast Airlines, the local service carrier operating just to the north of Southwest Airways' territory. The two airlines met at Medford, Oregon, Southwest's

CLOCKWISE FROM ABOVE: *The three successive liveries applied to Pacific's F-27s (original 1959 paint scheme, early 1960s livery, and late 1960s final scheme) are displayed here on N2770R, N2772R, and N2771R, respectively. (First two photos by Larry Smalley from the Tim Williams collection, third photo from the Bill Thompson collection)*

northernmost point, and West Coast's southernmost. It was a particularly weak "end of the line" city for feeder connections. If the two companies were allowed to merge, people from the smaller cities in Washington State and Oregon could travel through to points in California and likewise for the residents of small-cities in California who would have one-carrier access to Portland and Seattle. It was postulated that a merger would create generous savings and increased revenue so petition for such a union was presented to the CAB. The CAB denied the request, fearing that the creation of a single local airline whose route system would stretch from Bellingham to Los Angeles would compete with Western Airlines and United for traffic along the Pacific Coast.

But the CAB followed its denial of the Southwest/West Coast merger request with proposal of a merger between Southwest Airways and Bonanza Air Lines, one in which neither carrier would be a willing participant. Bonanza had been losing money while Southwest was profitable. The CAB felt that a merger would reduce Bonanza's reliance on subsidy. Lack of interest on the part of either airline caused the CAB to drop the matter but both carriers, along with West Coast, would be back at the bargaining table discussing merger many years later.

In 1952, Southwest boldly took the step to acquire larger, more modern equipment. Its aircraft of choice was the 40-passenger Martin 202. The move was bold because another local service carrier, Pioneer Air Lines, had recently replaced its entire fleet of DC-3s with Martins, to the displeasure of the CAB, which refused to underwrite the purchase with increased subsidy. Subsequently, Pioneer had to remove its Martins from service and lease more DC-3s. The fiasco put Pioneer into a spiral that eventually led to the company losing its identity through merger with Continental Air Lines, a trunk carrier. Southwest, on the other hand, purchased only four Martins to supplement its DC-3s, not to replace them, and initially added only two of the type to its schedule rotation. This more conservative approach to fleet upgrade had favorable results, making Southwest the first of the Locals to successfully add larger equipment to its fleet.

Southwest Airways continued on its path of progress by recording the highest passenger load factor among the Locals in 1954 and 1955. The carrier was a thorn in the side to much larger United Air Lines, whose authority to serve Santa Barbara, Monterey, Eureka and Red Bluff was temporarily suspended by the CAB in 1952, in order to turn these stations over completely to the local airline. United made an offer to the CAB: The trunk carrier proposed taking over Southwest and operating the feeder system itself without taking subsidy. The CAB declined. Had the CAB accepted United's offer, it may have set a precedent that could have led to the demise of the fledgling network of independent local airlines. Instead, 1955 brought permanent certification of the Locals with Southwest being the first carrier to receive one of the non-expiring certificates. Concurrent with this new recognition bestowed upon Southwest, United was allowed to re-enter the markets of Monterey, Santa Barbara and Eureka.

Southwest joined the ranks of carriers hiring female flight attendants as the ability of pursers to sort cargo and baggage was lost with the introduction of the Martins.

Southwest Martin 202 featured on a postcard. (From Aviation World via the author)

America's Local Service Airlines

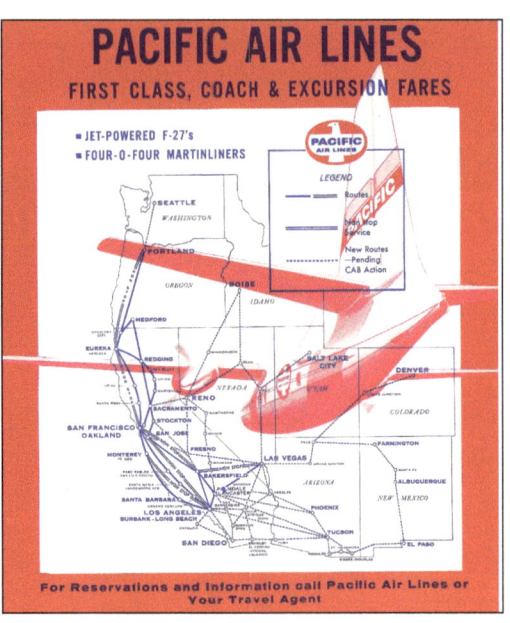

Left to Right: Southwest Airways officially became Pacific Air Lines in March 1958, as announced on this June 1, 1958 timetable cover. Pacific introduced turboprop Fairchild F-27s, branded as "Jethawks", into the fleet in 1959. The route map from December 1960 shows grand plans as Pacific applied for route extensions, most of which were not approved. The July 30, 1966 timetable announces the introduction of jets, Boeing 727s, into Pacific's fleet. (All from the author's collection)

Over the years, the company's route network was strengthened with liberalized operating authority allowing non-stop and limited-stop operation between various points on its system.

Las Vegas, Nev., became a Southwest Airways station in 1957, with service to the desert vacation oasis provided from Burbank via Palmdale/Lancaster. The company was now referring to itself in promotional material as "Southwest Airways, The Pacific Air Line."

On March 6, 1958, the company officially changed its name to Pacific Air Lines, an appellation more appropriate to the territory served.

In April 1959, Pacific entered the turboprop era by introducing Fairchild F-27s into service on its routes, referring to the brand new aircraft as *Jethawks*. Late in 1959, Pacific also began to replace the Martin 202s in its fleet with pressurized Martin 404s, purchased second-hand from TWA. Over the years, Pacific operated a fleet of 10 Martin 404s, in a 44-passenger configuration. One of the 404s was eventually converted to a cargoliner.

Also in 1959, the issue of having Medford, Ore., as the terminal point for two local service carriers was resolved when

Pacific began replacing Martin 202s with pressurized 404s in late 1959. N40432 is seen here in an early 1960s paint scheme. (Photo by Bill Thompson)

The Boeing 727-100 was too big and too costly to operate for Pacific's needs. They were a stopgap to be used until 737s became available. The 727s were eventually eliminated from the fleet of the new company, Air West, after Pacific merged with Bonanza and West Coast. The 737 order was cancelled. (Photo from PacificAirLinesPortolio.com)

As part of an image makeover after the introduction of jets, flight attendants were decked out in a trendy hot-pink uniform. On the right, Pacific's final timetable, effective April 28, 1968, announces the merger forming Air West. (From the author's collection)

Pacific's system was extended northward to Portland and West Coast was authorized to fly south to Sacramento, Oakland and San Francisco. Pacific's system was enlarged further in 1962 with the addition of Reno, Fresno, Long Beach and San Diego to the company's route map. Lake Tahoe was added the following year.

In 1963, Leland Hayward and John Connelly sold shares of Pacific stock to West Coast's Nick Bez, effectively giving that company a one-third interest in Pacific. The prospect of a merger between the two airlines was once again being pursued, but this time West Coast was the stronger of the two carriers. Making even more money now than either West Coast or Pacific was Bonanza Air Lines, which had once lagged behind with a weak network stretching through the Desert Southwest. The CAB launched an investigation into West Coast's acquisition of Pacific stock, which had been accomplished without permission of the CAB. The prospect of merger between Pacific and West Coast or between Pacific and Bonanza loomed in the background now as it had years before.

When the local service carriers started gearing up for the jet age, both Bonanza and West Coast chose the Douglas DC-9 as their jetliner of choice. Pacific's management decided to hold out for the Boeing 737, which was several years behind the DC-9 in development. As a stopgap measure, Pacific would take delivery, via lease, of five Boeing 727-100s to operate while awaiting production of its six ordered 737s.

The 727s arrived and two of them were immediately leased to National Airlines. The remaining three went on-line in July 1966. Pacific's most profitable non-stop route, San Jose – Los Angeles, had just been invaded by intrastate carrier, Pacific Southwest Airlines (PSA), bringing low-fare competition to Pacific's bread-and-butter market. The new jets were put into service on routes where the company felt they could make an impression and make money: San Francisco – Monterey – Santa Barbara – Los Angeles, San Francisco – Fresno – Bakersfield – Los Angeles, and, of course, San Jose – Los Angeles. Other markets eventually received service from the tri-jets.

With its new jets, Pacific wanted to boost traffic and generate attention. The company hired comedian and satirist, Stan Freberg, to create an advertising campaign that would create 'buzz' for Pacific Air Lines. Freberg's work was known for being unorthodox, and his work for Pacific Air Lines proved to be no exception. In a campaign he called "Sweaty Palms," introduced in May 1967 concurrent with the inaugural of non-stop Burbank – San Francisco service, Freberg played on the public's fear of flying. Print ads began with: "Hey there! You with the sweat in your palms," while flight attendants were instructed to announce after each landing, "We made it! How about that?" Hot pink lunch pails containing a rabbit's foot, a small security blanket and silly putty were passed out to passengers. There were plans to paint the exterior of one of the 727s to look like a steam locomotive. That particular aircraft was to be equipped with a train whistle and recorded train sounds were to be played in the cabin.

The campaign never made it as far as painting the jetliner to resemble a train. Some members of Pacific's board of directors were not pleased with the content of the ad program and the company's vice president of marketing and its director of advertising resigned. The campaign was withdrawn in June 1967.

Pacific stewardesses were clad in trendy new hot pink uniforms as part of the company's makeover.

The 727s entered more markets where the CAB allowed liberalized authority: non-stop San Jose – Las Vegas, Burbank – Las Vegas, and Monterey – Los Angeles. But losses were so great that management actually considered removing the jets from service. It was decided that such a move would do more harm than good to the public's perception of Pacific and, besides, the merger issue was now front-and-center.

On July 21, 1967, G. Robert Henry, former executive vice president of Bonanza Air Lines, took over as president of Pacific Air Lines in preparation for a three-way merger between Bonanza, Pacific, and West Coast. Pacific would be the surviving carrier and the company's name would be changed to Air West. Headquarters were to remain in San Francisco. The CAB gave its blessing and President Lyndon Johnson signed off on the merger because it involved international routes to Mexico (Bonanza) and Canada (West Coast).

Pacific, West Coast, and Bonanza officially became Air West on April 17, 1968, and the first integrated schedule of the three airlines was issued on July 1. Three of America's permanently-certificated local service carriers had just disappeared. ✈

CHAPTER 11

PIEDMONT AIRLINES

Winston-Salem, N.C., is in the heart of tobacco country. Two brands of cigarettes popular in the Twentieth Century took their monikers from the two halves of the city's name. The local airport, Smith Reynolds, was named after Zachary Smith Reynolds, the aviator son of R.J. Reynolds, founder of the tobacco company that bears his name. So it should be no surprise that the fixed-base operation (FBO) at that airport, which Tom Davis bought in 1940, was called Camel City Flying Service, named after one of the cigarette brands manufactured in Winston-Salem.

Z. Smith Reynolds' brother, Dick Reynolds, had formed Reynolds Aviation in 1927. By the late 1930s, the company's name had been changed to Camel City Flying Service and was under the management of Mac McGinnis, Reynolds' chief pilot. McGinnis hired Tom Davis, a young man from a prominent Winston-Salem family, to be an aircraft salesman for the company in 1939. The following year Davis purchased a controlling interest in the fixed base operation from Dick Reynolds and he renamed the enterprise Piedmont Aviation. The new name became effective on July 2, 1940, and Tom Davis was on his way to becoming one of the Twentieth Century's legendary figures in commercial aviation.

Piedmont Aviation established FBOs throughout the State of North Carolina. Then, during World War II, Piedmont took on the task of pilot training and aircraft maintenance for the military. The company's facility at Winston-Salem employed 100 people and instructed more than 1,000 pilots during the war years, including military students from South America.

When the Civil Aeronautics Board (CAB) began its process of creating America's feeder airline network, Piedmont Aviation was one of the applicants in the Southeastern States Case. Tom Davis and his team carefully prepared their presentation to the CAB, outlining fiscal plans for running an airline and noting the company's history as a successful fixed-base operator with many locations, emphasizing the contemplated airline's ability to handle much of its own maintenance. His original proposal for routes blanketed the state of North Carolina, covered much of Virginia and South Carolina, and reached into neighboring states.

The CAB issued its decision on April 4, 1947, selecting Piedmont to operate local services between the Ohio Valley and the Atlantic Coast area of Virginia and North Carolina. As was the case with successful feeder applicants in other parts of the country, undoubtedly working in Piedmont's favor was the added fact that the company had performed work for the government during the war. However, the route system awarded to Piedmont was much smaller and quite different than the one originally proposed by the company.

One of the other applicants in the case, State Airlines of Charlotte, filed an objection to the CAB's decision. State, founded in 1939 by Hank K. Gilbert, Jr., had performed an in-depth study of the transportation needs of the area, determining which cities would generate the greatest number of air travelers per capita. Gilbert's team had also estimated operating costs and had lined up financing. Obviously they were upset when Piedmont won the award as they felt they were better suited to operate a feeder airline in the region. State challenged the CAB's decision on a number of grounds including the award of routes to Piedmont that did not match those requested by the company.

State's challenge was accompanied by protests from Delta Air Lines and Eastern Air Lines. Both Delta and Eastern contended that they could operate the new feeder routes as part of their own systems. The feeder concept was brand new and unproven. The last thing that the established airlines wanted was for new airlines to be given authority that might eventually be expanded into competition.

State Airlines took the matter to the United States Court of Appeals and then, dissatisfied with the ruling from that body, all the way to the United States Supreme Court, which would not hear the case until 1949. In the meantime, the Court of Appeals and the CAB cleared Piedmont to begin operations. The Supreme Court settled the matter once and for all when they issued their decision on February 6, 1950, upholding the CAB's decision-making process and, thus, the CAB's award of the certificate to Piedmont.

Piedmont's network started out as a pattern of basically east – west routes, spanning the Appalachian Mountains. To quote the CAB, this experimental feeder system would connect "the industrial Midwest with the Middle Atlantic States of North Carolina and Virginia. Surface transportation [has] become highly developed in a north – south direction, but because of the natural barriers created by the Appalachian Mountain range slow and circuitous rail and highway systems [have] developed in an east – west direction."

Piedmont Aviation remained the name of the company performing fixed base services, while Piedmont Airlines was the designation given to the entity that would operate the feeder

Piedmont initiated operations in 1948 with three Douglas DC-3s. (Photo from the Tim Williams collection)

This January 20, 1949 timetable shows the initial route system awarded to Piedmont, while the advertisement touts the DC-3 fleet's style, comfort and performance. (From the author's collection)

network. Three Douglas DC-3s, one leased from Southern Airways of Atlanta, the other two purchased from Colonial Airlines, made up the airline's initial fleet.

Piedmont's inaugural flight departed Wilmington, N.C., at 7:15 a.m. on February 20, 1948, postponed one week from February 13 due to weather. After stops in Southern Pines, Charlotte, and Asheville, N.C.; Tri-Cities, Tenn. / Virginia; and Lexington, Ky., each involving a municipal celebration, the flight arrived at its terminus, Cincinnati, Ohio. The return to Wilmington took place after a luncheon at the Cincinnati airport commemorating the first flight.

Service over Piedmont's other authorized routes was phased in during the course of the next three months culminating with the Norfolk – Cincinnati route activated on May 14, 1948.

During its first few years of operation, Tom Davis saw to it that thriftiness was the company's guiding principle, while the employees worked hard to make sure that the airline, christened *The Route of the Pacemakers*, would be a success. The company performed all of its own maintenance in-house. Passenger count increased markedly year-by-year as the airline's flight completion factor hovered at 98 percent. The airline rose to the top among the Locals as it registered the lowest operating expense per revenue plane mile in 1950 among its peers operating exclusively with DC-3s for the entire year. Most impressive to the CAB was Piedmont's lower need for mail pay subsidy in comparison to the other Locals. When the airline's certificate came up for renewal, the Civil Aeronautic Board examiner recommended that it be extended for 10 years, an extraordinary recommendation for a type of air carrier still in the proving stages. The CAB renewed for seven years, which was still a powerful testament to the carrier's record.

Even though Piedmont ranked highest among the Locals in passenger revenue in 1953 and 1954 and its subsidy requirement was lower than that of other local service carriers, the company still relied on those government payments, as did all of its peers.

It came with the territory that short hops among small cities in aging airliners required more money than passenger and cargo revenue alone could provide.

Like all of the other local airlines, Piedmont got a boost in 1955 with permanent certification. Also that year the company's route system was extended to Washington, D.C., Columbus, Ohio, and Charlottesville, Va., all of which became high-volume stations for Piedmont.

At the end of 1955, Piedmont was flying 17 Douglas DC-3s, and the company acquired three more the following year. Better equipment was needed. In an interview with *American Aviation* magazine, Tom Davis referred to Convairs and to Martin 202s as "substitutes" for DC-3s, and not very suitable for local service. Davis had his eye set on the new-generation, pressurized, turbo-prop Fairchild F-27. In 1956, Piedmont ordered 12 of the type with an option for 12 more, the largest aircraft order placed by a local service airline up until that time. Piedmont's F-27s would be configured to carry 36 passengers.

In the same magazine interview mentioned above, Davis defended Piedmont's employment of male pursers as opposed to stewardesses, noting that the men were important in reducing time and expense at terminals by arranging baggage of deplaning passengers in advance of arrival, thereby expediting ramp work.

The new airplanes began arriving in late 1958, by which time Piedmont had reduced its order from 12 to 10. The ambitious plan to eventually purchase 24 F-27s was reduced to the reality of being able to afford eight, as two of the new planes were immediately sold to corporate customers. The Fairchilds entered service on November 14, 1958, and proved to be popular with passengers.

In March 1961, the CAB transferred Capital Airlines' route authority between Norfolk, Va., and Knoxville, Tenn., via

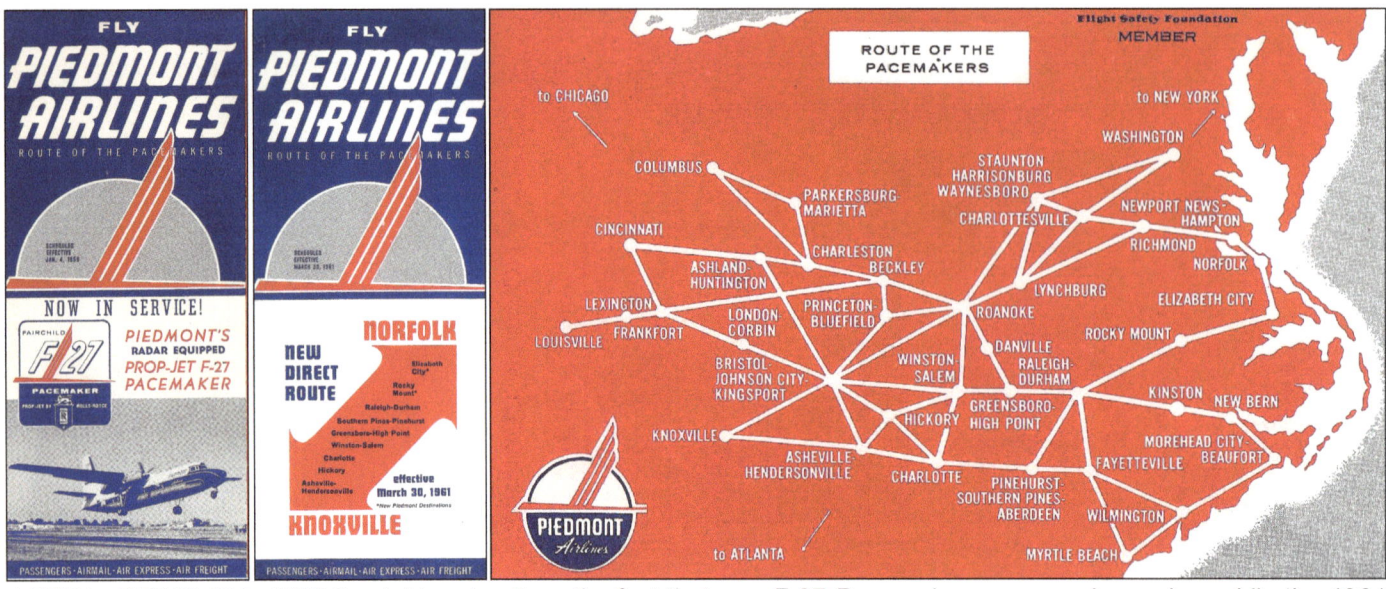

LEFT to RIGHT: *This 1959 timetable advertises the fact that new F-27 Pacemakers are now in service, while the 1961 issue announces the route transferred from Capital Airlines. This 1961 route map shows the extent of Piedmont's growth after 13 years in business.. (From the author's collection)*

intermediate points, to Piedmont, which added Elizabeth City and Rocky Mount, N.C., to the *Route of the Pacemakers*. This was overshadowed the following year by expansion of Piedmont's system south to Atlanta and north to Baltimore with yet more new stations added to the airline's network.

More aircraft were needed as Piedmont grew and the company's management wanted to phase out the DC-3s. In 1961, Piedmont purchased 17 Martin 404s from TWA, one of the two original operators of the type. These used aircraft were a lot less expensive than buying brand new F-27s, and Piedmont operated the 404s with 44-passenger interiors, eight seats more than were available on the Fairchilds. Although Piedmont is generally associated with the F-27 in this era it was actually the Martin that became the backbone of Piedmont's fleet. Piedmont would eventually buy and operate 36 Martin 404s over the years. One Martin 202 was purchased for spare parts.

With the arrival of the Martins, which went into service in January 1962, Piedmont began hiring female flight attendants to replace its all-male corps of pursers. The Martin's configuration eliminated the ability to arrange deplaning passengers' luggage in flight, thereby negating the advantage that the men had held.

As more Martins joined the fleet alongside the eight F-27s, Piedmont eased its DC-3s out of service. Finally, on February 20, 1963, the company operated its last DC-3 flight. A total of 23 *Gooney Birds* had served in the colors of Piedmont Airlines over the years.

With all of the Locals looking to the future and the looming need for turbojets, Tom Davis and his staff chose the Boeing 737 to be Piedmont's aircraft for entry into the ranks of pure-jet operators. However, the Boeing twin-jet would not be available until 1968. In the interim, the Boeing Co. leased two 727-100s to Piedmont, and it was these impressive airliners that would have

In 1958, Piedmont began to upgrade to the next generation of aircraft in the form of the Fairchild F-27. While the F-27 was a favorite of customers, it was the Martin 404 that would form the backbone of the fleet. (Piedmont publicity photo from the author's collection)

Piedmont Martin 404s photographed at Asheville, N.C., in August 1964, by the author in his teen years. Note the starboard engine running on the second aircraft. It was standard Local Airline practice at intermediate stops to leave the engine running that was opposite passenger activity.

LEFT to RIGHT: *Two Boeing 727-100s joined Piedmont's fleet in 1967 while the carrier waited for 737s to be delivered. In 1968, the Japanese-built Nihon YS-11 was introduced to replace Martins and Fairchilds. This July 1981 route map shows limited and well-reasoned growth almost 3 years after deregulation went into effect. Good planning helped Piedmont to survive and prosper. (From the author's collection)*

the honor of providing the first jet services along the *Route of the Pacemakers*. The airplanes were huge compared to anything Piedmont had operated previously. The airline had expanded north to New York's LaGuardia Airport in November 1966; consequently the 727s were christened the *Manhattan Pacemaker* and the *Empire State Pacemaker*.

The two Boeing tri-jets entered service on March 15, 1967. Four months later, the *Manhattan Pacemaker* was involved in a tragedy that brought unwanted attention to Piedmont. The aircraft was climbing out of Asheville / Hendersonville, N.C., around noon on July 19, 1967, when it was hit by a Cessna 310 being flown by a private pilot. As a result of the mid-air crash, all 79 aboard the 727 died as did the three occupants of the Cessna.

It would be the most deadly accident in Piedmont's history.

In addition to the 727s, Piedmont introduced another new type into its fleet in 1967, the FH-227B, an advanced and stretched version of the F-27. Ten of these 44-passenger aircraft replaced the smaller Fairchilds.

1968 would outpace 1967 for new aircraft acquisitions as the company made a bold move by placing a Japanese-built turboprop into service. The Nihon YS-11 was a twin-engine, 60 passenger airplane that offered better operating performance than the FH-227B for Piedmont's airports located in the Appalachians. The YS-11, with its increased capacity, could operate unrestricted out of every airport on the system and would replace the Martin 404s, helping to transform the Pacemaker fleet into an entirely

The combination of Fairchild F-27s and Martin 404s allowed Piedmont to phase out Douglas DC-3s. This F-27 was photographed at the Charlottesville, Va., airport in January 1959. (Company photo from the AAHS photo archives, AAHS-D003475)

America's Local Service Airlines

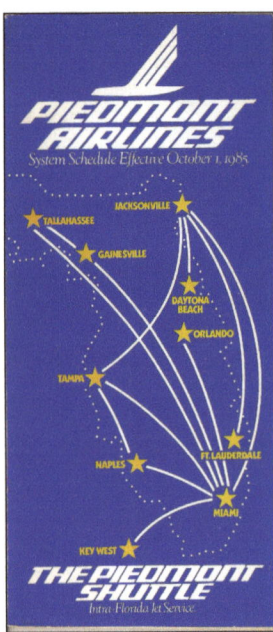  

Left to Right: By 1983, "feeder airline" Piedmont had established its own regional feeder operation. In 1986, Piedmont acquired Utica, N.Y.-based Empire Airlines. 1987 saw the airline become an international carrier with flights between Charlotte and London. (From the author's collection)

turbine-powered operation. More than 20 YS-11s eventually flew in Piedmont colors.

Finally, the Boeing 737-200s began arriving in 1968. The 737 would prove itself to be the standard aircraft for Piedmont as the years went by.

Piedmont had been a consistently profitable company, but like other Locals that were now being designated Regionals, the transition to the jet age while still carrying the responsibility of serving small cities started to take its toll.

The huge investment in new aircraft, the loss of one of the two 727s, escalating operating costs, a 1969 pilot strike over the three-man cockpit issue and, finally, a downturn in the economy, led to losses in 1968, '69, and '70. The dedicated effort of the company's employees turned the financial picture around but then the industry endured the 1973 oil crisis. Piedmont's management led the company through the lean years and faced the growing inevitability of deregulation.

In the late 1970s, Piedmont management, with the help of the company's advertising agency, instituted the *Careline* program, known for its slogan, "We Care." The purpose of the program was to motivate employees and inform the public that 'Piedmont cares.' The result was an inspired workforce made ready to face the challenges of a deregulated environment.

Unlike most other carriers, Piedmont thrived after deregulation as a result of good planning, good management, and, as always, good customer service. Piedmont developed what it referred to as its *Bypass Strategy*, putting it into effect after deregulation became a reality in 1978. Instead of jumping into big markets that other carriers were entering, Piedmont began offering non-stop service from cities on its own system to destinations that previously required a connection, bypassing the connecting terminal point.

Piedmont also adopted the hub-and-spoke system establishing, first, Charlotte, N.C., then Dayton, Ohio, as major connecting points where passengers inbound from 'spokes' could be transferred to other 'spokes.' The two airports were perfect hubs for the airline as Piedmont easily became the predominant carrier in both cities. The company went on to open hubs in Baltimore, Md., and Syracuse, New York. The Syracuse hub was established after the acquisition of Utica-based Empire Airlines in 1986.

The above strategies were accompanied by a commitment to advertising. A new agency was hired in 1979, the budget for advertising was increased by 70 percent and Piedmont soon became *The Up and Coming Airline*.

More 737s were acquired as needed, and the need was great. In 1981, Piedmont became the largest single operator of Boeing 737s in the world.

The Boeing 727 once again entered Piedmont's fleet in 1976 as extra lift was needed. Then, in 1982, the *Route of the Pacemakers* became an all-turbojet airline when the final YS-11 was withdrawn from service on March 14. With the 60-passenger YS-11 gone, Piedmont added the twin-jet, 65-passenger Fokker F-28 to its fleet in 1984.

Tom Davis stepped down as president in 1981, assuming the titles of Chairman and CEO. He then

Nihon YS-11s were added to the fleet in 1968 along with Boeing 737s. N164F was photographed at Washington National on November 19, 1968. (Photo from the Hufford collection of the AAHS archives, AAHS-37425)

Piedmont Boeing 727-95, N834N, departs Denver Stapleton airport in July 1982. (Raymond Rice photo from the AAHS photo archives, AAHS-D003473)

relinquished those positions in 1983, having built his little feeder operation into the tenth largest airline in the United States; 17th largest in the world.

Henson Aviation was acquired in 1983, to be operated as a subsidiary providing regional feed into what was now an airline that had grown well beyond the description of Local Service or Regional. Piedmont became a transcontinental carrier in 1984, achieving the status of a Major Airline with annual sales in excess of $1 billion.

Piedmont became a transatlantic operator in 1987, with the inaugural of Boeing 767 service from Charlotte to London. By this time all of the other original local service carriers had disappeared through merger or bankruptcy, with the exception of one – US Air, formerly Allegheny Airlines.

Piedmont's success had made it an attractive target for merger or acquisition in the chaotic takeover years of the 1980s. After fending off several other suitors, Piedmont succumbed to merger with its fellow ex-Local, US Air. The merger was finalized in 1989, and US Air became the surviving carrier.

Piedmont's demise reduced the ranks of the 'Original 13' down to one. But the *Route of the Pacemakers* left a proud legacy of service and Piedmont Airlines, gone but not forgotten, is still remembered fondly as one of America's finest airlines. ✈

Piedmont became the largest single operator of Boeing 737s in the world and continued to add newer versions up until the merger with US Air in 1989. This Boeing 737-401, N407US, was photographed at San Diego's Lindbergh Field in January 1989. (Photo from the AAHS photo archives, AAHS-D003474

America's Local Service Airlines

CHAPTER 12

SOUTHERN AIRWAYS

Frank W. Hulse already had a lot of aviation experience under his belt when he decided to apply for a feeder airline certificate from the Civil Aeronautics Board (CAB). He started out as an assistant mechanic with a fixed-base operation (FBO) called Southern Airways, in Augusta, Georgia. That company, founded in April 1929, was the first to use the Southern Airways name. In 1936, Hulse and his associate, Ike F. Jones, purchased a controlling interest in the FBO and Frank Hulse, now 24 years old, was named president. He was also the station manager for Delta Air Lines, C.E. Woolman's scheduled airline that operated two flights a day through Augusta.

The fixed base operation grew by installing facilities at other airports. In August 1939, Frank Hulse moved to Birmingham, Ala., when his company established a presence in that city under the title of Southern Airways Sales Company. The Southern Airways Sales Company of Alabama then took over operation of the TVA (Tennessee Valley Authority) airport at Muscle Shoals, Alabama. Also that year, Southern Airways (of Georgia) purchased the assets of Eastern Flying Schools, which operated a fixed-base service at Atlanta Municipal Airport, giving Southern Airways a foothold in the busy Atlanta area. To round out 1939, Southern Airways of South Carolina established a fixed-base operation at Anderson. Southern Airways was now the largest fixed-base operator in the South, and Frank Hulse was in charge of the entire organization. He was 27 years old.

During World War II, Hulse's companies trained thousands of pilots at facilities in Decatur, Ala., and Camden, South Carolina. By September 1944, the Southern Airways group of companies maintained facilities at Birmingham, Decatur, Huntsville and Muscle Shoals, Ala.; Atlanta and Augusta, Ga.; Anderson, Camden and Greenville, S.C.; and Charlotte, North Carolina.

Frank Hulse was quick to see the advantages looming in the feeder airline experiment proposed by the CAB. On

A typical Local Service Airline scene: Southern DC-3 N65A during a station stop at Pascagoula, Mississippi. Southern began serving Pascagoula in 1961. (Photo courtesy of David L. Weatherford)

America's Local Service Airlines

July 26, 1943, a new airline company named, appropriately, Southern Airways, Inc., was incorporated by Hulse and his associates. On January 5, 1944, Southern Airways, Inc., filed an application with the CAB for a Certificate of Public Convenience and Necessity to establish a feeder airline system in the southeastern United States.

In the Southeastern States Case, a decision was reached on April 4, 1947, awarding Southern a route extending from Memphis, Tenn., to Charlotte, N.C., via Atlanta and 10 other cities in Mississippi, Alabama, Georgia and South Carolina. Southern was also given a route from Atlanta to Jacksonville with stops at five Georgia airports along the way. An extension from Columbus, Ga., to Charleston, S.C., via intermediate points rounded out the designated network. In comments accompanying the award, the CAB made note of the Southern Airways organization's broad experience and praised Hulse and his associates for their organizational planning. Regarding the issue of antitrust practices, the CAB found that the relationship between Southern Airways, Inc., the proposed air carrier, and the five affiliated Southern companies run by Frank Hulse "does not present any question of monopoly or restraint of competition," noting that the airline planned to "use the facilities of its associated companies for the maintenance and overhaul of aircraft."

In the Mississippi Valley Case, decided December 18, 1947, Southern was selected to provide service south of Memphis to numerous points in Mississippi and Louisiana with routes extending to Mobile, Ala., and to New Orleans, Louisiana. The decision was challenged by other feeder airline applicants seeking to fly those routes and the entire case was reopened with Southern's award being cancelled. The CAB would eventually rule again in Southern's favor but it would not be until 1950 that Segments 4 and 5, extending from Memphis to New Orleans and from Columbus, Miss., to Mobile, Ala., respectively, were certificated to Southern Airways.

The new airline owned a Douglas DC-3, which it leased to Tom Davis's Piedmont Aviation in Winston-Salem, N.C., so that Davis could get his feeder airline, Piedmont Airlines, into operation. The lease provided much-needed revenue for Southern. More financing was obtained late in 1948 through the efforts of Birmingham, Ala., based investment firms. Southern was, in a sense, their hometown airline since Frank Hulse lived there and maintained his office there.

Southern Airways DC-3 N71SA at Memphis on April 7, 1967. This was the final livery to adorn Southern's DC-3s, which would be phased out of the fleet altogether in the next few months. (Photo from the Hufford collection, AAHS-37708)

Southern launched service on June 10, 1949, and continued to expand. By June 1951, the route system reached 31 airports in the southeastern US." (All timetables and route maps from the author's collection)

America's Local Service Airlines

The airline's route map changed slowly during the early 1950s, but by 1957 Southern was serving both Panama City and Eglin AFB on the Florida Gulf Coast, and Gulfport / Biloxi in Mississippi. In addition to businessmen, the company actively pursued military traffic and vacationers. (All from the author's collection)

But even though Hulse maintained his residence in Alabama's largest city, it was obviously Atlanta, Ga., with its busy airport, that would be the center of Southern's system. The company's base of operations would be Atlanta Municipal Airport while Frank Hulse continued to maintain the airline's executive office in the Brown-Marx Building in Birmingham. On January 1, 1949, Southern Airways opened an office in Atlanta to begin hiring personnel.

After Southern had completed a formal showing of adequacy for the airports to be served, the coveted Certificate of Public Convenience and Necessity was issued to the company by the CAB on February 8, 1949. The certificate was valid for three years. Once a feeder airline had received its certificate, service was expected to be inaugurated within the following three months.

Southern Airways was finally ready to take to the air with the first flight scheduled for June 10, 1949. The company's inaugural, Flight One, would operate from Atlanta to Memphis via Gadsden, Birmingham and Tuscaloosa, Ala., and Columbus, Mississippi. Southern's flights would carry a male *flight agent*, who could help with the boarding and deplaning of passengers, the loading and unloading of baggage and freight and he could also sell tickets in-flight.

According to a story in the *Southernaire*, the company newspaper, on the occasion of the airline's fifth anniversary in 1954, it was the weather in Gadsden, the first stop along the route of the inaugural flight, which caused a delay in the departure of Flight One from Atlanta. It was also reported that Frank Hulse received a call from the CAB in Washington asking him whether or not Southern Airways was actually going to get airborne that day. If not, the company's certificate may have been in jeopardy.

The weather in the Southeast improved and the inaugural flight, with Capt. George Bradford and S.C. Buchannan at the controls of DC-3, N61450, lifted off from Atlanta Municipal Airport on the morning of June 10 for its round-trip to Memphis via four intermediate cities. Eleven passengers were carried that day. "Handsome L.D. McDonald was in the cabin to welcome our first passengers aboard," the *Southernaire* reported in reference to the flight agent. Each intermediate landing was scheduled for a two-minute station stop, with the right engine always running, except for Birmingham, where five minutes were allowed at the gate. Southern Airways, Inc., the South's local service airline, was officially in business and ready to grow.

With more DC-3s coming into Southern's stable, service was inaugurated over the Atlanta to Jacksonville route on June 25, 1949. On August 5, the Atlanta – Charlotte part of the Memphis – Atlanta – Charlotte route was put into operation and two round-trip flights per day were now scheduled over every segment. Finally, on Sept. 15, 1949, the route from Columbus, Ga., to Charleston, S.C., was activated with the CAB commenting that "full operation of an airline system this size with two daily round trips, night and day service, in a period of less than 100 days constituted a new record in the local-service industry." The airline was now operating into 20 airports in the southeastern United States.

During those first months in 1949, Southern operated approximately 90 days under Visual Flight Rules (VFR) before receiving instrument authority. The Company did not receive authorization to operate under Instrument Landing System (ILS) parameters until January 27, 1950. Because of its own high safety standards, Southern did not operate under minimum ILS conditions until the winter of 1950-51, resulting in many cancelled and delayed flights that impacted traffic development during the first year and a half of operation.

The final awards in the CAB's Mississippi Valley Case were made in the summer of 1950 and Southern received its authority to start service to 10 new stations south of Memphis. Service was inaugurated over the new routes in stages with New Orleans coming on-line as a terminal city on January 15, 1951. After two daily round-trips had been established over all segments of the Mississippi Valley Case routes, Southern's revenues underwent a sudden upsurge. Regarding Hulse and his team, the CAB noted that "management has acted promptly and decisively in meeting the usual problems involved in starting up a feeder line operation."

In addition to businessmen and pleasure travelers, Southern wisely pursued military traffic, a strategy the company would continue throughout its existence. In 1952, 24 of Southern's 32 cities served 70 military installations and bases. If the company made itself indispensable to the military and, therefore, to the government, it was likely that the company would be looked upon favorably by the government's airline regulator, the CAB.

Southern progressed methodically during the 1950s. Tupelo, Miss., improved its airport to the point where it could accept DC-3s, and service was inaugurated there on June 15, 1951. Gulfport/Biloxi, Miss., was added to the system in 1952.

With the CAB's permission, in 1953 service was suspended on the route across central Georgia from Columbus to Charleston via Macon and Augusta, a segment that had never been profitable. Aside from that route, only three other stations were dropped from Southern's network in the 1950s: Hattiesburg, Miss. (which would see Southern return in 1960 after Delta Air Lines dropped service there), La Grange, Ga., and Clarksdale, Mississippi.

Meanwhile, Southern added service to Monroe, La., the birthplace of Delta Air Lines, in 1953; Dothan, Ala., and Panama City, Fla., in 1956; and Eglin Air Force Base, Fla., in 1957. Panama City and Eglin AFB were particularly important because they gave Southern access to the white sand tourist beaches along the Gulf of Mexico on the panhandle of Florida.

Eglin assured not only a source of military traffic but also a good supply of vacationers as the civilian terminal at the air force base served the tourist centers of Destin and Fort Walton Beach.

The biggest boost to the company came in 1955 with the granting of permanent certificates by the CAB to the 13 remaining local service airlines, including Southern Airways. Southern's permanent Certificate of Convenience and Necessity was presented to Frank Hulse by CAB chairman Ross Rizley during ceremonies held in a hangar at Atlanta's Municipal Airport on December 9, 1955. Mr. Rizley was introduced to the audience in attendance by Atlanta mayor William B. Hartsfield, whose name would grace the city's airport 25 years later.

In August of 1957, Southern Airways boarded its one millionth passenger, Mrs. Robert Coleman, in Charlotte, North Carolina.

1958 saw the transfer of air service at Greenwood, Miss., from Delta Air Lines to Southern Airways, a process that demonstrated one of the true purposes of local service airlines, to replace trunk carriers at smaller stations.

On December 1, 1958, Southern inaugurated service to two cities in Alabama with important military installations. Anniston had never had scheduled air service before. The city was the site of Fort McClellan, at the time home of the Women's Army Corps (WAC). Fort McClellan was also site of the Chemical Corps School, an Army facility devoted to chemical warfare training. Southern's DC-3s began landing at Anniston Municipal Airport four times a day as an intermediate stop between Gadsden and Atlanta. Of even greater significance was Southern's inauguration of service on the same day at Huntsville, the location of Redstone Arsenal. Huntsville and the arsenal were becoming famous at the time as the home of America's space flight program and the United States Army Ordinance Missile Command. Huntsville had been served by Eastern Air Lines and Capital Airlines for years when Southern was allowed into the market. The airline's blue and yellow DC-3s

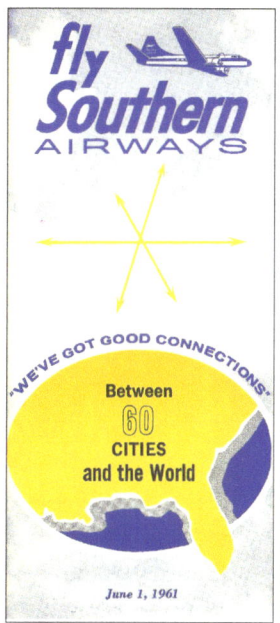
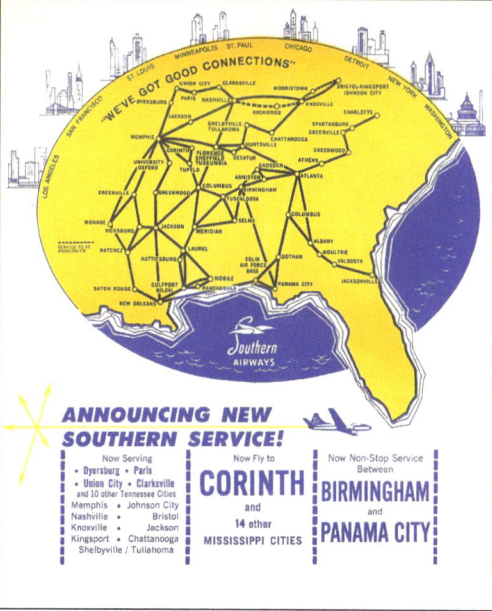

Southern's Dec. 1, 1958 timetable introduces service to two cities in Alabama with important military installations: Anniston and Huntsville. The June 1, 1961 route map shows dynamic growth during the preceding two years with Southern now serving 14 airports in Mississippi and blanketing the state of Tennessee. (All from the author's collection)

Southern's management announced the intended purchase of second-hand Martin 404s from Eastern Air Lines in 1960. Partly due to a pilots' strike, the Martin acquisition was delayed and the type entered service on October 29, 1961. (Photo from the AAHS archives)

began transporting passengers from Huntsville non-stop to both Atlanta and Memphis.

Southern's tenth anniversary was celebrated in 1959, and two more stations were added to the airline's network that year: University/Oxford, Miss., home of the University of Mississippi, and Bogalusa, Louisiana. Southern closed out the decade with a fleet of 20 Douglas DC-3s and 700 employees.

Frank Hulse's airline, which had grown slowly and methodically in the 1950s, would blossom in the early 1960s, adding new cities, new routes and more aircraft. The number of revenue passengers flown annually would nearly double in the first three years of the decade.

But with this expansion came growing pains. When contract negotiations between Southern's pilots and the company broke down, the Air Line Pilots Association (ALPA) called a strike that all but shut down the company's operations on June 5, 1960. In addition to a basic pay increase request, one issue causing contention was a demand by pilots for a guarantee of a minimum of one hour of pay for every four hours away from their base, commonly referred to in the industry as *trip rig*. In 1960, Frank

The company referred to its Martin 404s as Southern 'Aristocrats'. The aircraft brought air-conditioning and pressurization to Southern's customers for the first time. N144S (above left) was photographed June 9, 1977, at an undisclosed location. The brochure at right, promoting the Martin's features, was issued when the Aristocrats were introduced in 1961. (Photo of the Martin from the Tim Williams collection)

Hulse and Southern's management looked upon this request as "featherbedding."

When the ALPA-represented pilots walked out, Southern began hiring non-union pilots to take their places. Despite threats from ALPA that they would "shut down the entire Southeast" by asking member pilots from other airlines serving the area to walk out on a sympathy strike, Southern continued to reinstate service as more non-union pilots were hired. On July 29, the union-represented pilots retracted their demands and agreed to accept the contract that had been offered to them by Southern's management on the condition that all striking pilots be returned to duty with their full seniority. The Company refused to dismiss the newly-hired non-union pilots who had kept the airline flying during the strike. Furthermore, management stated that striking pilots would be returned to duty as needed with the non-union pilots holding date-of-hire seniority and the returning pilots given new seniority numbers based on the date that they returned to work. This was, obviously, a no-win situation for everyone involved, particularly for the pilots who had helped build the company during its first 11 years. The issue was not resolved until 1962 when the government pressured Southern management to end the stalemate and rehire most of the striking pilots.

In spite of the strike, Southern grew in 1960. On February 26, prior to the walkout, Southern inaugurated service to Nashville, Tenn., and Muscle Shoals (Florence / Sheffield / Tuscumbia), Ala., providing the first through flights between Nashville and New Orleans. On April 1, Decatur, Ala., was added to the network, and later that month Selma, Ala., and Meridian, Miss., came on-line as part of a transfer of some local services from Delta to Southern as Delta began to phase out the last of its DC-3s (Delta's last DC-3 flight took place on October 29, 1960). Part of the Delta route transfer included returning Hattiesburg to the Southern system.

Later in 1960, with its pilot corps back to pre-strike levels, Southern began service to Jackson, Tenn., a city that had lost its air service when intrastate carrier, Southeast Airlines, ceased operations on July 31. Southern also received authority to serve Knoxville, Chattanooga, Bristol/Kingsport/Johnson City (Tri Cities) and other eastern Tennessee cities previously served by Southeast.

Having started operations in 1957 as a subsidiary of Mason and Dixon Truck Lines, Southeast Airlines operated under state of Tennessee authority, without a federal certificate and without the benefit of government subsidy, serving cities throughout the state with a fleet of DC-3s and Convair 240s. Southeast applied to the CAB for a Certificate of Public Convenience and Necessity, claiming that it would continue to operate its Tennessee system without subsidy. But the award of a federal certificate to operate Southeast's routes was given to Southern instead. One member of the CAB, G. Joseph Minetti, objected to choosing Southern over Southeast noting that, if Southeast was given the federal certificate, that company could then interline traffic with connecting certificated carriers and earn revenue from carrying the U.S. mail, albeit at the unsubsidized rate. But Southern won. The company knew how to make and keep friends in high places.

In 1960, Southern Airways management unveiled the company's *New Look* campaign, which included the announcement that five Martin 404s would be joining the fleet. The company hoped to have the 'new' aircraft, to be purchased second-hand from Eastern Air Lines, in service by July of 1960. The pilots' strike postponed the purchase until the following year.

In 1961, the reassignment of the Southeast Airlines system to Southern Airways was complete with the former company's western Tennessee routes put into operation by Southern. The new cities in this area included Clarksville, Paris, Dyersburg and Union City.

Pascagoula and Corinth were also added to the network in

DC-3 N66SA, msn 11631, was photographed at Memphis in July 1965. This aircraft operated Southern's first scheduled flight on June 10, 1949, when it was registered N61450. (Photo from the Tim Williams collection)

DC-9s entered service with Southern in 1967. In 1969, the first of the company's stretched DC-9-31s joined the fleet (N89S is pictured here). With jets in the fleet, Southern asked for, and received, permission from the CAB to offer some longer-range flights. (Photo from the Tim Williams collection)

1961, bringing to 14 the total number of airports in Mississippi served by Southern Airways.

On October 29, 1961, Southern Airways introduced the Martin 404s into service. Dubbed *Aristocrats* by the public relations department, the 40-passenger, tricycle-gear aircraft brought air-conditioning and pressurization to Southern's passengers for the first time.

Southern continued to add more Martin 404s to its fleet during 1962. Also that year, the airline added three stations in South Carolina, inaugurating service to Columbia, the state capital, Myrtle Beach and, once again, Southern entered the Charleston market. On October 28, Rockwood, Tenn., became a Southern station, bringing to 13 the total number of airports served by the airline in the state of Tennessee.

While Southern was regularly applying for authority to serve new cities and new routes, it was also ready to abandon stations that had not lived up to the company's boarding expectations or to the CAB's "Use It or Lose It" criteria. On November 30, 1963, the airline withdrew its service from Corinth, Miss.; Selma, Ala.; Morristown, Dyersburg, Union City, Paris and Clarksville, Tennessee.

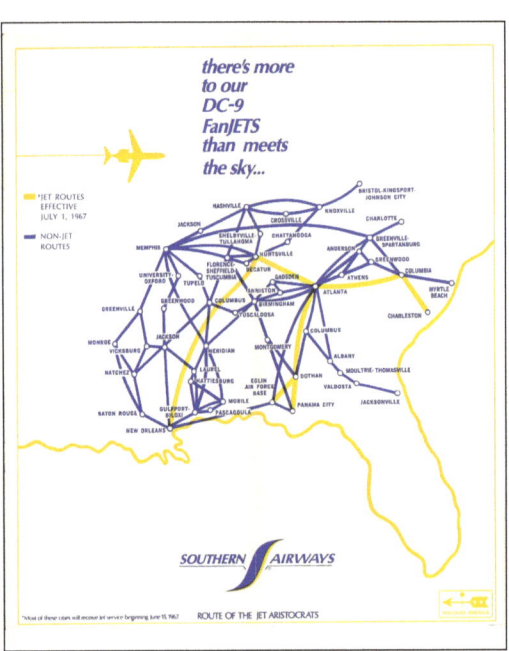

FAR LEFT: *This June 15, 1967 route map shows Southern's initial jet service routes printed in gold ink.*

MIDDLE: *By the summer of 1968, marketing was focused on Southern's jet service although most flights were still operated with Martin 404s.*

RIGHT: *In June 1969, Southern celebrated its 20th anniversary of scheduled service.*
(All from the author's collection)

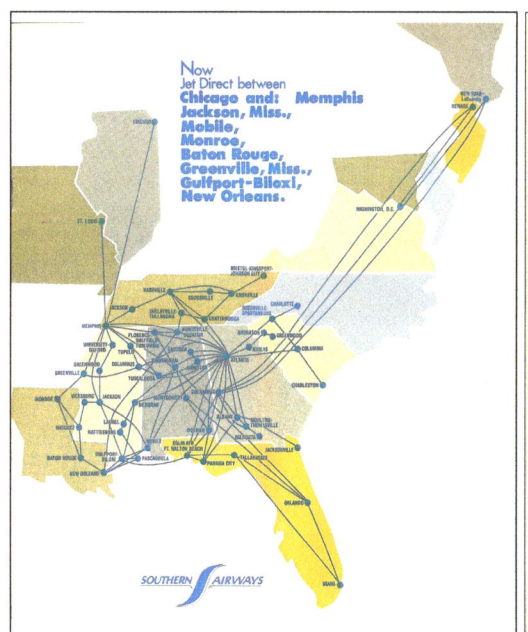 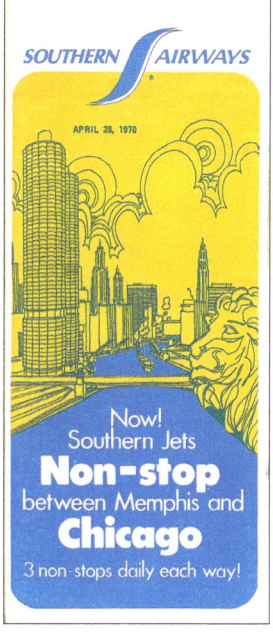 

Far Left: By 1970, the CAB was granting Local Service Carriers expanded authority. Southern was flying from the Southeast to Washington, DC and New York, and to Chicago.
Middle: The company's April 26, 1970 timetable announces the new service to Chicago (Midway).
Right: In 1971 Southern resurrected the 'Nighthawk' name, originally used by Capital Airlines, for its short-lived night coach service along the Mississippi Valley. (All from the author's collection)

By November 1963, Southern's load factor averaged 41.24 percent and the fleet consisted of 37 aircraft: 14 Martin 404s and 23 Douglas DC-3s.

In 1964, Southern was awarded a route from Memphis to Panama City via Muscle Shoals, Birmingham and Montgomery, bringing the Alabama state capital onto the airline's system. Southern became the sole carrier serving the Muscle Shoals Airport when this route went into service, as the CAB terminated Eastern's authority to serve the point. Southern also replaced Eastern at Anderson, S.C., on October 25, 1964.

In December 1964, Southern Airways boarded its four millionth passenger.

With a perfect safety record, increasing income, passenger boardings going up and a growing load factor, it was time for the company to take the next step. On August 24, 1965, Frank Hulse announced an initial order for three Douglas DC-9 FanJets, with an option to buy three more. The first three jets were expected to arrive early in 1967. In making his announcement, Hulse reported that Southern connected more of its passengers to and from trunk carriers than any of the other 12 Local Service Airlines. With DC-9s, Southern could provide its customers connecting to and from the 'big' airlines "jet service with equally modern and comfortable equipment."

Southern Airways got a taste of the big time in 1966. Mechanics represented by the International Association of Machinists (IAM) went on strike at five major airlines simultaneously (Eastern, National, Northwest, TWA and United) and Southern stepped in to help fill the void. The IAM was bargaining for pay increases at all five carriers. The strike lasted for 43 days, from July 8 through August 19, bringing 60 percent of the nation's airline network to a virtual standstill. At first Southern was given expedited permission by the CAB to fly non-stop segments over its own system to fill in for service gaps left by the striking carriers. Then NASA requested that Southern be given permission to transport passengers between Huntsville, Al., location of NASA's Marshall Space Flight Center, and Washington, D.C., the nation's capital. With United and Eastern on strike, Southern was Huntsville's only operating airline. Southern was given permission to operate daily service temporarily between Huntsville and Washington via Greenville/Spartanburg, S.C., using Martin 404s. The space agency then expressed the need to connect Huntsville with west coast points via a connection in St. Louis, and with Cape Kennedy (Cape Canaveral) via Orlando. Southern was given temporary authority to operate daily from Orlando, Fla., to St. Louis via Tallahassee, Florida's capital city, and Huntsville, commencing August 4. Tallahassee, normally served only by Eastern and National, which were both on strike, had been without air service for nearly a month. During the strike Southern boarded 141,964 passengers and received many kudos from government agencies, corporations and cities and towns impacted positively by Southern's extra service.

The company started off 1967 by introducing a new trademark, *Accent S*. Designed by advertising agency, Harris & Weinstein Associates, the symbol, in "royal blue and gleaming gold," was described as "sleek," "graceful" and "elegant." This was followed by a new uniform for Southern's 100 stewardesses, created by French designer, Pierre Balmain. An apricot-colored ensemble with a pill box hat, worn with an *Accent S* pin instead of traditional crew wings, the new uniform was considered to be very modern. Chief Stewardess, Kay Davison, commented: "Our stewardesses are becoming members of the 'jet-set' and we want them to look and feel the part." The new uniform went 'on-line' on June 15, the first day of jet service.

Southern's final livery, featuring the 'FlightMark' symbol on the aircraft tail, is illustrated here on DC-9-14 N3302L (fleet #971). Date and location unknown. (From the David L. Weatherford collection)

Generating appropriate publicity, the delivery flight of Southern's first DC-9-15, N91S, from Long Beach, Calif., to Charleston, S.C., set an official speed and distance record for the type on May 9, 1967: 4 hours, 13 minutes and 12 seconds for the coast-to-coast hop. Serving as first officer aboard the flight was George Bradford, captain of Southern's very first scheduled flight back in 1949.

As a poignant counterpoint to the introduction of the DC-9 FanJets, Southern operated its last scheduled DC-3 service, Flight 240, from Dothan, Ala., to Memphis, Tenn., via Montgomery, Birmingham and Muscle Shoals, Al., on July 31, 1967.

When Southern introduced its new 75-passenger Douglas DC-9s, Frank Hulse asked the CAB to reexamine Southern's service pattern. In particular, he requested the removal of restrictions to allow more non-stop and skip-stop authority so that Southern's jets could achieve maximum potential providing longer hauls. The introduction of jets into the fleets of the Local Service Carriers brought about the inevitable need for these airlines to infringe on the territory previously reserved for trunk airlines. No longer were the Locals hopping along a string of small cities with DC-3s, picking up passengers along the way to be deposited at a hub airport for the continuation of their journeys aboard the jet aircraft of 'big' airlines. Yes, that transfer of passengers from small towns to big city airports was still their main reason for being. But now the Locals had their own jets... expensive, new jets... that required flights of longer duration to achieve their maximum revenue potential. The era of second-hand aircraft performing service for these hard-working airlines was slowly coming to a close. Now this group of air carriers was being courted by the sales representatives of Douglas, Boeing and British Aircraft Corporation as potential customers for their new generation of jets. The Locals were all grown-up now.

The CAB took its task seriously and went about handling the situation in an interesting manner. The trunk carriers took passengers between the nation's major markets, such as Atlanta to New York and Atlanta to Washington. The Locals would dutifully deliver their passengers from places like Columbus, Ga.; Dothan, Al.; and Eglin AFB, Fla., to the hub airport (in this case, Atlanta) where they would transfer to Eastern, Delta or United for their onward journey to the Big Apple or to the nation's capital. What if the CAB allowed Southern to fly their expensive new DC-9s on a typical up-and-down hop from Eglin to Dothan to Columbus collecting passengers, and then, instead of flying the last 82 miles into Atlanta, how about avoiding the congestion of Atlanta altogether and operating that DC-9 non-stop from Columbus to Washington and then on to New York? The loss of passengers to Delta, Eastern and United out of Atlanta would be minimal but the long-haul from Columbus to Washington and then on to New York could be a money-maker for Southern. And the convenience of having direct flights to the nation's most important cities was certainly a boon for places like Dothan and Columbus. To make Southern a less-desirable alternative for passengers just flying between Washington and New York in competition with the big boys, Southern's flights to Washington would operate via Dulles Airport, 26 miles from downtown Washington, as opposed to close-in National Airport. The CAB gave this route authority to Southern and declared it to be "subsidy ineligible."

Southern was awarded new routes in 1969 non-stop between Memphis and St. Louis and between Memphis and Chicago, albeit via Midway Airport instead of O'Hare. Southern would now compete head-to-head with Delta in these two major markets. These would not be the last of Southern Airways' long-distance awards.

Southern received the first of its stretched Douglas DC-9-30s in 1969. Before entering scheduled service on June 1, the aircraft flew a charter for the New Mexico Amigos, a goodwill ambassadors group. Southern now had authority to operate charter flights throughout the United States, to Canada and the Bahamas and, during 1969 Southern flew one million aircraft miles in charter operations carrying, among others, the athletic teams of 35 colleges and universities.

On February 15, 1970, Southern inaugurated service to Tallahassee, Orlando and Miami, Fla., and the new Chicago (Midway) non-stop from Memphis began on April 1. Southern's system now stretched from Miami to Chicago and from New

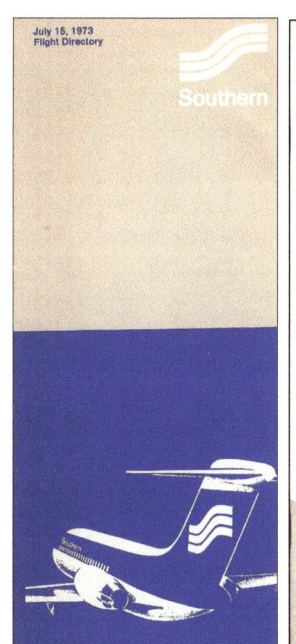 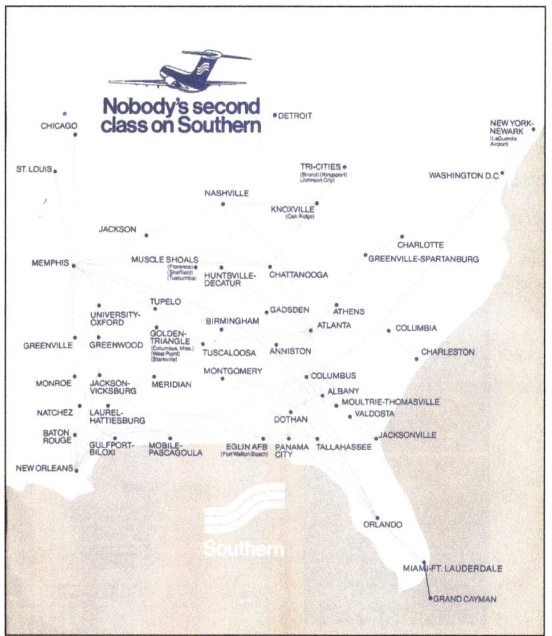 

LEFT: *Southern's new 'Flightmark' branding is introduced with the July 15, 1973 timetable. Middle: By December 1974, Southern's system had been extended north to Detroit and south to Grand Cayman. RIGHT: The August 8, 1977 timetable introduces the Swearingen Metro II, which was the type chosen to replace the Martin 404s. The Metro's shortcomings quickly made themselves apparent. (All from the author's collection)*

Orleans to New York. The company began referring to itself as a regional carrier, a moniker more appropriate to its range of operations than the term local airline. By the summer of 1970, more than 75 percent of Southern's passengers were being flown aboard DC-9s while the dependable Martin 404s continued to provide service to smaller stations such as Anniston, Pascagoula and Moultrie.

In 1972, the airline announced a fanciful new ad campaign. Taking advantage of the 'smiley face' image and the slogan, *Have a Nice Day*, which were famous elements of pop culture at the time, each of the DC-9s had a smiley face painted on its radome encircled by the words, *Have A Nice Day, Southern Airways*. To round out the ad campaign, the phrase "We serve the nicest people the very nicest way we know" became the company slogan.

As Southern's 25th anniversary approached in 1974, the company began its preparation for the future. A new corporate identity was developed and Southern's new "signature" was the *FlightMark*, described as a combination of "the letter S with a graphic simulation of the flow of air over a wing – the basic mechanism enabling aircraft flight." A new paint scheme was designed incorporating two colors, blue and white, and featuring the FlightMark on the tail (vertical stabilizer) of the aircraft. The new livery would not be applied to the Martin 404s, which were slowly being phased out of service.

The company was recommended for route extensions to Detroit and to the Cayman Islands. Meanwhile, in 1974, Southern sought to terminate service at five of its least productive stations: Natchez, Mississippi; Anderson and Greenwood, S.C.; Crossville and Shelbyville/Tullahoma, Tennessee. All of these requests were eventually approved by the CAB.

With the introduction of service to Grand Cayman, Southern became the U.S.

This is Southern's final timetable, issued April 29, 1979. The extent of the company's network before merger with North Central Airlines is illustrated in the route map. (From the author's collection)

flag carrier on this route and played the part well. Advertised as Southern's "Grand Flight to Grand Cayman," inflight service featured individual sandwich baskets plus tall glasses of Southern's own rum punch garnished with fruit kabobs for those who cared to imbibe. The feeder airline that started out by flying passengers from Gadsden and Tuscaloosa to Atlanta was now an international carrier. And it was still serving the needs of Tuscaloosa and Gadsden customers.

Southern's advertising campaign in the mid-1970s stressed the one-cabin, standard class layout aboard the company's aircraft, promising that *Nobody's Second Class on Southern*. Humorous radio and television commercials touting this theme brought much attention to the regional airline.

The company was profitable and reported another good financial year in 1976. But the satisfaction of maintaining a profitable and growing operation was tempered by the news that Southern suffered its second fatal crash on April 4, 1977. Douglas DC-9-31, N1335U (fleet number 934), operating as flight 242 between Huntsville and Atlanta, attempted an emergency landing on a rural Georgia highway after losing power in both engines while transiting a violent hailstorm. 72 people, including eight on the ground, perished in the crash.

A replacement type had to be found for the aging Martin 404s. There were still several communities on Southern's system that did not generate enough traffic to warrant DC-9 service and a few whose airports could not accommodate the jets. But it was getting more difficult and more expensive to maintain the old piston-engine airliners as spare parts were becoming harder to find. In a move that turned out to be a rather poor choice, Southern selected the Swearingen Metro II as the Martin's replacement. This 19-passenger aircraft, which did not carry a flight attendant, entered service on August 8, 1977. Its shortcomings quickly made themselves apparent. If a full complement of passengers boarded the aircraft on hot days Down South, it was sometimes necessary to leave baggage behind due to weight restrictions. The last Martin 404 operated right up until the day that the type's FAA authorization for operation by a certificated carrier expired, April 30, 1978. Some of the Martins went on to an after-life serving a few more years with intrastate carriers in Florida.

At the opposite end of the spectrum, Southern became the first U.S. airline to place a firm order for the Douglas DC-9 Super 80, a stretched version of the DC-9 that would later be called the MD-80. Frank Hulse signed a $60 million dollar contract in 1977 for four aircraft, estimating delivery in 1980.

Hulse had formed Southern Airways and remained at its helm, first as president, then as chairman, for the entire duration of its existence. With deregulation looming on the horizon, Hulse and his team saw it as imperative that Southern merge with another carrier. The bigger the better would be a survival tactic in the brave new world of deregulated airlines. Long before the Airline Deregulation Act of 1978 became law, Frank Hulse and Southern's management team began discussion with Hal N. Carr, chairman of North Central Airlines, one of the other surviving Local Service Carriers, about the possibility of merger. The route systems of the two airlines were not exactly a perfect match. North Central had a network of local routes in the northern tier of states stretching from North Dakota to Ohio. Southern's system was concentrated in the Southeast. There was a large amount of territory separating the two distinct areas of service. The airlines' networks met at several points that were at the ends of long-distance routes for one carrier or the other (or both): Denver, Minneapolis/St. Paul, Milwaukee, Chicago, Detroit, Atlanta and New York. On July 13, 1978, several months before the deregulation act was signed into law, Frank Hulse and Hal Carr announced their intent to merge the two companies. While 2.2 shares of North Central common stock would be exchanged for each share of Southern stock, North Central would be the surviving carrier, although a new name would be chosen.

On July 1, 1979, the new airline was born. Republic Airlines now operated the routes of the former North Central Airlines and Southern Airways while the names of those two carriers were relegated to the history books. What had seemed an unusual pairing turned out to be a good bet on the part of Mr. Hulse and Mr. Carr. Republic lasted for seven years, during which time it absorbed Hughes Airwest and became a major carrier. In 1986, Republic was purchased by Northwest Airlines, which in turn merged with Delta Air Lines 22 years later. ✈

CHAPTER 13

TRANS-TEXAS AIRWAYS

Aviation Enterprises started out like so many other feeder airline predecessors, as a fixed base operator (FBO). Founded in 1940, Aviation Enterprises, Ltd. chartered, repaired and sold aircraft and offered flying lessons at Houston's Municipal Airport (later renamed William P. Hobby Airport). During WWII, the company trained hundreds of ferry pilots for the Women Air Force Service Pilots (WASP) program at Avenger Field in Sweetwater, Texas.

In 1943, the company's founder, R. Earl McKaughan, along with his associates, applied to the Civil Aeronautics Board (CAB) for feeder routes blanketing the State of Texas and extending as far as New Orleans, Memphis, Kansas City, St. Louis and Salt Lake City. The Board divided the company's request into two parts: the proposed service within the States of Texas and Oklahoma, plus the route to Salt Lake City, would be considered in the Texas – Oklahoma Case, while the application for routes to New Orleans, Memphis, St. Louis and Kansas City were to be dealt with in the Mississippi Valley Case. The company's proposed routes in the Texas – Oklahoma Case alone encompassed a staggering 10,792 miles. In November 1944, the airline applicant officially became Aviation Enterprises, Inc., a separate entity from Aviation Enterprises, Ltd.

The company had no luck in the Mississippi Valley Case, but the Texas – Oklahoma proceeding was a different story. When the decision was handed down on December 14, 1946, only two applicants were awarded feeder routes in the states under consideration. Central Airlines received authority to serve a network of routes primarily in Oklahoma, and Aviation Enterprises took the prize for local service routes within Texas.

As with many of the other outfits selected to perform feeder airline service after the war, the company's massive pilot-training effort for the military during the conflict carried weight when the CAB made its decision. Also working in Aviation Enterprises' favor was its selection of James V. Allred, former governor of Texas, as one of the airline's vice presidents. And it didn't hurt the firm's prospectus that the officers of the company had pockets deep enough to finance the start of operations.

The award handed down by the CAB was for a network much smaller than the one applied for. No route to Salt Lake City would be forthcoming. In fact, the new airline's entire certificated system would be confined to the State of Texas. Five routes serving 28 Texas airports were assigned to Aviation Enterprises.

Like most of the Local Service carriers, Trans-Texas Airways initiated service with Douglas DC-3s. N25673 is seen here in the late-1940s paint scheme. (Photo from the author's collection)

America's Local Service Airlines

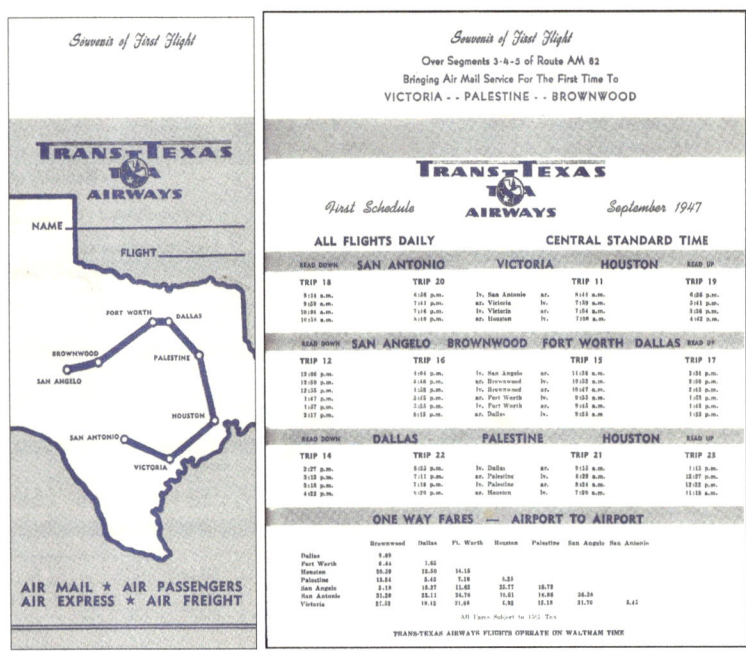
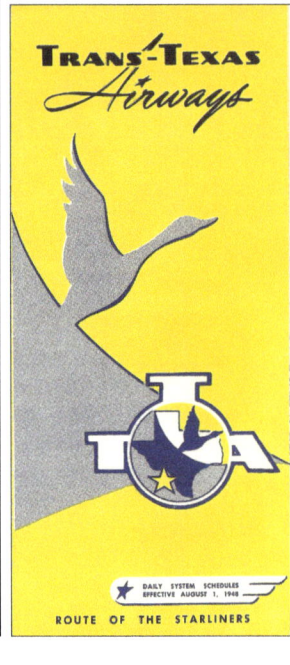

FAR LEFT: *The cover of TTA's first timetable, issued in September 1947, as a "souvenir of first flight."*

MIDDLE: *Schedules from the first timetable.*

RIGHT: *Cover of a 1948 timetable displaying the slogan, "Route of the Starliners."*

(From the author's collection)

They stretched from Dallas to Houston and westward to El Paso via intermediate points, and a branch extended south along the Rio Grande from Eagle Pass to Brownsville, again serving cities in between.

Preparations got underway to get the company airborne. Instead of using Beech D-18s, which the officers of the corporation had originally contemplated when the application was filed, it was evident that DC-3s, with their 21 passenger seats, would be more appropriate for the type of operation to be conducted. A more suitable name was also needed, one that would catch the public's attention. The perfect moniker was chosen and in June 1947, several months before the first flight took off, the bland-sounding Aviation Enterprises, Inc. officially became Trans-Texas Airways (TTA).

Quoted in the employee newspaper, *The Starliner*, on the occasion of the airline's 30th anniversary in 1977, one of TTA's first pilots, A.J. High, recalled: "We didn't even have an airplane when I first came to work (in 1947). For three weeks until we got our first DC-3, I helped put together crew manuals, build a fence at the Victoria airport, and drive a jeep all over Texas to deliver ramp equipment to our stations."

Delays were faced, like they were at the other feeder airlines, while aircraft were secured, airports were prepared, and final clearance was sought from the Civil Aeronautics Authority affirming that all safety requirements would be met. A "souvenir timetable" for the proposed first flight was issued in September 1947, but scheduled service did not get underway until October 11, when two DC-3s inaugurated schedules to eight Texas cities.

In 1942, a new song entitled "Deep in the Heart of Texas" rose to the top of "Your Hit Parade's" popularity list. The lyrics stated that "The stars at night are big and bright deep in the heart of Texas," and TTA dubbed its DC-3s "Starliners"

when they first took to the air. They would be referred to that way for years to come.

The first Starliner flights carried stewards tending to the needs of passengers, but the company soon began hiring young women to serve as hostesses. Keeping with the Texas image that the airline was trying to promote, a 'cowgirl' uniform consisting of traditional hat, vest, blouse, neck scarf, skirt and boots was selected for the female flight attendants. It was a style that was modified over the years, but TTA stewardesses still wore a modernized western-style uniform into the 1960s.

In 1948, McKaughan hired a man who would become a legend in the airline industry to join TTA's management team. M. Lamar Muse became the company's acting secretary-treasurer, and his innovative financial practices, including the selection of a permanent subsidy rate for TTA as opposed to the temporary rates preferred by other Locals, would serve the airline well during its early years. He created a desperately-needed business plan to help Trans-Texas squeeze profits out of serving places like Eagle Pass, Del Rio and Carrizo Springs / Crystal City. Muse would eventually move on to become a vice president of Southern Airways, president of Central Airlines, president of Southwest Airlines, and founder of his own company, Muse Air.

TTA's statistics were so dismal during its first year of operation that the CAB instituted an early investigation to determine whether or not the airline's Certificate of Public Convenience and Necessity should be renewed. Ex-Governor Allred, now the company's general counsel (chief attorney), set his political connections into motion. Forty-four U.S. senators and congressmen wrote to the Board expressing support for TTA. The company needed a chance to prove itself. And the failure of another certificated feeder carrier after the demise of Florida Airways, an under-performer based in Orlando whose

  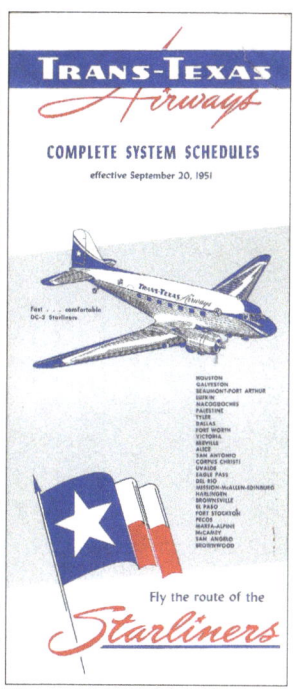

TTA flight attendants ("hostesses") were provided with "cowgirl" uniforms, variations of which were employed until the 1960s. LEFT: December 1, 1949 timetable cover featuring a flight attendant. ABOVE: An early TTA hostess class sits on the horizontal stabilizer of a DC-3. RIGHT: TTA's September 20, 1951 timetable cover listing cities served, all in Texas. (From the author's collection)

certificate had not been renewed, would give fuel to the skeptics who questioned the integrity of the entire local service airline experiment. Allred argued TTA's case before the Board noting that the airline's passenger count was growing dramatically, revenue was steadily increasing and the smaller cities and towns that had paid for airport improvements to accommodate TTA's DC-3s deserved the opportunity to show that they would use the air service. Trans-Texas Airways survived the scrutiny and, when the company's temporary certificate came up for renewal in 1950, the route system, with some adjustments, was certificated for another three years.

James V. Allred left TTA in 1949 when he was appointed to a federal judgeship by President Harry S. Truman. He was replaced in his position as general counsel for TTA by John B. Connally, a future governor of Texas and the man who gained notoriety by being the other person shot while riding in President Kennedy's limousine in Dallas in 1963.

TTA finally received authority to expand outside the State of Texas in 1953. In addition to Shreveport, La., and Memphis, Tenn., service was inaugurated to nine airports in Arkansas and to six new stations in Texas, including Austin, the state capital. The airline was allowed to suspend operations at the underperforming cities of Alice, Nacogdoches and McCamey.

Also that year, the fleet underwent a cabin modernization program as 26 "deep rubber-foam full-reclining seats" were installed in the DC-3s, along with "new color harmonies and rich walnut paneling."

Confirming its steady climb in popularity, TTA celebrated its half-million passenger mark when it boarded its 500,000th customer on October 27, 1954, in San Angelo. Just the year

TTA's DC-3 Starliners were rechristened "Super Starliners" after undergoing a 'Maximizer' upgrade in the late 1950s, which included the installation of wheel-well doors. N28391 is seen here at Dallas (Love Field) in June 1962. (Photo from the Tim Williams collection)

America's Local Service Airlines

TTA DC-3 N18105 (built as a DST), is seen at Dallas (Love Field) in September 1966. By this time, the livery had been simplified. (Photo from the Tim Williams collection)

before, Jim Beck, TTA's Interline and Agency Manager had written in *The Starliner Banner*, the employee newspaper, that the region's "surface transportation at its best was never very good (and) in the past few years a number of passenger trains have been discontinued completely." People were learning to rely on the airplane for their intercity transportation.

This was the 'sweet spot' in the history of America's Local Service Airlines, as passenger train service was being cut back and before the Interstate Highway System had started to spread. The Locals were truly filling a need by carrying passengers across distances of 50-to-250 miles, connecting smaller communities with big cities and their busy airports.

In January 1956, TTA expanded further by linking Laredo with San Antonio, Austin, Fort Worth and Dallas, and by inaugurating service to Lake Charles and Lafayette, La., from Shreveport, Dallas and several East Texas cities. The CAB also allowed the company to offer improved service over its existing network by approving nonstops between Dallas and Beaumont / Port Arthur, a big market for the airline, and between Fort Worth and San Angelo. Waco and Temple became the newest Texas stations on the Trans-Texas route map.

McKaughan and his team began upgrading the efficiency of the company's DC-3s by having a newly designed high-performance package installed on each aircraft. The "Maximizer" upgrade included the installation of wheel-well doors, a redesigned engine cowling and oil cooler package, a

TTA's route adjustments and expansion between 1949 and 1953 are presented in the three system maps below. The illustrations are from December 1949, September 1951, and August 1953, respectively. The last of the three maps shows TTA's first expansion outside the State of Texas, across Louisiana and Arkansas, to Memphis, Tennessee. (From the author's collection)

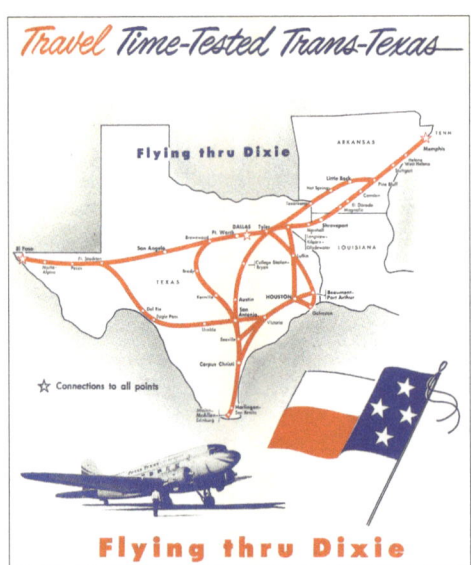

 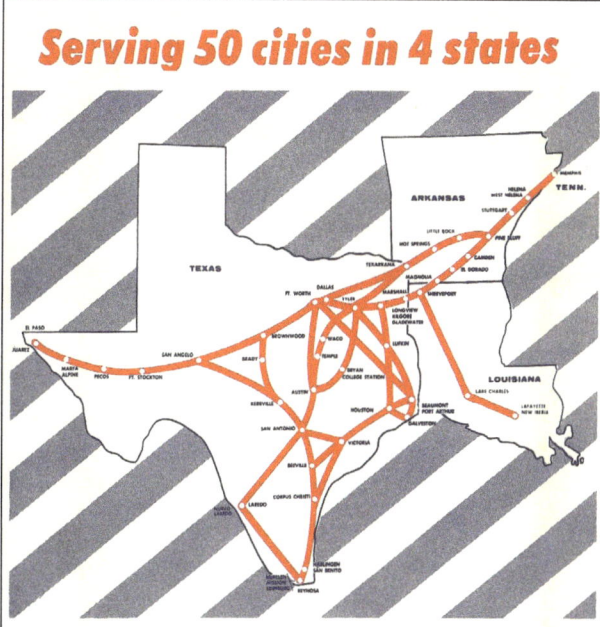 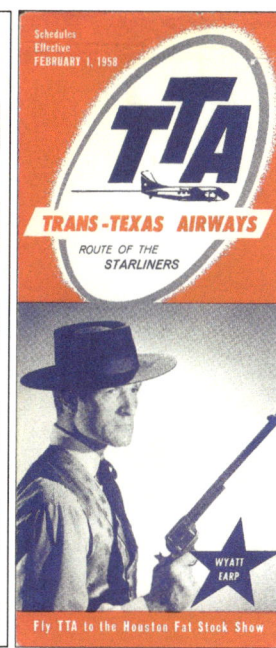

FAR LEFT: *TTA's October 1, 1957 timetable celebrated the airline's 10th anniversary.*
MIDDLE: *October 1, 1957 route map boasted service to 50 cities in 4 states.*
RIGHT: *January and February 1958 timetables promoted Fort Worth and Houston livestock shows featuring TV characters Annie Oakley (Gail Davis) and Wyatt Earp (Hugh O'Brian). (From the author's collection)*

tail wheel-well enclosure, and what was referred to as a Siamese exhaust system. The entire retrofit increased the aircraft's cruising speed by at least 20 mph in addition to improving the range, payload and economy of the Starliners, turning the fleet of 20 DC-3s into what would now be dubbed "Super Starliners." Among those announcing the upgrade program to an audience at the company's Houston headquarters in 1957 was R.E. "Dick" McKaughan Jr., director of flight operations and son of R. Earl McKaughan.

TTA aggressively sought new route authority and, in 1957, the map of proposed routes stretched as far east as Jacksonville, Fla., Atlanta, Ga., and Tri-Cities, Tenn., and as far north as Cincinnati and St. Louis, with dozens of points designated in between. It was a map of wishful thinking as the CAB denied TTA's requests for such extensive expansion.

Oddly, in the Southeastern Area Local Service Case, TTA had applied for routes serving a couple of dozen cities that were firmly in Southern Airways' service area. It was no surprise, then, when those routes were awarded to Southern instead of Trans-Texas.

TTA was also anxious to connect Memphis with New Orleans via University/Oxford, Greenwood and Jackson, Miss., and Bogalusa, Louisiana. The Ole Miss Airport at University/Oxford was dedicated on May 9, 1957, and a TTA Super Starliner, provided by the company to fly dignitaries to the dedication, was the first multi-engine aircraft to land on the brand new runway. Aboard the plane were R. Earl McKaughan and other TTA officials plus a large group of influential Mississippi politicians

TTA began supplementing its DC-3 fleet with larger Convair 240s, in service from April 1, 1961. One of the company's 240s is pictured above, with shadows accentuating the red lettering on the aircraft. (From the author's collection)

America's Local Service Airlines

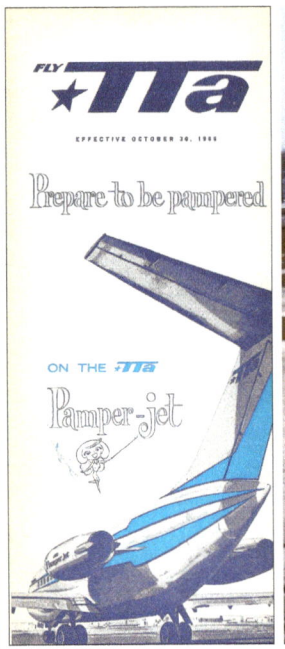

1966 was a milestone year for TTA. LEFT to RIGHT: Convair 600s were introduced on March 1, and pure-jet service was inaugurated with DC-9 'Pamper Jets' on October 30. One of the company's Rolls-Royce Dart powered 'Silver Cloud' Convair 600s is pictured. (Timetables from the author's collection, photo from the Tim Williams collection)

and businessmen who had boarded in Jackson and Greenwood. Despite the attempts to woo favor from these VIPS, this route was also awarded to Southern, instead of TTA, in the South Central Area Local Service Case, decided in March 1959.

Despite losing the Memphis to New Orleans route, TTA won big in the South Central Area decision. The company was awarded seven new stations, stretching its system eastward to the terminal points of Jackson, Miss., and New Orleans with service authorized to Natchez, Miss., and to Alexandria, Monroe, DeRidder and Morgan City, Louisiana. Flights were inaugurated in June 1959 to each of the new stations except Morgan City, which came on-line two years later.

1959 also saw the inauguration of nonstop service between both Houston and San Antonio on the one hand, and the Rio Grande Valley (Harlingen, Tex.) on the other. Midland/Odessa, Tex., became a TTA station in August of that year.

As the company settled down to operating its expanded route system, the issue of acquiring larger aircraft came to the forefront. A few of the Locals had upgraded their fleets by purchasing the new turboprop Fairchild F-27. Others had found their larger airliners by obtaining used Convair twins or Martins from trunk carriers disposing of the types. TTA chose the latter strategy, buying a fleet of 25 Convair 240s from American Airlines, with deliveries scheduled over a period of several years. It was apparently a dispute over this transaction that caused a parting of the ways between R. Earl McKaughan and Lamar Muse. Muse left Trans-Texas in 1960. His legacy of sound financial planning lived on in the pages of the company's 1960 annual report as the aircraft purchase was reported thusly: "An agreement was reached in 1960 with American Airlines for the purchase of a fleet of Convair aircraft, resulting in your company being the first local service carrier to secure modern equipment without earlier requesting a guaranteed loan from the CAB or diluting existing shareholders' equity through the issuance of convertible debentures to finance equipment."

The first Convairs entered service on April 1, 1961, accompanied by a new 'Silverliner Buffet' offered on Convair evening flights and continental breakfast on morning flights. New Neiman-Marcus hostess uniforms included 'Convair red' coats and western ties.

The next couple of years were stable for TTA as more Convairs came on-line and the route map remained unchanged. But the airline was bracing for the results of one of the CAB's last major investigations into local service. This one encompassed the heart of TTA's service area. Dubbed the Southwestern Area Local Service Case, the investigation dealt not only with requests for new service from Trans-Texas, but also with the possibility of transferring routes embracing many medium-sized and smaller cities from trunk carriers, particularly Continental, to local service operators like TTA.

Trans-Texas Airways was awarded the biggest route expansion in its history with the decision of the Board in the Southwestern Area Local Service Case in 1963. Replacing trunk carrier service, TTA gained 13 new stations. The CAB also allowed more liberalized operating authority over the existing system permitting nonstop service over several important routes, most notably Dallas – Houston. The CAB was gradually allowing the Locals into more lucrative markets in order

Left: DC-9-15MC N1303T is pictured in TTA's blue-and-silver livery. Right: Trans-Texas Airways became Texas International Airlines on April 1, 1969, and new corporate colors of purple, white and gray were applied to the fleet, seen here on DC-9-14 N1302T. (Photos from the Tim Williams collection)

to offset the need for subsidy on other routes. The trunk carriers that TTA was replacing had operated into the previously mentioned 13 stations without benefit of subsidy from U.S. taxpayers. Now Trans-Texas, a local service line, would require more than $1 million a year from the public coffers in order to serve the same cities.

TTA had been a consistently profitable operation for most of its existence and the company continued that proud record through the early 1960s.

The next advancement came when TTA management decided to convert the entire fleet of Convairs to prop jets. The Convair twins were well-suited for turboprop conversion. Many of the 340 and 440 models in service with other airlines were retrofitted with engines manufactured by the Allison Division of General Motors. The resulting product was christened the Convair 580. Allison's engines were considered too powerful for use on the earlier model Convair 240s that TTA flew. The Convair Division of General Dynamics, manufacturers of the original aircraft, developed a conversion for the 240s using Rolls-Royce Dart engines. The resulting airliner was dubbed the Convair 600. There were only two airlines that chose to convert their 240s to 600 standards: TTA and its neighboring local service carrier, Central Airlines, which had also acquired its 240s from American Airlines. Trans-Texas chose to perform all of its conversions 'in house' using kits supplied by Convair. Introduced into service on March 1, 1966, TTA referred to its jazzed-up Convairs as 'Silver Cloud 600s.'

The Convair conversions were just an interim measure. All of the Locals were jumping on the 'pure jet' bandwagon and, in order to remain competitive, TTA also needed to climb aboard. Remaining competitive had not been an issue for local service airlines in the early years as they were barred and protected from competition with trunk carriers by the CAB. But the public was not going to settle for a Convair, jet-prop

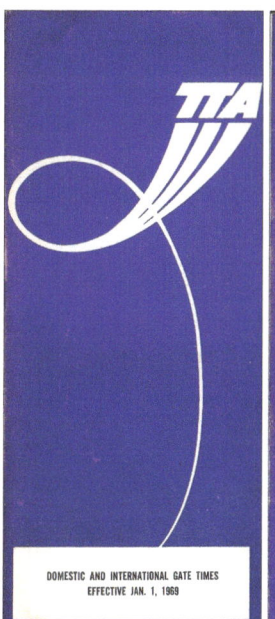

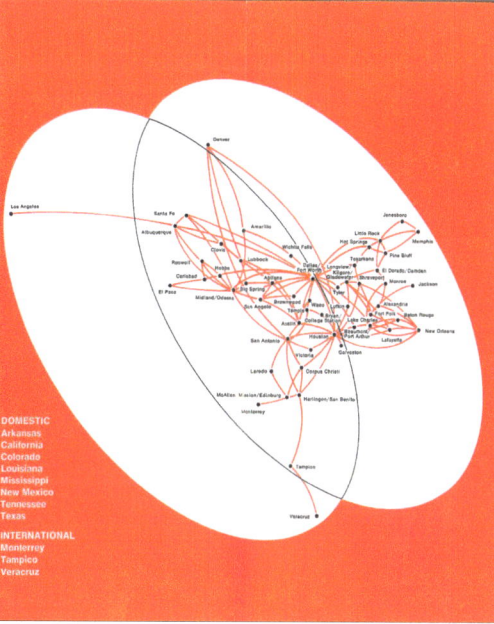

LEFT to RIGHT: Change is in the air as revealed by the cover of this TTA January 1, 1969 timetable presenting the new corporate colors. The April 1, 1969 timetable announces the name change to Texas International with the slogan, 'It's a whole new airline.' Finally, the route map from the October 26, 1969 timetable shows a system that stretches west to Los Angeles and south to Veracruz. (From the author's collection)

America's Local Service Airlines

Frank Lorenzo's Jet Capital Corp. purchased Texas International in 1972, and introduced yet another livery change, which harkened back to TI's roots. The Texas state flag's colors of red, white and blue were applied to the fuselage and a lone star was painted on the tail of the aircraft. The attractive paint scheme is displayed on a DC-9-30 (left) and a Convair 600 (right). (Photos from the Tim Williams collection)

or not, between Houston and Dallas when the competition was flying newer, more modern aircraft. And passengers on TTA's own Beaumont/Port Arthur to Dallas flights deserved to be accommodated on an airliner similar to the jets that they would be connecting to in Dallas.

Trans-Texas ordered seven Douglas DC-9s, including DC-9-14s and DC-9-15MCs (Minimum Change for conversion to cargo aircraft). TTA referred to its new DC-9s as 'Pamperjets,' introducing them into service on October 30, 1966.

R. Earl McKaughan turned over the reins of his company to his son, R.E. "Dick" McKaughan Jr., who became president of the airline in 1966, while the senior McKaughan was designated chairman of the board.

TTA's string of profitable years came to an end as the staggering cost of the Convair conversion and jet purchase programs made their presence known on the balance sheet despite increasing passenger loads. Lamar Muse was no longer there to help keep expenses in check. But TTA was not the only local service carrier that took a blow after transitioning its entire fleet in the late Sixties. Some other Locals were forced to merge when the flow of red ink overwhelmed them.

Increasing its status among America's airlines, Trans-Texas Airways became an international carrier with the addition of Monterrey, Tampico and Veracruz, Mexico, to its route map in late 1966. TTA was flying four different types of equipment in 1967: DC-9s, Convair 600s, Convair 240s, which had yet to be retrofitted, and reliable old DC-3s

After 20 years of running the airline, the McKaughans were receptive to an offer made by Carl Pohlad and his Minnesota Enterprises, Inc. (MEI) to purchase TTA. The deal was finalized in 1968 and changes were about to take place.

Trans-Texas had been a great name for a local service airline serving routes primarily within Texas and its neighboring states.

LEFT to RIGHT: *After deregulation, Texas International focused on a two hub system oriented around Houston and Dallas / Ft. Worth, as seen in this April 1981 route map. Lorenzo created Texas Air Corp., a holding company which owned TI. In 1982, Texas Air purchased Continental Airlines and merged the two carriers. Although Texas International was technically the surviving company, the Continental Airlines name was retained. The merger is reflected in these two timetables effective June 1, 1982.*

But, like the other Locals, TTA was now flying jets, and it was the U.S.-designated flag carrier to three destinations in Mexico. The term 'regional airline' was now more appropriate than 'local service carrier.' In a move to keep the identification with the State of Texas alive while embracing the wider market being served, TTA shareholders agreed to change the company's name to Texas International Airlines.

The name change officially took place on April 1, 1969, and with it came new corporate colors of purple, white and gray, which were applied to the aircraft fleet.

The company name and corporate colors were not the only change that took place. The McKaughans were gone and MEI had installed Robert J. Sherer as the airline's president in July 1968. Sherer would be replaced by W.L. Lane in 1970.

By the end of 1969, Texas International (TI) was flying its DC-9s to Denver and Los Angeles, once again as a result of the CAB's efforts to boost revenue among the 'Locals,' and to reduce the reliance on subsidy.

The first of the company's stretched Douglas DC-9-31s was delivered in 1969 and the next year TI undertook an experiment following in the footsteps of other Locals that had replaced service at less-productive stations with smaller aircraft. The airline invested in several 15-passenger Beech 99A 'Skylarks' to offer frequent service between Houston and Galveston, and to replace the larger Convair 600s at places like Lufkin and Victoria. The aircraft was not a popular type with passengers and was removed from the fleet a few years later.

The Denver route was extended to Salt Lake City in 1970. Mexico City received service starting in 1972; it would be the last new station added to TI's network before deregulation.

But the company was in desperate financial trouble, rapidly heading towards bankruptcy. With a $6 million per year loss recorded since 1968 and past debts due of $20 million, a new savior had to be found. MEI had problems of its own and, obviously, had not provided the solution to the company's financial predicament.

Jet Capital Corp., owned by Francisco "Frank" Lorenzo and Robert J. Carney, purchased the airline in 1972 and began the process of turning it around. Another new paint scheme was selected, this one once again honoring the airline's heritage with the Texas 'lone star' painted on the tail of aircraft sporting a red, white and blue livery.

Frank Lorenzo implemented changes that focused the airline's routes on Houston and Dallas/Fort Worth. He was helped immensely by the sudden 'sunbelt' growth boom, with Houston at its center, after the Arab oil embargo of 1973. In 1976, the company posted a profit of $3.2 million, quite a turnaround from the dark days of 1972.

Texas International Airlines was competing head-to-head with low-cost carrier Southwest Airlines and Lorenzo successfully petitioned the CAB to allow TI the flexibility of offering reduced fares on major routes. Dubbed "Peanuts Fares," Texas International made itself known in the U.S. domestic airline market with introduction of the lower fares in 1977. By August of that year, TI's load factor reached 63.1 percent, the highest among any of the still-labeled local service carriers.

Deregulation became a reality in October 1978 and Frank Lorenzo became the poster boy for airline leaders making the most of the new business environment. In 1980 he created Texas Air Corporation as a holding company under whose umbrella Texas International Airlines was placed. In 1982 Texas Air purchased Continental Airlines, one of several carriers that had not fared well in the deregulated industry. Texas International was merged with Continental and, although TI was technically the surviving carrier, the Continental name was retained. On June 1, 1982, it was the end of the line for yet another of the nation's 13 permanently certificated local service airlines. ✈

CHAPTER 14
WEST COAST AIRLINES

Nick Bez was the epitome of The American Dream come true, a self-made man in the Horatio Alger tradition. He arrived in New York from his native Dalmatia in 1910, a teenager alone and penniless but determined to make his way in the 'new world.' Thirty-six years later he was the founder and president of one of America's certificated local service airlines.

After reaching the United States, Bez made his way to the Pacific Northwest where he knew there was a Dalmatian community involved in the fishing industry. Having grown up on the Adriatic, Nick Bez knew a thing or two about the sea and fishing. Hard work, determination to succeed and thrifty ways eventually gave him enough money to buy his own boat. His fleet grew and he engaged in a battle for control of the Alaska salmon fishing industry and came out a winner.

Nick Bez entered the airline business when he founded Alaska Southern Airways in the early 1930s with a Loening Air Yacht. Later, he acquired two Lockheed Vegas from the assets of Alaska-Washington Airways. The airline was a sideline as Bez's primary business continued to be the fishing and canning industry. Alaska Southern offered service from Juneau to Seattle via Ketchikan and, on November 13, 1934, Bez sold the airline to Pacific Alaska Airways, a Pan American subsidiary.

Nick Bez was becoming a very wealthy man. A staunch supporter of the Democratic Party, Bez gained a degree of fame when he was photographed in 1945 rowing a boat in Puget Sound aboard which President Harry S. Truman was fishing for salmon. The two men became good friends.

Bez began canning fish aboard a large ship, a converted freighter, owned by the U.S. government in a project financed by the Reconstruction Finance Corporation. The purpose was to prove that Americans could replicate the work previously done by the Japanese who had been very active in using floating canneries before WWII.

Amidst all of his commercial and government-sponsored fishing activities, Nick Bez decided to get back into the airline business. West Coast Airlines (WCA) was incorporated on March 14, 1941, for the purpose of obtaining a certificate to operate service along the Pacific coast. The Civil Aeronautics Board (CAB) put a moratorium on route applications for the duration of the war but, during that time, the Board created the classification of carriers known as feeder airlines.

On May 22, 1946, the CAB issued its decisions in the West Coast Service Case, authorizing Nick Bez's WCA to operate local

Classic shot of a West Coast DC-3 on the ramp at Yakima. The 1950s paint scheme was green and white, appropriate for the "Evergreen Empire." (Photo by John Elott via Ed Davies)

LEFT to RIGHT: *WCA's February 1, 1949 timetable shows the initial north-south system in Washington State and Oregon. The first timetable issued reflecting the West Coast Airlines and Empire Air Lines merger was effective September 28, 1952. The temporary use of the West Coast Empire name and the route map of the merged company are illustrated in that timetable. (From the author's collection)*

services in the states of Washington and Oregon on a north-south network stretching from Bellingham to Medford.

Bez apparently had no problem raising capital as he got his airline up and running with two Douglas DC-3s on December 5, 1946, over the Seattle – Portland section of his award. West Coast operated two routes between these major cities: one inland and one along the coast, each serving communities en route. The following year, with three more "Gooney Birds" in the fleet, flights were inaugurated over the remainder of the system, from Bellingham to Seattle with two stops along the way, from Port Angeles to Seattle, and from Portland south to Medford via several cities in Oregon. The company proudly touted its slogan, "Serving the Evergreen Empire."

West Coast added a sixth DC-3 in 1949, however, the airline's utilization of each aircraft in revenue service that year averaged a surprisingly low four hours and 41 minutes per day.

The CAB was coping with its feeder airline experiment trying to nurture the new breed of carrier while figuring out the best ways to save money for taxpayers. Subsidy was an enormous part of the local airline equation and Congress would be holding the CAB accountable if the Board did not try to reduce the amount of financial aid flowing to the feeders. One of the new certificated carriers, Florida Airways, had already gone belly-up and others had to be given permission to use single-engine equipment just to get them off of the ground. The Board encouraged mergers among the feeders if the result would be route improvements, cost savings and economies of operation. A three-way merger among Monarch Airlines, Challenger Airlines and Arizona Airways, approved in 1950, was the perfect example of this philosophy in action. Previously, Arizona Airways had not been able to start operations under the terms of its federal certificate but the resources of the newly formed triumvirate, now called Frontier Airlines, put the entire system, stretching through the Rocky Mountain States, into a coordinated service pattern that worked very well.

Nick Bez met with Jack Connelly, the president of Southwest Airways, in 1949 to negotiate terms of a merger between the two airlines. Southwest was the certificated feeder carrier operating a network in the territory just to the south of West Coast's. Southwest's system stretched from Medford, Oregon, down to Los Angeles and, if a merger was accomplished, Southwest would be the surviving carrier. Nick Bez would, of course, benefit financially under the terms of the agreement. The CAB entered into "extensive proceedings" to consider the matter and in the end decided that merger of the two airlines would be "adverse to the public interest." Had the merger been approved, Southwest could have become a huge local service operation extending from Bellingham, Wash., to Phoenix, Ariz., since the Board had tentatively approved Southwest for a route from Los Angeles to Phoenix. Southwest was so confident of the merger and of the Phoenix route award being certified that the airline published its timetables with the projected route structure printed on the covers. As it was, the Board was afraid of creating a behemoth of a local airline along the Pacific Coast, one that might step on the toes of trunk carriers Western and United, which operated in the same region. Not only was the merger denied but another hearing was held and the Los Angeles to Phoenix local service route was reassigned to Bonanza Air Lines, which the Board felt had a very weak route structure to begin with.

In denying the merger, the Board suggested that perhaps Southwest should merge with Bonanza instead and that West Coast Airlines might consider a merger with Empire Air Lines, the local service carrier based in Boise that operated in Idaho, eastern Oregon and Washington State. Neither Southwest nor Bonanza was the least bit interested in pursuing merger talks with each other but Nick Bez knew a good opportunity when he saw one. First of all, West Coast's and Empire's systems did not connect so, in order to effect a merger, the CAB would have to give West Coast significant east-west routes across Washington

LEFT: *Nick Bez was a Horatio Alger success story, having risen from poor immigrant to founder and leader of West Coast Airlines.* RIGHT: *Except for minor tweaks, the WCA system remained relatively unchanged between 1952 and 1959. The November 1955 route map is illustrated..*

connecting the two networks and creating a local service airline stretching across the three northwestern states, from Port Angeles to Pocatello. Second, since the Board had suggested the marriage, the Board's approval was almost assured if a deal could be reached between the two feeders.

After several rounds of negotiations, an agreement was reached and the CAB instituted its hearings, which happened to coincide with the certificate renewal hearings for Empire. The merger was approved along with the expected connecting routes eastward from both Seattle and Portland via the important point of Yakima and and by way of other cities, to Spokane, Pasco, Pendleton, Walla Walla and the rest of the Empire system.

The merger took effect on September 28, 1952, when the first joint timetable was issued with the title "West Coast Empire Airlines" on the cover. A through-flight was instituted between Seattle and Idaho Falls, from one end of the system to the other, with 11 stops in between. The name West Coast Empire was employed on timetables and promotional material for a year, although the true corporate name remained West Coast Airlines. The company's updated slogan was "Building a New West Coast Empire."

In the 1953 annual report, Nick Bez outlined some of the problems encountered in merging the two airlines. Selecting the best service patterns, consolidating maintenance facilities and the need for more headquarters space were the three issues at the top of the list. A favorable lease on a hangar formerly occupied by Pan American at Boeing Field in Seattle solved the maintenance and headquarters issue, centralizing everything in a spacious facility.

Boeing Field had been West Coast's base of operation since its inception but, in an odd situation unique to West Coast Airlines among all of the Locals, Bez kept West Coast's Seattle operation anchored at that airport after all of the other airlines serving Seattle had moved to Seattle-Tacoma International Airport (SeaTac). West Coast had Boeing Field all to itself after Pan Am finally joined the other carriers serving Seattle over at Sea-Tac in

LEFT: *This post card view captures two West Coast DC-3s on the ramp at Yakima.* RIGHT: *In the 1950s, West Coast used a mythical figure as its advertising mascot, employing the slogan: Serving Paul Bunyan's Empire.*

LEFT: *West Coast Airlines made history in 1958 as the first airline in the world to fly the F-27.* RIGHT: *With the new F-27s came a new paint scheme, which was also applied to the DC-3s, as seen here on N2025A at Seattle in November 1959. (Photo from the Tim Williams collection)*

1953. This meant that anyone connecting between West Coast and other airlines would have to make the 7.5 mile land journey between the two airports, with a minimum connecting time of one hour. This certainly hampered one of the main purposes of a feeder airline, to feed traffic to other carriers.

As West Coast steadily maintained its operation during the mid-1950s, the airline took on a new advertising slogan. Covering both the Evergreen Empire of the Pacific Northwest and the Inland Empire of the former Empire Air Line's network, WCA employed a mythical figure to be its mascot and claimed that the company was "Serving Paul Bunyan's Empire."

Nick Bez pulled off a coup when he inked a deal with Fairchild Aircraft Corp. to purchase four American-built versions of the new turboprop Fokker Friendship, to be called the Fairchild F-27. West Coast also held options for four additional F-27s.

Delivery of the first aircraft, anticipated in late 1957, was delayed until 1958, entering service on September 28 of that year. But the delayed deliveries did not matter. West Coast still received worldwide publicity as the first operator of the type, designed specifically for local service, short-haul operators. WCA became the first of the 13 permanently certificated local service airlines in America to put a brand new, factory-fresh turboprop airplane into service.

1959 proved to be another news-making year for West Coast as the CAB awarded 17 new stations to the airline along with routes stretching into three new states, California, Utah and Montana. The important terminal points of San Francisco and Salt Lake City were brought onto WCA's route map.

In 1960, West Coast became an international airline as service was inaugurated between Spokane and Calgary, Alberta,

West Coast was the first of the 13 Locals to place factory-fresh turboprop aircraft into service. The F-27s would be repainted into a final WCA livery in the mid-1960s to coordinate with the new DC-9 paint scheme. N2702 is pictured here. (Photo from the Robert Hufford collection in the AAHS archives, AAHS-40815)

WCA signed an order for four Douglas DC-9-14s to be delivered in 1966 and 1967, allowing WCA to enter the "jet age." The first aircraft delivered was N9101 that made its first revenue flight on September 26, 1966. Tragically, five days later it crashed on Mt. Hood while descending to land at Portland, Oregon. Eighteen people were killed in the first crash ever of a Douglas DC-9. (Photo from the Tim Williams collection)

Canada. Nick Bez's little airline that started out hugging the Pacific Coast in two states now connected more than 60 cities in six states and Canada.

The Paul Bunyan slogan was replaced with the simpler "WCA is Going Your Way," and, once again, West Coast settled into a steady routine operating its enlarged route system with F-27s and DC-3s. The next big step in the airline's progress would be its ascent into the jet age in the company of all of the other Locals that were taking that same big step.

But before the jets came into the picture, there was one more distraction to be dealt with. Even though the CAB had squelched plans for West Coast to merge with Southwest Airways back in 1950, Nick Bez was still interested in a merger. Southwest had changed its corporate name to Pacific Air Lines in 1958, and, in 1963, Leland Hayward and Jack Connelly, founders and former chairman and president of that airline, quietly sold 34 percent of Pacific's common stock to Nick Bez. The CAB opened an investigation claiming that this had been an illegal attempt by one airline to take over another. Before the hearings began in May 1964, Bez sold the Pacific shares to a group calling itself Seton Associates. The Board wanted to know if there was any connection between West Coast and Seton, but by selling the shares, Nick Bez had cleverly removed himself and West Coast from any threat of prosecution.

West Coast was a profitable airline in 1965, but it still relied heavily on Public Service Revenue (subsidy) to cover its operations serving smaller cities. Nevertheless, West Coast had to keep up with all of its contemporaries and Nick Bez signed an order for four Douglas DC-9-14s to be delivered in 1966 and '67.

In what can only be described as the most tragic of circumstances, West Coast's very first DC-9 to be delivered, a

West Coast introduced Piper Navajo "MiniLiners" to replace aging DC-3s on lightly traveled routes as reflected in this April 1967 advertisement. On the right, Navajo N11133 is pictured preparing to board passengers at Boise, Idaho, March 21, 1968. (Photo from the Hufford collection of the AAHS archives, AAHS-40856)

Even the remaining DC-3s got the new paint scheme introduced with the DC-9s, as seen here on N65351. West Coast was the only one of the three airlines combining in 1968 to form Air West that was still operating Gooney Birds *at the time of the merger. N1051N is pictured here with West Coast window band and Air West titles. WCA's final timetable, effective April 28, 1968, announces that the company is 'soon to become Air West." (Photo of N65351 by Curt Hulslander via the author, N1051N from the AAHS archives)*

brand new $3 million turbojet proudly carrying the local airline's livery, crashed in the Mt. Hood National Forest in Oregon on descent for landing in Portland, while operating a scheduled flight. The aircraft had only been in service for six days, inaugurating West Coast's first jet operations on September 26, 1966. The accident took place on October 1. Eighteen people aboard the aircraft died in the first crash ever of a Douglas DC-9.

WCA needed an airplane to replace its aging DC-3s on thinly travelled routes and the company found an interesting solution in the form of three leased Piper Aztecs, which were put into service in 1966. The experiment with the Aztecs was promising, so the company purchased four of the larger Piper Navajos. Referring to them as "MiniLiners," WCA kept the small aircraft in its fleet to serve stations like Roseburg, Oregon, and Sun Valley, Idaho, until the end of the airline's existence.

And the end was not very far away. Nick Bez wanted a merger and he was about to get it. Pacific Air Lines, which had once been the very profitable Southwest Airways, was not doing well after introducing large Boeing 727s onto a route system that was facing strong competition from intrastate carrier, PSA, among others. Bonanza, which had once been looked upon as having a weak route system that hopped across the desert was now doing very well since that desert included the booming cities of Las Vegas and Phoenix.

West Coast itself was doing very well and, in a move that the CAB would approve this time, the three airlines agreed to merge. The new airline was to be called Air West, and Nick Bez was going to be the chairman of the board and chief executive officer. Bonanza's Edmund Converse who, like Bez, had nurtured his company from the very beginning would be vice chairman of the board.

The companies received the necessary blessings from the CAB and also from the president of the United States, whose approval was necessary since international routes were involved. On July 1, 1968, Air West came into being and three of America's permanently certificated local service carriers flew off into the sunset: Bonanza, Pacific, and West Coast Airlines. ✈

CHAPTER 15

NOT TO BE FORGOTTEN...

The local service carriers that received permanent certification in 1955 remained intact as a group of 13 until 1967, when two members of that group (Frontier and Central) merged, reducing the count to 12. By that time the Locals had saturated the continental United States with service to small cities and the nature of their operations had begun to change, prompted by the introduction of jets and the advancement of the Interstate Highway System.

Between 1945 and 1950, several other companies received temporary certification from the Civil Aeronautics Board (CAB) to operate as feeder carriers but, for one reason or another, these additional local service airlines did not survive to see their names printed upon one of the CAB's permanent Certificates of Public Convenience and Necessity issued in 1955.

A full list of the 25 companies that received feeder certificates is included in Chapter One, and the story of some of those outfits is briefly covered there. A few of the carriers never did get airborne under the terms of their federally-issued certificates while others did succeed in establishing service, only to disappear through merger or by refusal of the CAB to renew their certificates. It is this latter group of companies, the ones that also served as part of America's local service airline network, whose story will be told in this chapter.

PIONEER AIR LINES

Pioneer's history was a cautionary tale for the other Locals. All of these airlines relied on public service revenue (subsidy) for a substantial part of their income and, since they were receiving federal tax dollars and operating on an "experimental" basis, it was expected that their management teams would do nothing that could be considered financially risky.

Pioneer was known as Essair (the ESS standing for Efficiency, Safety and Speed) when the airline received the very first feeder certificate issued by the CAB in 1945. The company had been in existence for several years and had previously provided intrastate service within Texas for a brief period. On August 25, 1945, Essair began operations under its new feeder certificate, providing service between Houston and Amarillo, Tex., via four intermediate cities using 10-passenger Lockheed L-10A Electras.

The following year, 21-passenger Douglas DC-3s were introduced to replace the smaller Electras and the company management wisely changed the outfit's name to Pioneer Air Lines.

Pioneer proved to be a success story in the feeder airline experiment. The route system grew as the CAB authorized more mileage for the airline in both Texas and New Mexico. Revenue passenger miles flown more than doubled between 1947 and

A Pioneer DC-3 in updated livery rests on an unidentified ramp (red window-band, blue titles and blue tail). A company DC-3 wearing the original livery can be seen in the distance. (From the author's collection)

The acquisition of Martin 202s would eventually lead to Pioneer's downfall, precipitated by a management move to upgrade its fleet too quickly without careful study of the impact that this might have on operations and cash flow. (Photo from the author's collection)

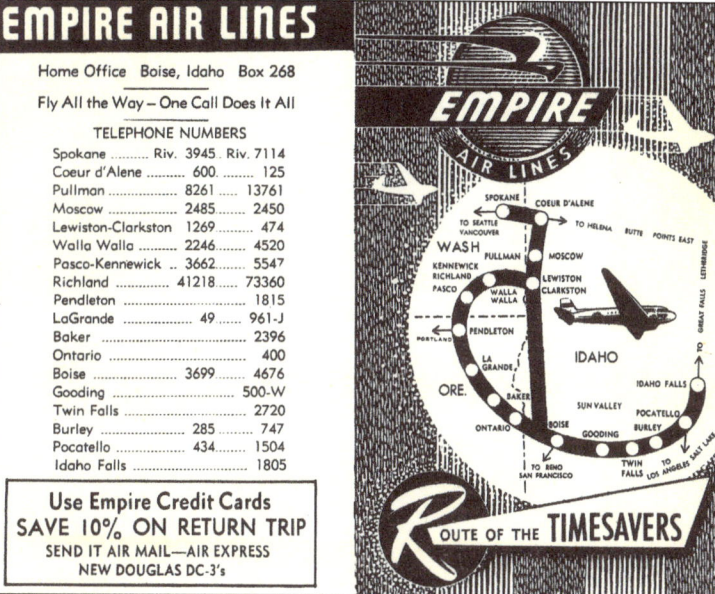

November 1, 1950, Empire timetable featuring route map. (Photo from the author's collection)

1950, while net profit climbed year-by-year during the same period. Charter traffic was so robust that an additional DC-3 was purchased for $55,000 in 1950 just to cater to that segment of the company's business. In his address to stockholders in the company's 1950 annual report, Pioneer's chairman of the board said: "I feel no hesitation in stating that our financial position is exceptionally sound, and that future prospects are brighter than anyone could have anticipated." Of course, the second largest source of revenue for Pioneer, 38 percent of its income in 1950, was "mail pay," the euphemism for payment by the Post Office for carrying the mail plus subsidy from tax dollars to cover the expense of bringing air mail and passenger service to smaller cities.

Pioneer's management was so confident of the company's prospects that they made a deal with the Glenn L. Martin Co. to acquire post-war, 36-passenger Martin 202As, which the manufacturer had on lease to TWA at the time. Pioneer would take delivery of the used 202As when they were returned to the Martin Co. by TWA in exchange for the newer, pressurized Martin 404s, which the trunk carrier was waiting for. When that transaction hit a snag in late 1951, Pioneer found what looked like a better deal. Northwest Airlines had decided to sell its fleet of Martin 202s and Pioneer snatched up nine of them. Pioneer sold its entire fleet of 11 DC-3s to help pay for the purchase.

That turned out to be the beginning of the end for Pioneer Air Lines.

Instead of augmenting its DC-3s with a couple of Martins, Pioneer had replaced its entire fleet. The company could proudly claim that it was the first feeder carrier to acquire aircraft larger than the DC-3, but it was a short-lived honor. The Martins were more expensive to operate than the DC-3s, so Pioneer asked the CAB for additional subsidy. The CAB refused to increase payments since the DC-3s had been serving adequately.

Losing money rapidly, Pioneer had no choice but to reinstate DC-3 service on its routes. The Martins were put up for sale through a company set up by Pioneer for that purpose, and 10 DC-3s were leased from the Navy. Short on cash, Pioneer asked the CAB to underwrite the lease agreement. The CAB refused, stating that Pioneer had owned a perfectly good fleet of DC-3s, which had been depreciated at public expense. The company chose to sell those airplanes and used the cash to buy bigger aircraft that proved to be too costly; now it was Pioneer's own fault that the company was in the mess that it was in.

The solution to Pioneer's problems was merger with a healthy company. The outfit that came to the rescue was a trunk carrier, Continental Air Lines. A deal was struck, and Continental officially absorbed Pioneer Air Lines into its system on April 1, 1955.

The irony of the merger date is that Pioneer's official demise took place less than two months before President Eisenhower signed the legislation granting permanent certificates to the existing local service carriers, which greatly increased their appeal to outside investors. Pioneer was to have been the 14th Local, but its permanent certificate was passed on to Continental instead. Of course, Continental already had a permanent operating certificate, which had been issued shortly after the CAB was created.

Had it not been for an unwise decision on the part of the company's management, Pioneer may have succeeded and thrived into the 1960s.

FLORIDA AIRWAYS

Thomas E. Gordon, doing business as Orlando Airlines, was awarded feeder routes in the State of Florida in the CAB's Florida Case, decided in March 1946. The name of the company was changed to Florida Airways and scheduled operations began on January 10, 1947.

The company had several things going against it right from the start. The airline's network was extremely weak, with routes heading north from Orlando to Tallahassee and Jacksonville. This was long before Orlando had become the tourist Mecca that it is today. The terminal points of Orlando and Tallahassee were served by certificated trunk carriers, Eastern and National, while Jacksonville was served by Eastern, National and Delta. The intermediate stations served by Florida Airways had weak traffic potential. Ocala and Gainesville were the most important en-route cities, while Sanford, Deland, Palatka, St. Augustine and Lake City were also served.

Florida Airways stuck with the Beech D-18 as its aircraft of choice to operate over its route system. Several other feeder carriers proposed using the 8-passenger twins, but most realized before they began operations that the Beechcraft product was not big enough to handle passenger loads into major stations.

The little Florida airline was infringing on the service area of Eddie Rickenbacker's Eastern Air Lines, and Ted Baker's National Airlines, both of whom would fight to the finish to keep Florida as their turf. There was no place for any other carrier, feeder or not, in the Sunshine State, as far as they were concerned.

By 1949, despite grand plans for expansion throughout the state, Florida Airways had added only two additional stations to its network, Perry and Leesburg, neither of which offered great potential as revenue producers. When it came time for the three-year review by the CAB to determine whether or not the airline's certificate should be extended, the CAB convened and decided against renewal. Despite the fact that the company claimed that it had completed 99.6 percent of its schedules, which it believed to be a record in the worldwide airline industry, Florida's Certificate of Convenience and Necessity was allowed to expire on March 28, 1949, and the little airline became the first of the feeders to cease operations.

An indication of the CAB's opinion of Florida Airways' management can be found in the record of the company's request for additional retroactive subsidy after it ceased operations. The Florida staff complained that their four Beech D-18s were not worth very much in the used aircraft market and they sold one at about half of the going rate in order to prove their point. The CAB noted in response that "... Florida's sales efforts were so inept that the amount received is hardly a reasonable indication of the fair residual value of its aircraft."

Eastern Air Lines was soon given permission to take over service at Ocala and Gainesville. None of the other intermediate points served by Florida Airways ever saw certificated service again.

EMPIRE AIR LINES

Empire Air Lines, founded by Bert Zimmerly and originally known as Zimmerly Air Lines, was already operating in Idaho when it received its federal certificate on May 22, 1946, to serve a route from Idaho Falls, Idaho, to Spokane, Wash., via a string of intermediate cities. Service under the CAB's jurisdiction began on September 28, 1946. Empire initially operated its schedules with 10-passenger Boeing 247Ds, but replaced them with five 21-passenger Douglas DC-3s in March 1948.

Though Empire was among the smallest of the new feeder carriers, its operation was particularly important for residents of Idaho. The ability to travel between Boise, the capital and largest city of the state, and points in northern Idaho (Lewiston, Moscow, and Coeur d'Alene) quickly by air, and the growth of traffic over the route after the company upgraded to DC-3s, was taken into consideration by the CAB when it came time for renewal of the company's operating authority in 1952. Empire carried 48,508 revenue passengers during the year ended June 30, 1951, and the CAB was ready to renew the airline's certificate for another five years.

Concurrent with the CAB's certificate renewal case for Empire Air Lines, the company came to an agreement with Nick Bez and his management staff at West Coast Airlines to merge the two local service carriers together. An account of the merger is included in the chapter of this book about West Coast Airlines.

Empire had become a successful, but small, local airline after it introduced DC-3s into its fleet, but the company disappeared

Empire initially employed Boeing 247Ds, but replaced them with DC-3s, one of which is seen here. Note the airstair door. (Photo from the author's collection)

into the network of West Coast Airlines after the two carriers were joined together in 1952.

MID-WEST AIRLINES

In a sense, Mid-West Airlines was doomed from the start. Although the CAB usually chose the right company for the job and selected the best routes for new feeder service after examining dozens of applications, once in awhile they created a flop.

The Iowa Airplane Co., a fixed base operator (FBO) in Des Moines, was selected by the CAB in December 1946 to operate three routes radiating from Omaha. One route meandered its way through Iowa and southern Minnesota to the Twin Cities of Minneapolis and St. Paul, but the other two routes had very weak terminals at their other ends: North Platte, Neb., and Huron, South Dakota.

Mid-West's certificate to serve many of its intermediate points was "subject to a further showing as to the adequacy of airport facilities." By 1949, many of the cities certificated for service did not have airports adequate for accommodating DC-3s. When the CAB passed its ruling that allowed feeders to begin service with single-engine equipment under certain conditions, Mid-West finally took to the air with Cessna 190s, an aircraft not intended for commercial airline use. While Mid-West's timetables claimed that four passengers could be accommodated aboard its little airplanes, the CAB classified the Cessnas as three-passenger aircraft. Apparently Mid-West's management expected three people to get very cozy, shoulder-to-shoulder, on the Cessna's aft bench-seat, while a fourth sat in the single seat up front next to the pilot.

While most of the other feeders that began operations with smaller-than-DC-3 aircraft quickly began to add the much larger *Gooney Birds* to their fleets, Mid-West struggled along with its single-engine Cessnas from the time of the company's first flight in 1949 until the CAB's hearing on whether or not to renew the company's certificate, in 1952.

There were obvious problems with an airline operating aircraft the size of the Cessna 190. First and foremost, these high-wing, general aviation-type tail-draggers did not inspire confidence in prospective passengers. If there were darkening clouds above the Great Plains, many people would feel safer in a bus or a railroad coach attached to terra firma than they would in a small, lightweight, single-engine aircraft. Then, of course, there was the issue of passenger capacity. Whether three or four customers were squeezed into Mid-West's aircraft, on a North Platte to Omaha trip there were six intermediate landings; seven between Omaha and Minneapolis/St. Paul. It's not hard to do the math and realize that not even one passenger destined for the final terminal could be boarded at each intermediate point.

In 1950, Mid-West carried only 6,940 revenue passengers and its "break-even need to commercial revenue" factor was almost 11 to 1.

That left the payment from the Post Office Department for transporting air mail, and its accompanying public service revenue (subsidy), as the primary source of income for Mid-West Airlines. In 1950, the government reduced Mid-West's subsidy payments to cover only one round-trip per day over each of its routes, as opposed to two. The reduction in service to just two flights per day at each station weakened Mid-West's passenger appeal even further.

The company's finances were in such bad shape that it was paying its pilots partly in the form of non-interest bearing notes that did not become due until two years after the date of execution. The CAB stepped in and ordered all pay to be issued in the form of cash or checks.

In 1951, Purdue University's Purdue Research Foundation offered to acquire Mid-West, partly to provide "Purdue University with a live laboratory to study airline transportation and its various ramifications." The purchase price was a mere $69,000. Purdue had the resources available to reinvigorate Mid-West and put DC-3s into operation over a streamlined and strengthened system. The CAB agreed to the acquisition late in 1951, but then took on the separate issue of whether or not to renew Mid-West's certificate after more than two years of poor performance.

In what must have been a frustrating blow to the Purdue Research Foundation, and to Mid-West employees, the CAB decided with a three to two vote not to renew Mid-West's certificate. Dissenting from that vote were CAB members Josh Lee and Joseph P. Adams, who thought that Mid-West should have been given a second chance under Purdue's guidance. They also concurred that the airline's network could be strengthened by extending the North Platte route to Denver, and transferring Mid-Continent Airlines' local service route between Sioux City and Chicago to Mid-West. With a local service system stretching from Chicago to Denver, and with Douglas DC-3s operating the schedules, Mid-West may have been able to succeed. But it was not to be. The local service airline's certificate was allowed to expire on May 16, 1952.

Not to be discouraged, Purdue University went on to extend its reach into the boardrooms of two other local service carriers, North Central Airlines and Lake Central Airlines.

WIGGINS AIRWAYS

E.W. Wiggins Airways was another carrier that was, in a sense, doomed from the start - not by a lack of passenger potential, but by a constrained service area and by using aircraft that were not big enough to meet the probable demand of the territory served.

Founded as a fixed base operator (FBO) in 1929, Wiggins received a CAB Certificate of Public Convenience and Necessity in June 1946 to operate a scheduled feeder airline in the New England area. Service began on September 29, 1949.

The problem with the Wiggins system was that it consisted of four different routes between the cities of Albany, N.Y., and Boston, Mass., each route serving different sets of intermediate

Wiggins operated twin-engine Cessna T-50s, which could only accommodate four passengers. (Photo from the Ed Coates collection)

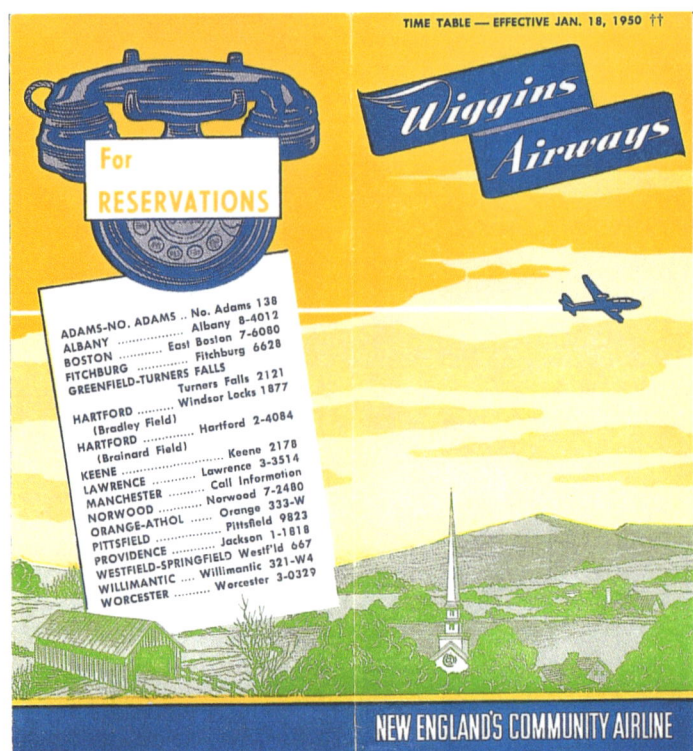

Wiggins Airways timetable effective January 18, 1950. The company billed itself as New England's Community Airline. (From the author's collection)

points. The area served was well-populated but not big enough to support the operation of an airline that would be expected to grow.

The aircraft type employed by Wiggins Airways was the four-passenger Cessna T-50. The advantage that the T-50 held over Cessna 190s and Beechcraft Bonanzas operated by some other feeders was the fact that it sported two engines. At least it was more reassuring to boarding passengers. But, again, if four passengers boarded at one station, the plane was full; there would be no room for more boarding passengers down-line.

Billing itself as *New England's Community Airline*, Wiggins managed to serve no fewer than 15 airports on its four routes between Boston and Albany. The airline wanted to expand southward to New York, which would have been a much stronger terminal point than Albany. But New York was already served from New England by Northeast Airlines, which operated Convairs and DC-3s over a network that surrounded the Wiggins system, yet Northeast still needed a lot of government subsidy to continue functioning. Wiggins was squeezed to its west by Robinson Airlines (later renamed Mohawk), a vibrant local service carrier that already had a fleet of DC-3s.

If the 19-passenger deHavilland Canada DHC-6 Twin Otter had existed at the time, it may have proven to be the most suitable airliner for the Wiggins system, but that design was still 15 years in the future. Like the other feeder carriers that started out with smaller aircraft, Wiggins, too, realized that it needed Douglas DC-3s. Unfortunately, Wiggins did not invest in any DC-3s before its certificate came up for renewal.

During the renewal hearings in 1952, the CAB decided that Wiggins was costing the government too much in subsidy for the service that was being provided. The CAB concluded that even if the company acquired DC-3s, Wiggins' operations would prove to be too costly. There really was no room for Wiggins.

Northeast Airlines and Robinson (Mohawk) could easily take over the little airline's service area. The CAB denied renewal and was ready to let Wiggins Airways die, effective January 1, 1953.

Wiggins fought back. The company challenged the CAB with 87 exceptions to the CAB examiner's findings and managed to postpone its own death until July 1953. On August 1, Mohawk Airlines inaugurated service through the heart of the former Wiggins territory, between Albany and Boston via three of the strongest stations on the former Wiggins system.

Though the certificated feeder carrier lasted only four years, the Wiggins organization continued to operate as a fixed base operation and contract freight carrier operating out of Manchester, N.H., until its acquisition by Ameriflight in December 2014. The company dabbled in scheduled commuter operations briefly in the late 1960s when it purchased and operated Cape & Islands Flight Service. In an unusual twist of events, the Wiggins organization sold Cape & Islands to Joe Whitney, who was in the process of establishing Air New England, which would be certificated as a local service carrier in 1975, 25 years after the last of the permanently-certificated Locals, Ozark Air Lines, had received its initial certificate. ✈

BIBLIOGRAPHY

In my airline history research I always try to rely on primary sources, such as company annual reports, contemporary aviation magazine articles from an era (Wayne W. Parrish's bi-weekly **American Aviation** magazine, **Airlift** magazine, and the U.S. publication, **Flight**, are particularly valuable resources), and material published by the airline itself, such as employee newspapers, etc. This is where the good stories and information are found... the stuff that you won't come across in a typical account of a company's history.

I particularly prefer to consult volumes of the **Civil Aeronautics Board Reports,** previously known as **Civil Aeronautics Board Reports - Economic Cases** (U.S. Government Printing Office). Volumes 4 through 78, covering Dec. 1942 – Sept. 1978, include all of the feeder/local airline cases up to deregulation. The **CAB Reports** were published like law books and they contain the record of each case heard by the Board. Reading through them, you will get a perspective of how much effort went into the process of choosing which companies would be certificated, which cities and routes would be served, and why. In the days of a regulated airline network in the United States, which produced the world's best air transportation system, there was a lot of examination, debate, and thoughtful consideration expended in the process of developing this industry. The members of the CAB were human, and sometimes the decisions they made were based more on political favors than on common sense. But the final outcome of the CAB's awards was made through a vote of majority opinion, thus the five Board members usually delivered the proper verdict.

Another good source of information is the series of books, **World Airline Record,** printed in seven successive editions between 1951 and 1972 (Roy R. Roadcap, Roadcap & Associates). Each volume contains brief histories and statistical information for individual airlines worldwide. These books are the next best thing to having separate annual reports for virtually every airline in the world.

I've been a collector of transportation books and ephemera my entire life, so I am fortunate to have a vast collection of timetables, annual reports, and other 'airline paper' at my disposal. In addition, the wonderful resources that I have had access to via research libraries and the kindness of individuals have been invaluable.

There have been several books written about 'The Locals' before this one, but this is the first to cover the history of each individual carrier in separate chapters. The following is a list of titles for those readers who wish to pursue the subject further.

BOOKS ABOUT THE INDIVIDUAL LOCAL SERVICE CARRIERS:

First and foremost, there are five books dealing with the history of individual Locals that I would highly recommend:

The Airway to Everywhere (W. David Lewis & William F. Trimble, University of Pittsburgh Press, 1988) is the detailed story of All-American Aviation, the predecessor of All-American Airways, which became Allegheny Airlines. While this is not the story of the actual local service carrier, the book gives an excellent portrayal of its predecessor company and the air mail pick-up service that it provided, detailing the events leading up to the decision to transform the company into a traditional feeder carrier.

Frontier Airlines: A History of the Former Frontier Airlines 1950-1986 (Gregory R. Stearns, Schiffer Publishing, 2012) is a labor of love written by a man whose parents both flew for Frontier. Stearns worked with material that was put on the shelves of the Western History Department of the Denver Public Library by Edward Gerhardt, a former employee of both Challenger and Frontier Airlines, who had embarked on a project to compile the history of Frontier in time for the company's 35th anniversary in 1981. That project was aborted when the airline pulled funding for it, but Stearns has done an admirable job of pulling it all together. Writing in a colloquial style, he has recorded the details of the company's history for posterity. The book is worth viewing for its wealth of previously-unpublished photographs alone.

Ceiling Unlimited: The Story of North Central Airlines (Robert J. Serling, Walsworth Publishing Co., 1973) was commissioned by the airline to mark its 25th anniversary. Serling was one of America's best known commercial aviation authors and his narrative of North Central's development was the first full-length corporate history of one of the Locals to be published.

Finally, the complete story of Piedmont Airlines has been the subject of two books:

Flight of the Pacemaker (Frank Elliott, The Piedmont Aviation Historical Society, 2006).

Piedmont Airlines: A Complete History, 1948-1989 (Richard E. Eller, McFarland & Co., 2008) are both well-done compilations of the company's history. Eller's work is more text-intensive while Elliott's big, hard-cover book is rich with photographs.

BOOKS ABOUT THE LOCALS, IN GENERAL:

There have been two books written on the general topic of America's certificated local service carriers:

The Local Service Airline Experiment (George C. Eads, The Brookings Institution, 1972) is a scholarly work dedicated to the examination of the Local Service Airlines as an economic experiment. Part of the 'Studies in the Regulation of Economic Activity' series, Eads reached the conclusion that the "experiment", in its original form, had been an economic failure.

In 2008, Stan Solomon released a wonderful little book entitled **Airlines for the Rest of Us: The Rise and Fall of America's Local Service Airlines** (iUniverse, Inc., 2008). His work covers the story of the Locals in a delightful, colloquial narrative.

OTHER BOOKS:

Aside from the above-mentioned, there are a few other books that deal specifically with one or more of the Locals. Among these are pilot memoirs, such as:

Frontier Airlines Captain Tex Searle's **The Golden Years of Flying, As We Remember"**, and **Meant to Fly: The Career of Captain A.J. High, Pilot for Trans-Texas Airways**.

Southern Airways has had two books written about drama and tragedy that affected the carrier: **Odyssey of Terror**, by Ed Blair with Captain William R. Haas, is a record of the thirty-hour 1972 hijacking of Southern Flight 49; and Sandy Purl's **Am I Alive?**, written with Gregg Lewis, is an account of the flight attendant's post-traumatic struggle after surviving the 1977 crash of Flight 242.

Author Terry Love published a hard-cover volume, **The Republic Airlines Story, 1945-1986** (Schiffer Publishing, 2012), which is best appreciated for its collection of photographs from each of that airline's predecessor companies. But beware of inaccurate captions.

Both Ozark and Hughes Airwest published hard-cover volumes that could be considered 'employee scrapbooks', and Arcadia Publishing, famous for its Images of America series of soft cover black-and-white photo histories, has issued a volume about US Airways and its predecessors, by William Lehman.

Airline Executives and Federal Regulation: Case Studies in American Enterprise from the Airmail Era to the Dawn of the Jet Age (edited by W. David Lewis, Ohio State University Press, 2000), contains a chapter dedicated to the story of Robert E. Peach and Mohawk Airlines, written by William M. Leary.

Finally, for information about the history of any of the world's airlines, I would direct the reader to all of the books written by R.E.G. (Ron) Davies, the late dean of commercial aviation historians. Davies' many titles encompass airline history around the world but, for information about the Locals, I suggest his **Airlines of the United States since 1914** (Smithsonian Institution Press, 1982; Paladwr Press, 1998).

www.ingramcontent.com/pod-product-compliance
Lightning Source LLC
Chambersburg PA
CBHW041118300426
44112CB00002B/18